msdn training

W9-BNI-821

2389B: Programming with Microsoft® ADO.NET

Course Number: 2389B
Part Number: X10-28183
Released: 02/2002

END-USER LICENSE AGREEMENT FOR MICROSOFT OFFICIAL CURRICULUM COURSEWARE –STUDENT EDITION

PLEASE READ THIS END-USER LICENSE AGREEMENT ("EULA") CAREFULLY. BY USING THE MATERIALS AND/OR USING OR INSTALLING THE SOFTWARE THAT ACCOMPANIES THIS EULA (COLLECTIVELY, THE "LICENSED CONTENT"), YOU AGREE TO THE TERMS OF THIS EULA. IF YOU DO NOT AGREE, DO NOT USE THE LICENSED CONTENT.

1.　　　**GENERAL.** This EULA is a legal agreement between you (either an individual or a single entity) and Microsoft Corporation ("Microsoft"). This EULA governs the Licensed Content, which includes computer software (including online and electronic documentation), training materials, and any other associated media and printed materials. This EULA applies to updates, supplements, add-on components, and Internet-based services components of the Licensed Content that Microsoft may provide or make available to you unless Microsoft provides other terms with the update, supplement, add-on component, or Internet-based services component. Microsoft reserves the right to discontinue any Internet-based services provided to you or made available to you through the use of the Licensed Content. This EULA also governs any product support services relating to the Licensed Content except as may be included in another agreement between you and Microsoft. An amendment or addendum to this EULA may accompany the Licensed Content.

2.　　　**GENERAL GRANT OF LICENSE.** Microsoft grants you the following rights, conditioned on your compliance with all the terms and conditions of this EULA. Microsoft grants you a limited, non-exclusive, royalty-free license to install and use the Licensed Content solely in conjunction with your participation as a student in an Authorized Training Session (as defined below). You may install and use one copy of the software on a single computer, device, workstation, terminal, or other digital electronic or analog device ("Device"). You may make a second copy of the software and install it on a portable Device for the exclusive use of the person who is the primary user of the first copy of the software. A license for the software may not be shared for use by multiple end users. An "Authorized Training Session" means a training session conducted at a Microsoft Certified Technical Education Center, an IT Academy, via a Microsoft Certified Partner, or such other entity as Microsoft may designate from time to time in writing, by a Microsoft Certified Trainer (for more information on these entities, please visit www.microsoft.com). WITHOUT LIMITING THE FOREGOING, COPYING OR REPRODUCTION OF THE LICENSED CONTENT TO ANY SERVER OR LOCATION FOR FURTHER REPRODUCTION OR REDISTRIBUTION IS EXPRESSLY PROHIBITED.

3.　　　**DESCRIPTION OF OTHER RIGHTS AND LICENSE LIMITATIONS**

　　　3.1　　*Use of Documentation and Printed Training Materials.*

　　　　　3.1.1　　The documents and related graphics included in the Licensed Content may include technical inaccuracies or typographical errors. Changes are periodically made to the content. Microsoft may make improvements and/or changes in any of the components of the Licensed Content at any time without notice. The names of companies, products, people, characters and/or data mentioned in the Licensed Content may be fictitious and are in no way intended to represent any real individual, company, product or event, unless otherwise noted.

　　　　　3.1.2　　Microsoft grants you the right to reproduce portions of documents (such as student workbooks, white papers, press releases, datasheets and FAQs) (the "Documents") provided with the Licensed Content. You may not print any book (either electronic or print version) in its entirety. If you choose to reproduce Documents, you agree that: (a) use of such printed Documents will be solely in conjunction with your personal training use; (b) the Documents will not republished or posted on any network computer or broadcast in any media; (c) any reproduction will include either the Document's original copyright notice or a copyright notice to Microsoft's benefit substantially in the format provided below; and (d) to comply with all terms and conditions of this EULA. In addition, no modifications may made to any Document.

　　　　　Form of Notice:

　　　　　© 2002. Reprinted with permission by Microsoft Corporation. All rights reserved.

　　　　　Microsoft and Windows are either registered trademarks or trademarks of Microsoft Corporation in the US and/or other countries. Other product and company names mentioned herein may be the trademarks of their respective owners.

　　　3.2　　*Use of Media Elements.* The Licensed Content may include certain photographs, clip art, animations, sounds, music, and video clips (together "Media Elements"). You may not modify these Media Elements.

　　　3.3　　*Use of Sample Code.* In the event that the Licensed Content includes sample code in source or object format ("Sample Code"), Microsoft grants you a limited, non-exclusive, royalty-free license to use, copy and modify the Sample Code; if you elect to exercise the foregoing rights, you agree to comply with all other terms and conditions of this EULA, including without limitation Sections 3.4, 3.5, and 6.

　　　3.4　　*Permitted Modifications.* In the event that you exercise any rights provided under this EULA to create modifications of the Licensed Content, you agree that any such modifications: (a) will not be used for providing training where a fee is charged in public or private classes; (b) indemnify, hold harmless, and defend Microsoft from and against any claims or lawsuits, including attorneys' fees, which arise from or result from your use of any modified version of the Licensed Content; and (c) not to transfer or assign any rights to any modified version of the Licensed Content to any third party without the express written permission of Microsoft.

3.5   *Reproduction/Redistribution Licensed Content.* Except as expressly provided in this EULA, you may not reproduce or distribute the Licensed Content or any portion thereof (including any permitted modifications) to any third parties without the express written permission of Microsoft.

4.   **RESERVATION OF RIGHTS AND OWNERSHIP.** Microsoft reserves all rights not expressly granted to you in this EULA. The Licensed Content is protected by copyright and other intellectual property laws and treaties. Microsoft or its suppliers own the title, copyright, and other intellectual property rights in the Licensed Content. You may not remove or obscure any copyright, trademark or patent notices that appear on the Licensed Content, or any components thereof, as delivered to you. **The Licensed Content is licensed, not sold.**

5.   **LIMITATIONS ON REVERSE ENGINEERING, DECOMPILATION, AND DISASSEMBLY.** You may not reverse engineer, decompile, or disassemble the Software or Media Elements, except and only to the extent that such activity is expressly permitted by applicable law notwithstanding this limitation.

6.   **LIMITATIONS ON SALE, RENTAL, ETC. AND CERTAIN ASSIGNMENTS.** You may not provide commercial hosting services with, sell, rent, lease, lend, sublicense, or assign copies of the Licensed Content, or any portion thereof (including any permitted modifications thereof) on a stand-alone basis or as part of any collection, product or service.

7.   **CONSENT TO USE OF DATA.** You agree that Microsoft and its affiliates may collect and use technical information gathered as part of the product support services provided to you, if any, related to the Licensed Content. Microsoft may use this information solely to improve our products or to provide customized services or technologies to you and will not disclose this information in a form that personally identifies you.

8.   **LINKS TO THIRD PARTY SITES.** You may link to third party sites through the use of the Licensed Content. The third party sites are not under the control of Microsoft, and Microsoft is not responsible for the contents of any third party sites, any links contained in third party sites, or any changes or updates to third party sites. Microsoft is not responsible for webcasting or any other form of transmission received from any third party sites. Microsoft is providing these links to third party sites to you only as a convenience, and the inclusion of any link does not imply an endorsement by Microsoft of the third party site.

9.   **ADDITIONAL LICENSED CONTENT/SERVICES.** This EULA applies to updates, supplements, add-on components, or Internet-based services components, of the Licensed Content that Microsoft may provide to you or make available to you after the date you obtain your initial copy of the Licensed Content, unless we provide other terms along with the update, supplement, add-on component, or Internet-based services component. Microsoft reserves the right to discontinue any Internet-based services provided to you or made available to you through the use of the Licensed Content.

10.   **U.S. GOVERNMENT LICENSE RIGHTS**. All software provided to the U.S. Government pursuant to solicitations issued on or after December 1, 1995 is provided with the commercial license rights and restrictions described elsewhere herein. All software provided to the U.S. Government pursuant to solicitations issued prior to December 1, 1995 is provided with "Restricted Rights" as provided for in FAR, 48 CFR 52.227-14 (JUNE 1987) or DFAR, 48 CFR 252.227-7013 (OCT 1988), as applicable.

11.   **EXPORT RESTRICTIONS.** You acknowledge that the Licensed Content is subject to U.S. export jurisdiction. You agree to comply with all applicable international and national laws that apply to the Licensed Content, including the U.S. Export Administration Regulations, as well as end-user, end-use, and destination restrictions issued by U.S. and other governments. For additional information see <http://www.microsoft.com/exporting/>.

12.   **TRANSFER.** The initial user of the Licensed Content may make a one-time permanent transfer of this EULA and Licensed Content to another end user, provided the initial user retains no copies of the Licensed Content. The transfer may not be an indirect transfer, such as a consignment. Prior to the transfer, the end user receiving the Licensed Content must agree to all the EULA terms.

13.   **"NOT FOR RESALE" LICENSED CONTENT.** Licensed Content identified as "Not For Resale" or "NFR," may not be sold or otherwise transferred for value, or used for any purpose other than demonstration, test or evaluation.

14.   **TERMINATION.** Without prejudice to any other rights, Microsoft may terminate this EULA if you fail to comply with the terms and conditions of this EULA. In such event, you must destroy all copies of the Licensed Content and all of its component parts.

15.   <u>**DISCLAIMER OF WARRANTIES.**</u> **TO THE MAXIMUM EXTENT PERMITTED BY APPLICABLE LAW, MICROSOFT AND ITS SUPPLIERS PROVIDE THE LICENSED CONTENT AND SUPPORT SERVICES (IF ANY)** *AS IS AND WITH ALL FAULTS,* **AND MICROSOFT AND ITS SUPPLIERS HEREBY DISCLAIM ALL OTHER WARRANTIES AND CONDITIONS, WHETHER EXPRESS, IMPLIED OR STATUTORY, INCLUDING, BUT NOT LIMITED TO, ANY (IF ANY) IMPLIED WARRANTIES, DUTIES OR CONDITIONS OF MERCHANTABILITY, OF FITNESS FOR A PARTICULAR PURPOSE, OF RELIABILITY OR AVAILABILITY, OF ACCURACY OR COMPLETENESS OF RESPONSES, OF RESULTS, OF WORKMANLIKE EFFORT, OF LACK OF VIRUSES, AND OF LACK OF NEGLIGENCE, ALL WITH REGARD TO THE LICENSED CONTENT, AND THE PROVISION OF OR FAILURE TO PROVIDE SUPPORT OR OTHER SERVICES, INFORMATION, SOFTWARE, AND RELATED CONTENT THROUGH THE LICENSED CONTENT, OR OTHERWISE ARISING OUT OF THE USE OF THE LICENSED CONTENT. ALSO, THERE IS NO WARRANTY OR CONDITION OF TITLE, QUIET ENJOYMENT, QUIET POSSESSION, CORRESPONDENCE TO DESCRIPTION OR NON-INFRINGEMENT WITH REGARD TO THE LICENSED CONTENT. THE ENTIRE RISK AS TO THE QUALITY, OR ARISING OUT OF THE USE OR PERFORMANCE OF THE LICENSED CONTENT, AND ANY SUPPORT SERVICES, REMAINS WITH YOU.**

16.   <u>**EXCLUSION OF INCIDENTAL, CONSEQUENTIAL AND CERTAIN OTHER DAMAGES.**</u> **TO THE MAXIMUM EXTENT PERMITTED BY APPLICABLE LAW, IN NO EVENT SHALL MICROSOFT OR ITS SUPPLIERS BE LIABLE FOR ANY SPECIAL, INCIDENTAL, PUNITIVE, INDIRECT, OR CONSEQUENTIAL DAMAGES WHATSOEVER (INCLUDING, BUT NOT**

LIMITED TO, DAMAGES FOR LOSS OF PROFITS OR CONFIDENTIAL OR OTHER INFORMATION, FOR BUSINESS INTERRUPTION, FOR PERSONAL INJURY, FOR LOSS OF PRIVACY, FOR FAILURE TO MEET ANY DUTY INCLUDING OF GOOD FAITH OR OF REASONABLE CARE, FOR NEGLIGENCE, AND FOR ANY OTHER PECUNIARY OR OTHER LOSS WHATSOEVER) ARISING OUT OF OR IN ANY WAY RELATED TO THE USE OF OR INABILITY TO USE THE LICENSED CONTENT, THE PROVISION OF OR FAILURE TO PROVIDE SUPPORT OR OTHER SERVICES, INFORMATION, SOFTWARE, AND RELATED CONTENT THROUGH THE LICENSED CONTENT, OR OTHERWISE ARISING OUT OF THE USE OF THE LICENSED CONTENT, OR OTHERWISE UNDER OR IN CONNECTION WITH ANY PROVISION OF THIS EULA, EVEN IN THE EVENT OF THE FAULT, TORT (INCLUDING NEGLIGENCE), MISREPRESENTATION, STRICT LIABILITY, BREACH OF CONTRACT OR BREACH OF WARRANTY OF MICROSOFT OR ANY SUPPLIER, AND EVEN IF MICROSOFT OR ANY SUPPLIER HAS BEEN ADVISED OF THE POSSIBILITY OF SUCH DAMAGES. BECAUSE SOME STATES/JURISDICTIONS DO NOT ALLOW THE EXCLUSION OR LIMITATION OF LIABILITY FOR CONSEQUENTIAL OR INCIDENTAL DAMAGES, THE ABOVE LIMITATION MAY NOT APPLY TO YOU.

17.   **LIMITATION OF LIABILITY AND REMEDIES.** NOTWITHSTANDING ANY DAMAGES THAT YOU MIGHT INCUR FOR ANY REASON WHATSOEVER (INCLUDING, WITHOUT LIMITATION, ALL DAMAGES REFERENCED HEREIN AND ALL DIRECT OR GENERAL DAMAGES IN CONTRACT OR ANYTHING ELSE), THE ENTIRE LIABILITY OF MICROSOFT AND ANY OF ITS SUPPLIERS UNDER ANY PROVISION OF THIS EULA AND YOUR EXCLUSIVE REMEDY HEREUNDER SHALL BE LIMITED TO THE GREATER OF THE ACTUAL DAMAGES YOU INCUR IN REASONABLE RELIANCE ON THE LICENSED CONTENT UP TO THE AMOUNT ACTUALLY PAID BY YOU FOR THE LICENSED CONTENT OR US$5.00. THE FOREGOING LIMITATIONS, EXCLUSIONS AND DISCLAIMERS SHALL APPLY TO THE MAXIMUM EXTENT PERMITTED BY APPLICABLE LAW, EVEN IF ANY REMEDY FAILS ITS ESSENTIAL PURPOSE.

18.   **APPLICABLE LAW.** If you acquired this Licensed Content in the United States, this EULA is governed by the laws of the State of Washington. If you acquired this Licensed Content in Canada, unless expressly prohibited by local law, this EULA is governed by the laws in force in the Province of Ontario, Canada; and, in respect of any dispute which may arise hereunder, you consent to the jurisdiction of the federal and provincial courts sitting in Toronto, Ontario. If you acquired this Licensed Content in the European Union, Iceland, Norway, or Switzerland, then local law applies. If you acquired this Licensed Content in any other country, then local law may apply.

19.   **ENTIRE AGREEMENT; SEVERABILITY.** This EULA (including any addendum or amendment to this EULA which is included with the Licensed Content) are the entire agreement between you and Microsoft relating to the Licensed Content and the support services (if any) and they supersede all prior or contemporaneous oral or written communications, proposals and representations with respect to the Licensed Content or any other subject matter covered by this EULA. To the extent the terms of any Microsoft policies or programs for support services conflict with the terms of this EULA, the terms of this EULA shall control. If any provision of this EULA is held to be void, invalid, unenforceable or illegal, the other provisions shall continue in full force and effect.

Should you have any questions concerning this EULA, or if you desire to contact Microsoft for any reason, please use the address information enclosed in this Licensed Content to contact the Microsoft subsidiary serving your country or visit Microsoft on the World Wide Web at http://www.microsoft.com.

Si vous avez acquis votre Contenu Sous Licence Microsoft au CANADA :

DÉNI DE GARANTIES. Dans la mesure maximale permise par les lois applicables, le Contenu Sous Licence et les services de soutien technique (le cas échéant) sont fournis *TELS QUELS ET AVEC TOUS LES DÉFAUTS* par Microsoft et ses fournisseurs, lesquels par les présentes dénient toutes autres garanties et conditions expresses, implicites ou en vertu de la loi, notamment, mais sans limitation, (le cas échéant) les garanties, devoirs ou conditions implicites de qualité marchande, d'adaptation à une fin usage particulière, de fiabilité ou de disponibilité, d'exactitude ou d'exhaustivité des réponses, des résultats, des efforts déployés selon les règles de l'art, d'absence de virus et d'absence de négligence, le tout à l'égard du Contenu Sous Licence et de la prestation des services de soutien technique ou de l'omission de la 'une telle prestation des services de soutien technique ou à l'égard de la fourniture ou de l'omission de la fourniture de tous autres services, renseignements, Contenus Sous Licence, et contenu qui s'y rapporte grâce au Contenu Sous Licence ou provenant autrement de l'utilisation du Contenu Sous Licence. PAR AILLEURS, IL N'Y A AUCUNE GARANTIE OU CONDITION QUANT AU TITRE DE PROPRIÉTÉ, À LA JOUISSANCE OU LA POSSESSION PAISIBLE, À LA CONCORDANCE À UNE DESCRIPTION NI QUANT À UNE ABSENCE DE CONTREFAÇON CONCERNANT LE CONTENU SOUS LICENCE.

EXCLUSION DES DOMMAGES ACCESSOIRES, INDIRECTS ET DE CERTAINS AUTRES DOMMAGES. DANS LA MESURE MAXIMALE PERMISE PAR LES LOIS APPLICABLES, EN AUCUN CAS MICROSOFT OU SES FOURNISSEURS NE SERONT RESPONSABLES DES DOMMAGES SPÉCIAUX, CONSÉCUTIFS, ACCESSOIRES OU INDIRECTS DE QUELQUE NATURE QUE CE SOIT (NOTAMMENT, LES DOMMAGES À L'ÉGARD DU MANQUE À GAGNER OU DE LA DIVULGATION DE RENSEIGNEMENTS CONFIDENTIELS OU AUTRES, DE LA PERTE D'EXPLOITATION, DE BLESSURES CORPORELLES, DE LA VIOLATION DE LA VIE PRIVÉE, DE L'OMISSION DE REMPLIR TOUT DEVOIR, Y COMPRIS D'AGIR DE BONNE FOI OU D'EXERCER UN SOIN RAISONNABLE, DE LA NÉGLIGENCE ET DE TOUTE AUTRE PERTE PÉCUNIAIRE OU AUTRE PERTE

DE QUELQUE NATURE QUE CE SOIT) SE RAPPORTE DE QUELQUE MANIÈRE QUE CE SOIT À L'UTILISATION DU CONTENU SOUS LICENCE OU À L'INCAPACITÉ DE S'EN SERVIR, À LA PRESTATION OU À L'OMISSION DE LA 'UNE TELLE PRESTATION DE SERVICES DE SOUTIEN TECHNIQUE OU À LA FOURNITURE OU À L'OMISSION DE LA FOURNITURE DE TOUS AUTRES SERVICES, RENSEIGNEMENTS, CONTENUS SOUS LICENCE, ET CONTENU QUI S'Y RAPPORTE GRÂCE AU CONTENU SOUS LICENCE OU PROVENANT AUTREMENT DE L'UTILISATION DU CONTENU SOUS LICENCE OU AUTREMENT AUX TERMES DE TOUTE DISPOSITION DE LA U PRÉSENTE CONVENTION EULA OU RELATIVEMENT À UNE TELLE DISPOSITION, MÊME EN CAS DE FAUTE, DE DÉLIT CIVIL (Y COMPRIS LA NÉGLIGENCE), DE RESPONSABILITÉ STRICTE, DE VIOLATION DE CONTRAT OU DE VIOLATION DE GARANTIE DE MICROSOFT OU DE TOUT FOURNISSEUR ET MÊME SI MICROSOFT OU TOUT FOURNISSEUR A ÉTÉ AVISÉ DE LA POSSIBILITÉ DE TELS DOMMAGES.

<u>LIMITATION DE RESPONSABILITÉ ET RECOURS.</u> MALGRÉ LES DOMMAGES QUE VOUS PUISSIEZ SUBIR POUR QUELQUE MOTIF QUE CE SOIT (NOTAMMENT, MAIS SANS LIMITATION, TOUS LES DOMMAGES SUSMENTIONNÉS ET TOUS LES DOMMAGES DIRECTS OU GÉNÉRAUX OU AUTRES), LA SEULE RESPONSABILITÉ 'OBLIGATION INTÉGRALE DE MICROSOFT ET DE L'UN OU L'AUTRE DE SES FOURNISSEURS AUX TERMES DE TOUTE DISPOSITION DEU LA PRÉSENTE CONVENTION EULA ET VOTRE RECOURS EXCLUSIF À L'ÉGARD DE TOUT CE QUI PRÉCÈDE SE LIMITE AU PLUS ÉLEVÉ ENTRE LES MONTANTS SUIVANTS : LE MONTANT QUE VOUS AVEZ RÉELLEMENT PAYÉ POUR LE CONTENU SOUS LICENCE OU 5,00 $US. LES LIMITES, EXCLUSIONS ET DÉNIS QUI PRÉCÈDENT (Y COMPRIS LES CLAUSES CI-DESSUS), S'APPLIQUENT DANS LA MESURE MAXIMALE PERMISE PAR LES LOIS APPLICABLES, MÊME SI TOUT RECOURS N'ATTEINT PAS SON BUT ESSENTIEL.

À moins que cela ne soit prohibé par le droit local applicable, la présente Convention est régie par les lois de la province d'Ontario, Canada. Vous consentez Chacune des parties à la présente reconnaît irrévocablement à la compétence des tribunaux fédéraux et provinciaux siégeant à Toronto, dans de la province d'Ontario et consent à instituer tout litige qui pourrait découler de la présente auprès des tribunaux situés dans le district judiciaire de York, province d'Ontario.

Au cas où vous auriez des questions concernant cette licence ou que vous désiriez vous mettre en rapport avec Microsoft pour quelque raison que ce soit, veuillez utiliser l'information contenue dans le Contenu Sous Licence pour contacter la filiale de succursale Microsoft desservant votre pays, dont l'adresse est fournie dans ce produit, ou visitez écrivez à : Microsoft sur le World Wide Web à http://www.microsoft.com

Contents

About This Course

This section provides you with a brief description of the course, audience, suggested prerequisites, and course objectives.

Description

This course teaches developers to build data-centric applications and Web services with Microsoft® ADO.NET, Microsoft SQL Server™ 2000, and the Microsoft .NET Framework.

Audience

This course is designed for the professional platform developer who is responsible for designing and building data-centric, distributed applications for his or her organization. It is designed for developers who have component and Web-application development skills and who have previously built solutions by using Microsoft Visual Studio®.

Typically, these individuals will have the following skills:

- Experience with a .NET language such as Microsoft Visual Basic® .NET, Microsoft Visual C#™, or Microsoft Visual C++®
- An understanding of object oriented concepts and terminology
- Experience developing distributed applications
- Experience developing Web-based applications hosted on Internet Information Server

Typically, these individuals perform the following key activities:

- Develop, design, and create interface specifications
- Create and test prototypes
- Design site security measures
- Develop application and data models
- Write supporting codeDevelop supporting relational databases

Student prerequisites

This course requires that students meet the following prerequisites:

Prerequisite skill	This skill can be fulfilled by taking
Basic understanding of database concepts including tables, rows, columns, primary keys, foreign keys, constraints, and views	Course 1609, *Designing Data Services and Data Models*
Understanding of database query concepts and SQL statements including SELECT, INSERT, UPDATE, and DELETE	Course 2071, *Querying Microsoft SQL Server 2000 with Transact-SQL*
Development experience using the Microsoft Visual Studio .NET development environment and the Microsoft .NET Framework	Course 2373, *Programming with Microsoft Visual Basic .NET* or Course 2124, *Introduction to C# for the Microsoft .NET Platform*
Programming experience with Visual Basic .NET or Visual C#	Course 2373, *Programming with Microsoft Visual Basic .NET* or Course 2124, *Introduction to C# for the Microsoft .NET Platform*
Ability to build a Microsoft Windows® or Web application	Course 1303A, *Mastering Microsoft Visual Basic 6 Fundamentals* or Course 1017A, *Mastering Web Application Development Using Microsoft Visual InterDev 6*

The course assumes that students have the following skills:

- Understanding of relational database concepts: table, row, column, primary keys, foreign keys, constraints, and views

- Data query and modification experience, including experience with SELECT, INSERT, UPDATE, and DELETE commands

- Exposure to XML documents, style sheets, and schemas

- Experience with Visual Basic .NET, Visual Basic for Applications, or previous versions of Visual Basic

- Experience building user interfaces, including Web applications or Windows applications

Course objectives

After completing this course, the student will be able to:

- Describe data-centric applications, ADO.NET architecture, and ADO.NET and XML.

- Connect to SQL Server and other data sources.

- Perform connected database operations including executing SELECT commands, database definition commands, dynamic SQL commands, and commands that return data from a SQL Server database in XML.

- Build a DataSet schema, populate it with data, and modify the data programmatically.

- Build a DataSet from an existing Data Source.

- Use XML techniques while working with DataSets, including table and column mapping, creating XML Schema Definition Language (XSD) schemas, building strongly typed DataSets, and interacting with XMLDataDocuments.

- Build a Web service that uses ADO.NET to query and update a data source.

- Troubleshoot errors within an ADO.NET application.

Student Materials Compact Disc Contents

The Student Materials compact disc contains the following files and folders:

- *Autorun.exe.* When the compact disc is inserted into the CD-ROM drive, or when you double-click the **Autorun.exe** file, this file opens the compact disc and allows you to browse the Student Materials compact disc.

- *Autorun.inf.* When the compact disc is inserted into the compact disc drive, this file opens Autorun.exe.

- *Default.htm.* This file opens the Student Materials Web page. It provides students with resources pertaining to this course, including additional reading, review and lab answers, lab files, multimedia presentations, and course-related Web sites.

- *Readme.txt.* This file explains how to install the software for viewing the Student Materials compact disc and its contents and how to open the Student Materials Web page.

- *2389B_ms.doc.* This file is the Manual Classroom Setup Guide. It contains a description of classroom requirements, classroom setup instructions, and the classroom configuration.

- *Appendix.* This folder contains appendix files for this course.

- *Democode.* This folder contains demonstration code.

- *Flash.* This folder contains the installer for the Macromedia Flash 5.0 browser plug-in.

- *Fonts.* This folder contains fonts that are required to view the Microsoft PowerPoint® presentation and Web-based materials.

- *Labs.* This folder contains files that are used in the hands-on labs. These files may be used to prepare the student computers for the hands-on labs.

- *Media.* This folder contains files that are used in multimedia presentations for this course.

- *Mplayer.* This folder contains the setup file to install Microsoft Windows Media™ Player.

- *Practices.* This folder contains files that are used in the hands-on practices.

- *Sampcode.* This folder contains sample code that is accessible through the Web pages on the Student Materials compact disc.

- *Webfiles.* This folder contains the files that are required to view the course Web page. To open the Web page, open Windows Explorer, and in the root directory of the compact disc, double-click **Default.htm** or **Autorun.**exe.

- *Wordview.* This folder contains the Word Viewer that is used to view any Word document (.doc) files that are included on the compact disc.

Document Conventions

The following conventions are used in course materials to distinguish elements of the text.

Convention	Use
◆	Indicates an introductory page. This symbol appears next to a topic heading when additional information on the topic is covered on the page or pages that follow it.
bold	Represents commands, command options, and syntax that must be typed exactly as shown. It also indicates commands on menus and buttons, dialog box titles and options, and icon and menu names.
italic	In syntax statements or descriptive text, indicates argument names or placeholders for variable information. Italic is also used for introducing new terms, for book titles, and for emphasis in the text.
Title Capitals	Indicate domain names, user names, computer names, directory names, and folder and file names, except when specifically referring to case-sensitive names. Unless otherwise indicated, you can use lowercase letters when you type a directory name or file name in a dialog box or at a command prompt.
ALL CAPITALS	Indicate the names of keys, key sequences, and key combinations—for example, ALT+SPACEBAR.
monospace	Represents code samples or examples of screen text.
[ ]	In syntax statements, enclose optional items. For example, [*filename*] in command syntax indicates that you can choose to type a file name with the command. Type only the information within the brackets, not the brackets themselves.
{ }	In syntax statements, enclose required items. Type only the information within the braces, not the braces themselves.
|	In syntax statements, separates an either/or choice.
▶	Indicates a procedure with sequential steps.
...	In syntax statements, specifies that the preceding item may be repeated.
. . .	Represents an omitted portion of a code sample.

msdn training

Introduction

Contents

Introduction

- Name
- Company or Organization Affiliation
- Title and Job Function
- Job Responsibility
- Development Experience
- Experience with ADO, XML, and Related Technologies
- Expectations for the Course

Course Materials

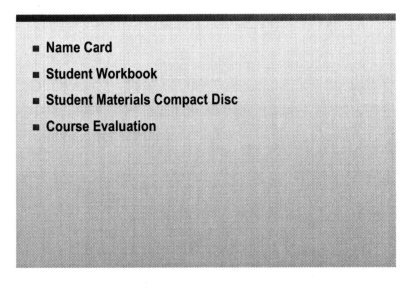

- Name Card
- Student Workbook
- Student Materials Compact Disc
- Course Evaluation

The following materials are included with your kit:

- *Name card.* Write your name on both sides of the name card.

- *Student workbook.* The student workbook contains the material covered in class, in addition to the hands-on lab exercises.

- *Student Materials compact disc.* The Student Materials compact disc contains the Web page that provides you with links to resources pertaining to this course, including additional readings, review and lab answers, lab files, multimedia presentations, and course-related Web sites.

Note To open the Web page, insert the Student Materials compact disc into the CD-ROM drive, and then in the root directory of the compact disc, double-click **Autorun.exe** or **Default.htm**.

- *Course evaluation.* To provide feedback on the course, training facility, and instructor, you will have the opportunity to complete an online evaluation near the end of the course.

  To provide additional comments or inquire about the Microsoft Certified Professional program, send e-mail to mcphelp@microsoft.com.

Prerequisites

- **Database basic concepts**
- **XML concepts and implementation**
- **Microsoft Visual Basic .NET or Visual C# .NET**
- **Microsoft Visual Studio .NET development environment**
- **Distributed application architecture**
- **User interface design**

This course requires that you meet the following prerequisites:

- Understanding of database basics: tables, rows, columns, primary keys, foreign keys, constraints, and views

- Awareness of concepts including SELECT, INSERT, UPDATE, and DELETE from tables

- Exposure to XML documents, style sheets, and schemas

- Familiarity with the Microsoft Visual Studio® .NET development environment, Microsoft Visual Basic® .NET, or Microsoft Visual C#™ .NET

- Ability to describe distributed application architecture

- Experience building user interface Web applications or Microsoft Windows® applications

Course Outline

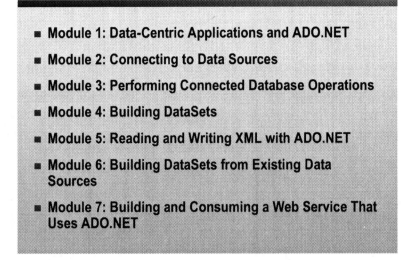

- Module 1: Data-Centric Applications and ADO.NET
- Module 2: Connecting to Data Sources
- Module 3: Performing Connected Database Operations
- Module 4: Building DataSets
- Module 5: Reading and Writing XML with ADO.NET
- Module 6: Building DataSets from Existing Data Sources
- Module 7: Building and Consuming a Web Service That Uses ADO.NET

Module 1, "Data-Centric Applications and ADO.NET" After completing this module, you will be able to diagram the architecture of data-centric applications, give examples of storage options, choose a connected or disconnected environment based on application requirements, diagram the ADO.NET object model, use the System.Data namespaces in applications, analyze typical business scenarios, and describe the use of XML in ADO.NET.

Module 2, "Connecting to Data Sources" After completing this module, you will be able to choose a .NET data provider, connect to SQL Server, connect to OLE DB data sources, manage a connection, handle common connection exceptions, and implement and control connection pooling.

Module 3, "Performing Connected Database Operations" After completing this module, you will be able to build command objects, execute commands that return a single value, execute commands that return rows, execute commands that do not return rows, and use transactions.

Module 4, "Building DataSets" After completing this module, you will be able to build a DataSet and a DataTable, bind a DataSet to a DataGrid, create a custom DataSet by using inheritance, define a data relationship, modify data in a DataTable, find and select rows in a DataTable, and sort and filter a DataTable by using a DataView.

Module 5, "Reading and Writing XML with ADO.NET" After completing this module, you will be able to generate an XML Schema Definition Language (XSD) schema from a DataSet by using graphical tools, identify the purpose and uses of the **XmlDataDocument** object, save a DataSet structure to an XSD schema file, create and populate a DataSet from an XSD schema and XML data, load data and schemas simultaneously into a DataSet, save DataSet data as XML, and write and load changes by using a **DiffGram**.

Module 6, "Building DataSets from Existing Data Sources" After completing this module, you will be able to configure a DataAdapter to retrieve information, populate a DataSet by using a DataAdapter, configure a DataAdapter to modify information, persist data changes to a server, and manage data conflicts.

Module 7, "Building and Consuming a Web Service That Uses ADO.NET" After completing this module, you will be able to build and consume a Web service and troubleshoot errors in an ADO.NET application.

Microsoft Certified Professional Program

- **Microsoft Certified Systems Administrator (MCSA)**
- **Microsoft Certified Systems Engineer (MCSE)**
- **Microsoft Certified Solution Developer (MCSD)**
- **Microsoft Certified Database Administrator (MCDBA)**
- **Microsoft Certified Professional (MCP)**
- **Microsoft Certified Trainer (MCT)**

Introduction

Microsoft Training and Certification offers a variety of certification credentials for developers and IT professionals. The Microsoft Certified Professional program is the leading certification program for validating your experience and skills, keeping you competitive in today's changing business environment.

MCP certifications

The Microsoft Certified Professional program includes the following certifications.

- MCSA on Microsoft Windows 2000

  The Microsoft Certified Systems Administrator (MCSA) certification is designed for professionals who implement, manage, and troubleshoot existing network and system environments based on Microsoft Windows 2000 platforms, including the Windows .NET Server family. Implementation responsibilities include installing and configuring parts of the systems. Management responsibilities include administering and supporting the systems.

- MCSE on Microsoft Windows 2000

  The Microsoft Certified Systems Engineer (MCSE) credential is the premier certification for professionals who analyze the business requirements and design and implement the infrastructure for business solutions based on the Microsoft Windows 2000 platform and Microsoft server software, including the Windows .NET Server family. Implementation responsibilities include installing, configuring, and troubleshooting network systems.

- MCSD

  The Microsoft Certified Solution Developer (MCSD) credential is the premier certification for professionals who design and develop leading-edge business solutions with Microsoft development tools, technologies, platforms, and the Microsoft Windows DNA architecture. The types of applications MCSDs can develop include desktop applications and multi-user, Web-based, N-tier, and transaction-based applications. The credential covers job tasks ranging from analyzing business requirements to maintaining solutions.

- MCDBA on Microsoft SQL Server 2000

  The Microsoft Certified Database Administrator (MCDBA) credential is the premier certification for professionals who implement and administer Microsoft SQL Server databases. The certification is appropriate for individuals who derive physical database designs, develop logical data models, create physical databases, create data services by using Transact-SQL, manage and maintain databases, configure and manage security, monitor and optimize databases, and install and configure SQL Server.

- MCP

  The Microsoft Certified Professional (MCP) credential is for individuals who have the skills to successfully implement a Microsoft product or technology as part of a business solution in an organization. Hands-on experience with the product is necessary to successfully achieve certification.

- MCT

  Microsoft Certified Trainers (MCTs) demonstrate the instructional and technical skills that qualify them to deliver Microsoft Official Curriculum through Microsoft Certified Technical Education Centers (Microsoft CTECs).

Certification requirements

The certification requirements differ for each certification category and are specific to the products and job functions addressed by the certification. To become a Microsoft Certified Professional, you must pass rigorous certification exams that provide a valid and reliable measure of technical proficiency and expertise.

For More Information   See the Microsoft Training and Certification Web site at http://www.microsoft.com/traincert/.

You can also send e-mail to mcphelp@microsoft.com if you have specific certification questions.

**Acquiring the skills
tested by an MCP exam**

Microsoft Official Curriculum (MOC) and MSDN® Training Curriculum can help you develop the skills that you need to do your job. They also complement the experience that you gain while working with Microsoft products and technologies. However, no one-to-one correlation exists between MOC and MSDN Training courses and MCP exams. Microsoft does not expect or intend for the courses to be the sole preparation method for passing MCP exams. Practical product knowledge and experience is also necessary to pass the MCP exams.

To help prepare for the MCP exams, use the preparation guides that are available for each exam. Each Exam Preparation Guide contains exam-specific information, such as a list of the topics on which you will be tested. These guides are available on the Microsoft Training and Certification Web site at http://www.microsoft.com/traincert/.

Facilities

msdn training

Module 1: Data-Centric Applications and ADO.NET

Contents

Microsoft

Overview

- **Design of Data-Centric Applications**
- **ADO.NET Architecture**
- **ADO.NET and XML**

Introduction

This module describes the design of data-centric applications, the Microsoft® ADO.NET architecture, and the integration between ADO.NET and XML.

Objectives

After completing this module, you will be able to:

- Give examples of storage options.
- Diagram the architecture of data-centric applications.
- Choose a connected, disconnected, or mixed environment based on application requirements.
- Use the System.Data namespaces in applications.
- Diagram the ADO.NET object model.
- Analyze typical business scenarios.
- Explain how to use ADO.NET with XML.

Lesson: Design of Data-Centric Applications

- **Data Storage**
- **What Is a Connected Environment?**
- **What Is a Disconnected Environment?**
- **Data Access Application Models**

Introduction

This lesson describes the design of data-centric application architecture and data storage options.

Lesson objectives

After completing this lesson, you will be able to:

- Give examples of common types of data storage.
- Choose between a connected and disconnected application environment.
- Diagram how data access application models have evolved.

Data Storage

Active X Data Object, So outdated

System. Data = ADO.NET

> **ADO.NET supports the following types of data storage:**
>
> - **Unstructured**
>
> - **Structured, non-hierarchical data**
>   - Comma Separated Value (CSV) files, Microsoft Excel spreadsheets, Microsoft Exchange files, Active Directory files, and others
>
> - **Hierarchical**
>   - XML documents and others
>
> - **Relational database**
>   - SQL Server, Oracle, Access, and others

Definition of data storage

Data storage is a method of storing specific items that together constitute a unit of information. Individual data items themselves are of little use; they become value resources only when put into context with other data items.

Types of data storage

The following table describes different methods of data storage.

Type	Characteristics	Examples
Unstructured	Data has no logical order.	Simple memos
Structured, non-hierarchical	Data is separated into units, but the units are organized strictly by their order.	Comma Separated Value (CSV) files or tab-separated files, Microsoft Excel spreadsheets, Microsoft Exchange files, Microsoft Active Directory™ files, indexed sequential access method (ISAM) files
Hierarchical	Data is organized in a tree structure, with nodes that contain other nodes.	XML data documents
Relational database	Data is organized in tables, with columns containing a specific type of data and rows containing a single record. Tables can be related over columns with identical data.	Microsoft SQL Server™ and Microsoft Access databases, Oracle databases
Object-oriented database	Data is organized as objects.	Objectivity/DB

ADO.NET support

ADO.NET can support all of the data formats in the preceding table.

What Is a Connected Environment?

- **A connected environment is one in which users are constantly connected to a data source**
- **Advantages:**
  - Environment is easier to secure
  - Concurrency is more easily controlled
  - Data is more likely to be current than in other scenarios
- **Disadvantages:**
  - Must have a constant network connection
  - Scalability

Introduction

For much of the history of computers, the only environment available was the connected environment.

Definition

A connected environment is one in which a user or an application is constantly connected to a data source.

Advantages A connected scenario offers the following advantages:

- A secure environment is easier to maintain.
- Concurrency is easier to control.
- Data is more likely to be current than in other scenarios.

Disadvantages

A connected scenario has the following disadvantages:

- It must have a constant network connection.
- Scalability

Examples

The following are examples of connected environments:

- A factory that requires a real-time connection to monitor production output and storage
- A brokerage house that requires a constant connection to stock quotes

What Is a Disconnected Environment?

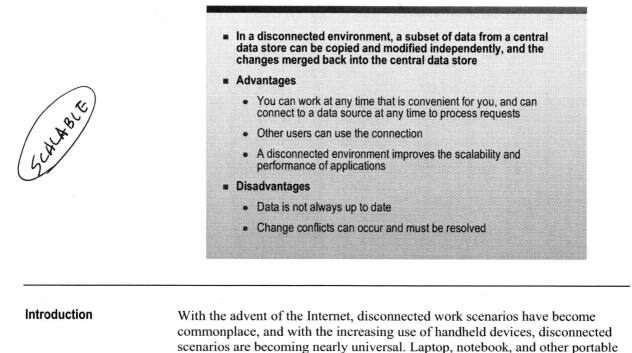

SCALABLE

- **In a disconnected environment, a subset of data from a central data store can be copied and modified independently, and the changes merged back into the central data store**
- **Advantages**
  - You can work at any time that is convenient for you, and can connect to a data source at any time to process requests
  - Other users can use the connection
  - A disconnected environment improves the scalability and performance of applications
- **Disadvantages**
  - Data is not always up to date
  - Change conflicts can occur and must be resolved

Introduction

With the advent of the Internet, disconnected work scenarios have become commonplace, and with the increasing use of handheld devices, disconnected scenarios are becoming nearly universal. Laptop, notebook, and other portable computers allow you to use applications when you are disconnected from servers or databases.

In many situations, people do not work entirely in a connected or disconnected environment, but rather in an environment that combines the two approaches.

Definition

A disconnected environment is one in which a user or an application is not constantly connected to a source of data. Mobile users who work with laptop computers are the primary users in disconnected environments. Users can take a subset of data with them on a disconnected computer, and then merge changes back into the central data store.

Advantages

A disconnected environment provides the following advantages:

- You can work at any time that is convenient for you, and can connect to a data source at any time to process requests.
- Other users can use the connection.
- A disconnected environment improves the scalability and performance of applications.

Disadvantages

A disconnected environment has the following disadvantages:

- Data is not always up to date.
- Change conflicts can occur and must be resolved.

Example

A farmer has a Microsoft Windows® CE device running SQL Server CE that he uses to keep track of livestock when animals are born.

Local copy — APP

Data Access Application Models

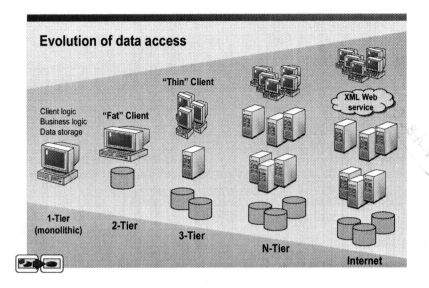

Introduction

Data access models have evolved with the evolution of computers, from highly localized to highly distributed. As the number of users and the amount of data increased, data access models evolved from a single user on a single application to multiple users on the Internet. The latest development in this evolution is the XML Web service model.

Definition of tier

Within a data access model, a tier is a logical level or layer at which the logical components of an application reside, not a physical tier. Tiers can reside on one or more computers, or physical tiers. The number of tiers refers to the number of levels, not the number of physical computers, into which services are divided. These levels typically include the following:

- Client tier, also known as the presentation or user services layer. This tier contains the user interface.

- Business logic tier, which contains the logic that interacts with the source of data. This "middle" tier contains the part of the application that interacts with the data; for example, creating a connection to the source of the data. The business logic tier is often physically implemented in all tiers; for example, as stored procedures in the data store, as classes within an application server, or as code within the client application.

- Data services tier, which contains the data that the business logic uses in the applications.

- Interoperability tier, which contains the logic that allows interaction between applications on different operating systems, or different types of data. For example, XML Web services can be hosted on any operating system.

Benefits of tiers

The major advantage of adding tiers is the ability to scale applications. Each additional tier allows you to add more users and isolate a level of application logic. Isolating the logic enables you to make changes to a specific area of an application without requiring changes to the other tiers.

For example, in a 1-tier application, a change to any level of logic requires that the entire application be recompiled and redistributed.

Evolution of access models

The following table compares the different types of data access models.

Model	Description	Advantages	Disadvantages
1-tier, or Monolithic	This model typically involves a single user and all three layers in a single computer. For example, an old-style Microsoft Access database with a single user.	Because everything is in one place, all components are easily accessible.	Program update requires source code to be modified, recompiled, and redistributed for every user. This model provides no real ability to scale.
2-tier – client/server	The user layer and business logic layer reside in one tier, data services on another. This model typically involves two or more computers. For example, a business personnel database. Often the business logic is split between the two tiers: some logic in the client application, and some as stored procedures in the data tier.	Provides some separation of functions.	Difficult to scale because the client is a "fat client" that contains both the presentation and business logic layers. Software distribution and maintenance problems.
3-tier	Each service is in a separate layer. Business logic moves into a new "Middle tier."	Good separation of functions. The client layer is a "thin client" that contains only the client logic, or presentation layer.	More complex to manage. Security is not as scalable/flexible as n-tier.
N-tier	An enterprise-level personnel database where several clients access a single application server. New tiers can be added as new logical needs occur.	Allows different applications on different operating systems to interact with both the user and the data.	Security issues. Remote procedure calls (RPC) cannot pass through firewalls.
N-tier with Web interface	Services are distributed between the Internet and intranet, with additional tier and additional servers dedicated to the network.	Zero client deployment costs. The only updates are to Web/application servers. HTTP can go through firewalls.	Security issues.

Balance

As a general guideline, keep in mind that as the number of tiers increases, the scalability and complexity of the data access model increase.

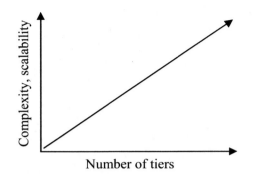

Practice

Group discussion. Ask a student to come to the front of the class, think of a database application that he or she has developed in the past, and then use the whiteboard to:

1. Draw a diagram showing the data access application model the database application used.

2. Draw the data storage formats the student needed to access.

Did the architecture use a connected or disconnected environment?

Lesson: ADO.NET Architecture

- **What Is ADO.NET?**
- **What Are the Data-Related Namespaces?**
- **Evolution of ADO to ADO.NET**
- **The ADO.NET Object Model**
- **Using ADO.NET Classes in a Connected Scenario**
- **Using ADO.NET Classes in a Disconnected Scenario**

Introduction

This lesson introduces ADO.NET and establishes its place in the Microsoft .NET Framework.

Lesson objectives

After completing this lesson, you will be able to:

- Explain how to use ADO.NET.
- Discuss how ADO.NET is divided into namespaces.
- Diagram the ADO.NET object model.

What Is ADO.NET?

ADO.NET is a set of classes for working with data. It provides:

- An evolutionary, more flexible successor to ADO

- A system designed for disconnected environments

- A programming model with advanced XML support

- A set of classes, interfaces, structures, and enumerations that manage data access from within the .NET Framework

---

Introduction

ADO.NET is the next step in the evolution of Microsoft ActiveX® Data Objects (ADO). It does not share the same programming model, but shares much of the ADO functionality.

Definition

ADO.NET is a set of classes for working with data.

Business use case

As application development has evolved, new applications have become loosely coupled based on the Web application model. An increasing number of applications use XML to encode data to be passed over network connections. ADO.NET provides a programming model that incorporates features of both XML and ADO.NET within the .NET Framework.

Benefits

ADO.NET provides the following advantages over other data access models and components:

- Interoperability. ADO.NET uses XML as the format for transmitting data from a data source to a local in-memory copy of the data.

- Maintainability. When an increasing number of users work with an application, the increased use can strain resources. By using n-tier applications, you can spread application logic across additional tiers. ADO.NET architecture uses local in-memory caches to hold copies of data, making it easy for additional tiers to trade information.

- Programmability. The ADO.NET programming model uses strongly typed data. Strongly typed data makes code more concise and easier to write because Microsoft Visual Studio® .NET provides statement completion.

- Performance. ADO.NET helps you to avoid costly data type conversions because of its use of strongly typed data.

- Scalability. The ADO.NET programming model encourages programmers to conserve system resources for applications that run over the Web. Because data is held locally in in-memory caches, there is no need to retain database locks or maintain active database connections for extended periods.

What Are the Data-Related Namespaces?

- **The data-related namespaces include:**
  - System.Data
  - System.Data.Common
  - System.Data.SqlClient
  - System.Data.OleDb
  - System.Data.SqlTypes
  - System.Xml
- **Practice**

Introduction

The .NET Framework divides functionality into logical namespaces, and ADO.NET is no exception. ADO.NET is implemented primarily in the System.Data namespace hierarchy, which physically resides in the System.Data.dll assembly. Some parts of ADO.NET are part of the System.Xml namespace hierarchy, for example the **XmlDataDocument** class.

The data-related namespaces

The following table describes the data-related namespaces.

Namespace	Description
System.Data	Core of ADO.NET. Includes classes that make up the disconnected part of the ADO.NET architecture. For example, the DataSet classes.
System.Data.Common	Utility classes and interfaces that are inherited and implemented by .NET data providers.
System.Data.SqlClient	SQL Server .NET Data Provider.
System.Data.OleDb	OLE DB .NET Data Provider.
System.Data.SqlTypes	Classes and structures for native SQL Server data types. A safer, faster alternative to other data types.
System.Xml	Classes, interfaces, and enumerations that provide standards-based support for processing XML. For example, the XmlDataDocument class.

Practice   ▶ **Reference the System.Data assembly, import the System.Data namespace, and declare an object variable**

1. Start the Visual Studio .NET development environment.

2. On the **File** menu, point to **New**, and then click **Project**.

3. In the **New Project** dialog box, select the following options, and then click **OK**.

Option	Selection
Project Types	Visual Basic Projects (or Visual C# Projects if you prefer)
Templates	Windows Application
Name	MyWindowsApplication
Location	<install folder>\Practices\Mod01

4. In the Solution Explorer, right-click the **References** folder and choose **Add Reference**.

5. Select the **System.Data.dll** assembly, click **Select**, and then click **OK**.

Note   Referencing the **System.Data** assembly is done by default in Windows Application projects, so the previous two steps are not usually necessary.

6. Open the code editor, and insert the following code before the existing code:

```
' Visual Basic
Imports System.Data
Imports System.Data.SqlClient

// Visual C#
using System.Data.SqlClient;
```

Note   Visual C# includes a **using System.Data;** statement by default in Windows Application projects (as well as a few other **using** statements), which is why that line is missing in the code above. If you add the preceding code to all subsequent classes, you will be able to declare object variables without having to explicitly specify the namespace.

7. Insert the following code in the **Form1_Load** event. Notice that you do not need to specify the namespace for the **DataSet** and **SqlConnection** classes:

```
' Visual Basic
Dim dsNorthwind As DataSet
Dim cnNorthwind As SqlConnection

// Visual C#
DataSet dsNorthwind;
SqlConnection cnNorthwind;
```

8. Save the changes to your project and close the Visual Studio .NET development environment.

Evolution of ADO to ADO.NET

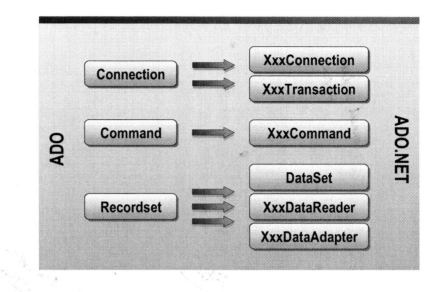

Introduction

Many changes have been made between ADO and ADO.NET. Most of these changes are a response to studies of how developers use (and misuse) ADO. Other changes have made ADO.NET more flexible, more powerful, and more scalable than ADO.

Divide and conquer

Because not all .NET data providers provide transactional functionality, ADO.NET moves that functionality into a separate class. This also means that the new ADO.NET connection object is more lightweight than the previous ADO connection object.

The ADO Recordset was a huge object in ADO. It provided the ability to support multiple types of cursors, from a fast, lightweight "firehose" cursor, to a disconnected client-side cursor that supported change tracking, optimistic locking, and automatic batch updates of a central database. However, all of this functionality was difficult (or impossible) to customize.

ADO.NET breaks the functionality of the old ADO Recordset into multiple classes, thereby allowing a focused approach to developing code. The Data Reader is the equivalent of a "firehose" cursor. The DataSet is a disconnected data cache with tracking and control binding functionality. The DataAdapter provides the ability to completely customize how the central data store is updated with the changes to a DataSet.

Reference

See Appendix B, "ADO and ADO.NET Comparison," for more information about the reasons for the changes between ADO and ADO.NET.

The ADO.NET Object Model

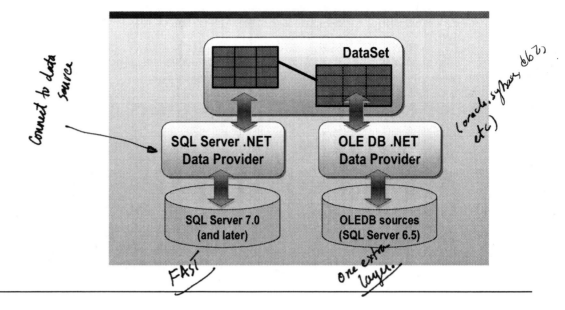

Handwritten annotations: Connect to data source → ; (oracle, sybase, db2, etc); FAST; One extra layer.

Introduction	The ADO.NET object model consists of two major parts:
	■ DataSet classes
	■ .NET data provider classes
The DataSet classes	The DataSet classes allow you to store and manage data in a disconnected cache. The DataSet is independent of any underlying data source, so its features are available to all applications, regardless of where the application's data originated.
The .NET data provider classes	The .NET data provider classes are specific to a data source. Therefore, the .NET data providers must be written specifically for a data source, and will work only with that data source. The .NET data provider classes provide the ability to connect to a data source, retrieve data from the data source, and perform updates on the data source. The ADO.NET object model includes the following data provider classes:
	■ SQL Server .NET Data Provider
	■ OLE DB .NET Data Provider
	■ Other .NET data providers

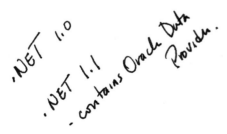

Handwritten annotations: .NET 1.0; .NET 1.1 - contains Oracle Data Provider.

Using ADO.NET Classes in a Connected Scenario

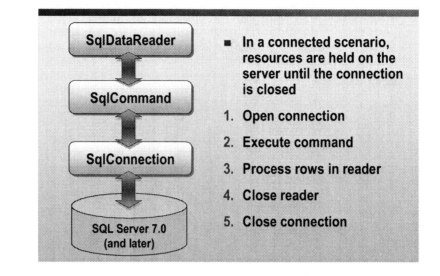

- In a connected scenario, resources are held on the server until the connection is closed

1. Open connection

2. Execute command

3. Process rows in reader

4. Close reader

5. Close connection

Introduction

The .NET data providers provide the ADO.NET classes that you will use in a connected scenario. The .NET data providers are designed to be lightweight. That is, they create a minimal layer between your code and the data source, to increase performance without sacrificing functionality.

Definition

The .NET Framework includes the following two data providers.

Data provider	Description
SQL Server .NET	Provides optimized access to SQL Server 2000 and SQL Server 7.0 databases.
OLE DB .NET	Provides access to SQL Server versions 6.5 and earlier. Also provides access to other databases, such as Oracle, Sybase, DB2/400, and Microsoft Access.

SQL Server .NET Data Provider

To use the SQL Server .NET Data Provider, you need to include the System.Data.SqlClient namespace in your applications. Using this provider is more efficient than using the OLE DB .NET Data Provider because it does not pass through an OLE DB or Open Database Connectivity (ODBC) layer.

OLE DB .NET Data Provider

To use the OLE DB .NET Data Provider, you need to include the System.Data.OleDb namespace in your applications.

Data provider classes

ADO.NET exposes a common object model for .NET data providers. In the SQL Server .NET Data Provider, the class names begin with the prefix **Sql**. For example, the connection class is named **SqlConnection**.

In the OLE DB .NET Data Provider, the class names begin with the prefix **OleDb**. For example, the connection class is named **OleDbConnection**.

In the future, more .NET data providers will be written with other prefixes. In the following table, these different prefixes are indicated with Xxx.

The following table describes the core classes that make up a .NET data provider, which are used in a connected scenario.

Class	Description
XxxConnection	Establishes a connection to a specific data source. For example, the **SqlConnection** class connects to SQL Server data sources.
XxxCommand	Executes a command from a data source. For example, the **SqlCommand** class can execute stored procedures or SQL statements in a SQL Server data source.
XxxDataReader	Reads a forward-only, read-only stream of data from a data source. For example, the **SqlDataReader** class can read rows from tables in a SQL Server data source. It is returned by the **ExecuteReader** method of the **XxxCommand** class, typically as a result of a SELECT SQL statement.

Example

The **XxxDataReader** class provides forward-only, read-only access to data in a data source. For example, to use a **SqlDataReader** to read data from a SQL Server database, you would perform the following steps:

1. Declare a **SqlConnection** object to connect to the SQL Server database.

2. Declare a **SqlCommand** object containing a SQL SELECT statement to query the database.

3. Declare a **SqlDataReader** object.

4. Open the **SqlConnection**.

5. Execute the **SqlCommand** object by using the **ExecuteReader** method, and assign the results to the **SqlDataReader** object.

6. Use the **Read** method of the **SqlDataReader** object to iterate forward through the data, and process the rows.

7. Close the **SqlDataReader**.

8. Close the **SqlConnection**.

Using ADO.NET Classes in a Disconnected Scenario

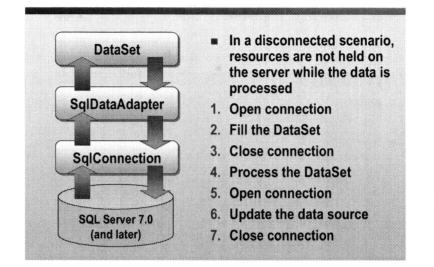

- In a disconnected scenario, resources are not held on the server while the data is processed
1. Open connection
2. Fill the DataSet
3. Close connection
4. Process the DataSet
5. Open connection
6. Update the data source
7. Close connection

Introduction

The ADO.NET classes that you will use in a disconnected scenario are provided by the .NET data providers and the System.Data namespace.

Data provider classes

ADO.NET exposes a common object model for .NET data providers. The following table describes the core classes that make up a .NET data provider, which are used in a disconnected scenario.

Class	Description
XxxDataAdapter	Uses the **Connection**, **Command**, and **DataReader** classes implicitly to populate a DataSet and to update the central data source with any changes made to the DataSet. For example, the **SqlDataAdapter** class can manage the interaction between a DataSet and a SQL Server 7 database.
XxxConnection	Establishes a connection to a specific data source. For example, the **SqlConnection** class connects to SQL Server data sources.
XxxCommand	Executes a command from a data source. For example, the **SqlCommand** class can execute stored procedures or SQL statements in a SQL Server data source.
XxxDataReader	Reads a forward-only, read-only stream of data from a data source. For example, the **SqlDataReader** class can read rows from tables in a SQL Server data source. It is returned by the **ExecuteReader** method of the **XxxCommand** class, typically as a result of a SELECT SQL statement.

Sequence of events

The following list describes the sequence you follow when working in a disconnected environment:

1. Open a connection.

2. Fill the DataSet by using the **Fill** method of a DataAdapter.

3. Close the connection.

4. Process the DataSet. You can sort, filter, summarize, or display the data in Web or Windows controls. The DataSet automatically tracks any changes to the data.

5. Open a connection. You can reuse the same connection that you used previously.

6. Update the data source with the changes in the DataSet by using the **Update** method of a DataAdapter.

7. Close the connection.

Lesson: ADO.NET and XML

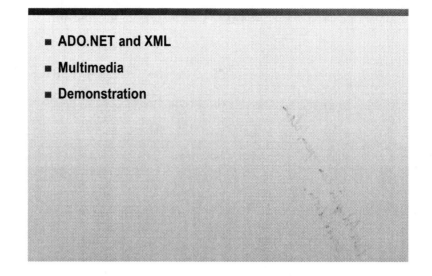

- ADO.NET and XML
- Multimedia
- Demonstration

Introduction

This lesson introduces the ADO.NET functions that relate to XML and XML Web services.

Lesson objectives

After completing this lesson, you will be able to:

- Explain how to use ADO.NET with XML.
- Describe how a simple XML Web service works with ADO.NET.

ADO.NET and XML

- ADO.NET is tightly integrated with XML
- Using XML in a disconnected ADO.NET application

Introduction

ADO.NET is tightly integrated with XML. The ADO.NET object model has been designed with XML at its core, rather than as an added extra, as in ADO 2.x. ADO.NET makes it easy for you to convert relational data into XML format. You can also convert data from XML into a collection of tables and relations.

Importance

XML is a rich and portable way of representing data in an open and platform-independent way. An important characteristic of XML data is that it is text-based. This makes it easier to pass XML data between applications and services, rather than passing binary data such as ADO Recordsets.

Scenario

You need to write an application that processes XML data. The XML data may come from an external business through an XML Web service, e-mail, Microsoft BizTalk™ Server, or many other sources.

Definition

The ADO.NET object model includes extensive support for XML. Consider the following facts and guidelines when using the XML support in ADO.NET:

- You can read data from a DataSet in XML format. This is useful if you want to pass data between applications or services in a distributed environment.

- You can fill a DataSet with XML data. This is useful if you receive XML data from another application or service, and want to update a database by using this data.

- You can create an XML Schema for the XML representation of the data in a DataSet. You can use the XML Schema to perform tasks such as serializing the XML data to a stream or file.

- You can load XML data into a Document Object Model (DOM) tree, from a stream or file. You can then manipulate the data as XML or as a DataSet. To do this, you must have an XML Schema to describe the structure of the data to the DataSet.

- You can create typed DataSets. A typed DataSet is a subclass of DataSet, with added properties and methods to expose the structure of the DataSet. Visual Studio generates an equivalent XML Schema definition for the typed DataSet, to describe the XML representation of the DataSet.

Example of using XML in a disconnected ADO.NET application

This example describes how to use XML in a disconnected ADO.NET application. You can use XML to pass data between the different parts of the system as follows:

1. The client application invokes an XML Web service, to request data from a database.
2. The XML Web service queries a data source, to obtain the requested data.
3. The XML Web service loads the results into a DataSet.
4. The XML Web service translates the data into XML format, and returns the XML data to the client application.
5. The client application processes the XML data in some way. For example, the client can load the XML data into a DataSet, and bind it to user-interface controls such as a DataGrid. When the client application is ready, it invokes an XML Web service to update the data source with the data changes.
6. The XML Web service loads the new XML data into a DataSet, and uses the new data to update the data source.

Reference

Module 5, "Using XML with ADO.NET," includes more details about the integration between ADO.NET and XML.

If you are interested in XML, you may also find the following Microsoft Official Curriculum courses beneficial:

- Course 1905B, *Building XML-Based Web Applications.*
- Course 1913A, *Exchanging and Transforming Data Using XML and XSLT.*
- Course 2091A, *Building XML-Enabled Applications using Microsoft® SQL Server™ 2000.*
- Course 2500A, *Introduction to XML and the Microsoft .NET Platform.*

Multimedia: ADO.NET and XML

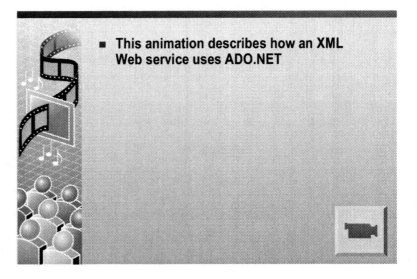

■ This animation describes how an XML
Web service uses ADO.NET

Introduction

This animation describes how a developer can use ADO.NET to create a
distributed solution to a business problem by building DataSets. The Visual
Studio .NET solution includes two projects. The first is an XML Web service,
and the second is a Windows application that uses the Web service.

Demonstration: ADO.NET and XML

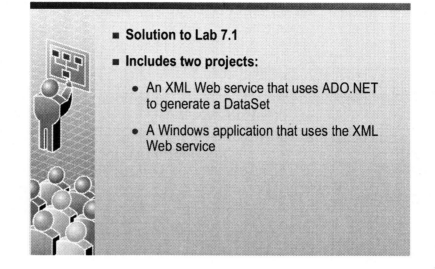

- Solution to Lab 7.1
- Includes two projects:
  - An XML Web service that uses ADO.NET to generate a DataSet
  - A Windows application that uses the XML Web service

Introduction

This demonstration shows how a developer can use ADO.NET to create a distributed solution to a business problem. The Visual Studio .NET solution includes two projects. The first is an XML Web service, and the second is a Windows application that uses the Web service.

Demonstration

▶ **To set up the XML Web service virtual directory**

1. Start the **Internet Services Manager**. It is one of the **Administrative Tools** installed with Windows 2000 Server.

2. Expand the **Default Web Site**.

3. Right-click the \2389\Labs\Lab07\Solution\VB\OnTheRoadWS\ virtual directory and choose **Properties**.

Note   If the 2389 virtual directory does not exist, run the **cvd2389.vbs** file in the <install_folder>\Labs\ folder.

---

4. Click **Create** to make the virtual directory into an application.

5. Click the **Directory Security** tab.

6. In the **Anonymous access and authentication control** section, click **Edit**.

7. Unselect the **Anonymous access** check box. Click **OK**.

8. Click **OK**.

9. Right-click the **OnTheRoadWS** virtual directory again, click **All Tasks**, and then click **Configure Server Extensions**.

Note   When creating an XML Web service by using the Visual Studio .NET development environment, these steps are completed automatically. When deploying an XML Web service to a production Web server, you need to manually configure the Web service, although automation using scripting is possible.

---

10. In the wizard, click **Next** until you see the final step, and then click **Finish**. This will use the default options for configuring the server extensions.

▶ **To set up the stored procedures**

1. Start the Microsoft SQL Server Query Analyzer.

2. Open the script named **lab6setup.sql** in the folder

    <install path>\2389\Labs\Lab06_1\

3. Run the script.

4. *On the Instructor machine only*: Open the script named **setuplab7.sql** in the following folder: <install path>\2389\Labs\Lab07\

5. *On the Instructor machine only*: Run the script.

6. Close the SQL Server Query Analyzer.

▶ **To open, rebuild, and test the XML Web service**

1. Start the Microsoft Visual Studio .NET development environment.

2. Open the existing solution named **OnTheRoad**, located at <install path>\2389\Labs\Lab07\Solution\VB\OnTheRoad\

3. View the **Solution Explorer** and browse the two projects. Notice that the XML Web service project is named **OnTheRoadWS**. The Windows Application project is named **OnTheRoad**.

4. Open the file **NWDataSet.xsd**. This file defines the schema used by the DataSet in this solution.

5. Open the file **SalesManager.asmx**. Right-click and select **Line Up Icons** if all of the data controls are not visible.

6. If the Instructor computer is not named London, select the **cnNorthwindInstructor** connection object and change the **data source** parameter to the name of the Instructor computer. For example, to use the local SQL Server, type **(local)**.

7. Right-click and select **View Code**. Notice that the class has two WebMethods named **GetDataSet** and **UpdateDatabase**.

8. To rebuild the XML Web service project, on the **Build** menu, click **Rebuild OnTheRoadWS**.

9. In the **Solution Explorer**, right-click the file **SalesManager.asmx** and click **Set As Start Page**.

10. In the **Solution Explorer**, right-click the project **OnTheRoadWS** and click **Set as StartUp Project**.

11. On the **Debug** menu, click **Start**.

Note The **SalesManager** Web service should now appear in Internet Explorer. You will see a Web page that describes the Web service and lists the two available methods. To manually test, run Internet Explorer and navigate to http://localhost/2389/Labs/Lab07/Solution/VB/OnTheRoadWS/SalesManager.asmx.

---

12. Click the **GetDataSet** link.

13. Enter **2** for the **iEmployeeID** value and **(local)** for the **sServerName** value.

14. Click the **Invoke** button.

15. The XML Web service should return an XML document containing all orders taken by that employee (Andrew Fuller).

16. Close the Internet Explorer windows.

► **To rebuild and test the Windows application**

1. In the Windows Application project named **OnTheRoad**, expand the **Web References** folder.

2. In the **Solution Explorer**, right-click **localhost** and choose Delete. Click Yes to confirm.

3. In the **Solution Explorer**, right-click the **Web References** folder and choose **Add Web Reference**.

4. Enter the URL for the XML Web service, http://localhost/2389/Labs/Lab07/Solution/VB/OnTheRoadWS/SalesManager.asmx, then click **Add Reference**. Notice that a copy of the Web service XSD file has been added to the project, and that WSDL and other files have been created.

5. In the **Solution Explorer**, right-click the project **OnTheRoad** and click **Set as StartUp Project**.

6. Open the **MainForm** class and notice the **mnuFill_Click** procedure that declares and calls the Web service.

7. To rebuild the solution, on the **Build** menu, click **Rebuild Solution**.

8. Close the Visual Studio .NET development environment.

26   Module 1: Data-Centric Applications and ADO.NET

▶ **To test the application settings**

1. Open Windows Explorer and navigate to the following folder:

   <install path>\2389\Labs\Lab07\Solution\VB\OnTheRoad\bin\

   You should see two files named **OnTheRoad.exe** (the application executable file) and **OnTheRoad.pdb** (the program debug database). If there is a file named **OnTheRoad.xml**, delete it. (This is where the data set is saved while you are working on the road.)

2. Double-click the executable file **OnTheRoad.exe** to run it.

   You will see a warning message stating that a DataSet was not found, and offering to connect to the central database to create one. Click **No**.

3. On the **Tools** menu, click **Options**. Notice that you can change the server name for the central database, and that it is currently set to **(local)**. Click **Cancel**. You do not want to change this option yet.

4. Close the application.

5. In Windows Explorer, notice that a file was created named **OnTheRoad.xml**. Double-click the file to open it in Microsoft Internet Explorer.

6. In Internet Explorer, review the contents of the file **OnTheRoad.xml**. Notice that it contains the ID of the currently selected employee (defaults to zero) and the server name for the central database.

7. Close Internet Explorer.

8. Double-click the executable file **OnTheRoad.exe** to run it again.

9. When you see the warning message, click **No**, because you are still not ready to connect to the central database.

10. On the **Tools** menu, click **Options**, and change the server name to the name of your computer. Click **OK**, to close the **Options** dialog box.

11. Close the application.

12. Double-click the file **OnTheRoad.xml** to open it in Internet Explorer again, and note that the server name has changed.

▶ **To test the local DataSet caching**

1. Rerun the executable file, and when you see the warning message, click **Yes**. This will connect you to the central database, and download a list of employees from the database.

2. In the **Get from central database** dialog box, choose **Dodsworth, Anne** for the employee name, and then click **OK**. You will see all of the customers (and their orders and order details) that are managed by this employee.

3. Close the application. This will automatically save the DataSet into the same XML file that stored the application settings.

4. In Internet Explorer, reopen the file **OnTheRoad.xml**.

5. On the **Edit** menu, click **Find (on This Page)** to search for the XML elements that begin with: <Products, <Employees, <Customers, <Orders, <OrderDetails, and <AppSettings. Review the contents.

6. Run the executable file again. Notice that you are no longer shown the warning message because the XML file contains a complete and valid DataSet.

7. In the data grid, expand the customer that has the company name **Around The Horn**. Notice that it currently has two orders. Change the order date of the first order to today's date.

8. Expand the first order and add a third order detail row, for a product ID **1**, with a unit price of **25** and a quantity of **4**. Click the first or second row to make sure that the change is made to the DataSet.

9. Click the **Update to central database** menu item. In the central database, one row will be added to the OrderDetails table, and one row in the Orders table will be modified.

10. Use the **Server Explorer** to verify that the changes were successfully made.

▶ **To remove the stored procedures used by the solution**

1. Start the Microsoft SQL Server Query Analyzer.

2. Open the script named **lab6reset.sql** in the folder

   <install path>\2389\Labs\Lab06_1\

3. Run the script.

4. Close the Microsoft SQL Server Query Analyzer.

Review

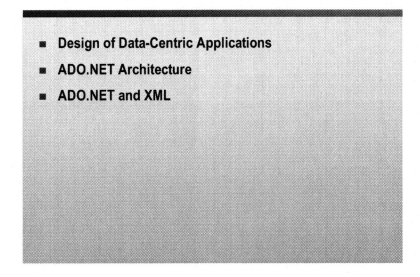

1. What are the characteristics of a connected architecture? Describe some scenarios where a connected architecture is appropriate.

2. What are the characteristics of a disconnected architecture? Describe a scenario where a disconnected architecture is appropriate.

3. What are the features and advantages of the XML Web service architecture?

4. How does ADO.NET increase the interoperability and scalability of disconnected systems?

5. What is a DataSet, and why is it important in ADO.NET?

6. Which .NET data providers are included in the .NET Framework?

Lab 1.1: Data-Centric Applications and ADO.NET

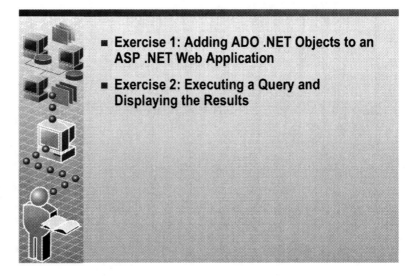

- **Exercise 1: Adding ADO .NET Objects to an ASP .NET Web Application**
- **Exercise 2: Executing a Query and Displaying the Results**

Objectives

After completing this lab, you will be able to:

- Identify the architecture of data-centric applications and storage options.
- Decide when to use different classes in the ADO.NET object model.
- Identify and use the System.Data namespaces and assemblies.
- Choose a connected or disconnected environment, based on application requirements.
- Propose an ADO.NET application architecture for typical business scenarios.

Prerequisites

Before working on this lab, you must have:

- The solution project files for this lab.
- The Northwind database installed.

Scenario

Northwind Traders needs to provide its customers and suppliers with an up-to-date product list. The company decides to develop a Web application to make this information available to as many users as possible.

The product data is held in a SQL Server 2000 database. The Web application will use the SQL Server .NET Data Provider because it provides optimized access to SQL Server 2000.

The Web application will use a connected ADO.NET architecture to retrieve the data, even though when the Web page is returned to the user, the application can be thought of as disconnected. Each time a user requests product data, the application performs the following tasks:

1. Open a connection to the database by using a **SqlConnection** object.

2. Query the database by using a **SqlCommand** object.

3. Create a **SqlDataReader** object, to read the results as efficiently as possible. The **SqlDataReader** object provides forward-only, read-only access to the data, and is the fastest way to process data in ADO.NET. Speed is an important design issue in Web applications, where demand can peak sharply.

4. Bind a DataGrid to the **SqlDataReader** object. This will cause the **SqlDataReader** object to loop through the data and populate the DataGrid with that data.

5. Close the **SqlDataReader** object.

6. Close the **SqlConnection** object.

This design ensures that the database connection is kept open for the shortest possible time. Releasing database connections quickly is an important requirement in many applications.

Starter and solution files   You will create a new Microsoft ASP.NET Web application in the folder *<install folder>*\Labs\Lab01\Starter\.

A Microsoft Visual Basic® solution is provided in the folder *<install folder>*\Labs\Lab01\Solution\VB\.

A Microsoft Visual C#™ solution is provided in the folder *<install folder>*\Labs\Lab01\Solution\CS\.

To use the solutions, you must first make the virtual directory containing the solution files into an ASP.NET application.

1. Start the **Internet Services Manager**. It is one of the Administrative Tools installed with Windows 2000 Server.

2. Expand the **Default Web Site**.

3. Right-click the \2389\Labs\Lab01\Solution\xx\MyWebApplication\ virtual directory and then click **Properties**. Note that *xx* represents VB or CS for the Visual Basic or Visual C# solution.

4. Click **Create** to make the virtual directory into an application.

5. Click the **Directory Security** tab.

6. In the **Anonymous access and authentication control** section, click **Edit**.

7. Unselect the **Anonymous access** check box. Click **OK**.

8. Click **OK**.

9. Right-click the **MyWebApplication** virtual directory again, click **All Tasks**, and then click **Configure Server Extensions**.

Note   When creating an ASP.NET application by using the Visual Studio .NET development environment, these steps are completed automatically. When deploying an ASP.NET application to a production Web server, you need to manually configure the Web service, although automation using scripting is also possible.

---

10. In the wizard, click **Next** until you see the final step, and then click **Finish**. This will use the default options for configuring the server extensions.

Estimated time to complete this lab: 30 minutes

Exercise 1
Adding ADO.NET Objects to an ASP.NET Web Application

In this exercise, you will select specific data from tables in the Northwind database.

▶ Create an ASP.NET Web application

In this procedure, you will create a new ASP.NET Web application in Microsoft Visual Studio .NET. You will examine the data-related assemblies that are referenced by default in the project.

1. Start Microsoft Visual Studio .NET.

2. On the **File** menu, point to **New**, and then click **Project**.

3. In the **New Project** dialog box, select the following options, and then click **OK**.

Option	Selection
Project Types	Visual Basic Projects (or Visual C# Projects if you prefer)
Templates	ASP.NET Web Application
Location	http://localhost/2389/Labs/Lab01/Starter/MyWebApplication

4. If the Solution Explorer is not visible, on the **View** menu, click **Solution Explorer**.

5. In the **Solution Explorer**, expand the **References** folder. Notice that the System.Data and System.XML assemblies are already referenced in the project, in addition to other core assemblies.

▶ Add a SqlConnection object to the application

In this procedure, you will add a **SqlConnection** object to your application. You will set its connection string to the Northwind database in SQL Server 2000.

1. On the **View** menu, click **Toolbox**.

2. In the **Toolbox**, select the **Data** tab.

   What data-related controls are available in this tab?

3. Drop a **SqlConnection** object onto the design surface of **WebForm1.aspx**. This action causes a **SqlConnection** object named **SqlConnection1** to appear beneath the form.

4. Right-click **SqlConnection1**, and then select **Properties**. The Properties window normally appears docked on the right side of the development environment.

5. In the Properties window, select the **ConnectionString** property. In the drop-down list for this property, select **<New Connection...>**.

6. The Data Link Properties dialog box appears. Enter the following information in this dialog box, and then click **OK**:

Field in dialog box	Enter this information
Server name	(local)
Information to log on to server	Use Windows NT® Integrated Security
Database on the server	Northwind

7. In the Properties window, examine the new value of the **ConnectionString** property.

▶ **Add a SqlCommand object to the application**

In this procedure, you will add a **SqlCommand** object to your application. You will configure the object to execute a SQL query, by using the database connection held in the **SqlConnection1** object.

1. In the **Toolbox**, select the **Data** tab, and then drop a **SqlCommand** object onto your Web form. This action creates a new object named **SqlCommand1** in your application.

2. In the Properties window, set the following properties for the **SqlCommand1** object. Set the properties in the order shown; you can use the Query Builder or type the SQL statement manually.

Property	Value
Connection	SqlConnection1
CommandText	SELECT ProductName, UnitPrice FROM Products

3. If you are prompted to regenerate the parameters collection, click **No** because there are no parameters in the command to regenerate.

▶ **Examine the code generated by the Web Form Designer**

When you add objects to your Web form, the Web Form Designer generates code to create and configure these objects in your application. In this procedure, you will examine the code that is generated for the **SqlConnection1** and **SqlCommand1** objects.

1. Right-click **WebForm1.aspx**, and then select **View Code**.

2. In the code editor, expand the gray box labeled **Web Form Designer Generated Code**.

3. Examine the code that the Web Form Designer has generated for the **SqlConnection1** and **SqlCommand1** objects. In the next few modules, you will learn in detail how this code works.

4. Verify that this code corresponds to the properties that you have set in the Properties window.

Caution   Do not modify the generated code in any way. You will lose these modifications the next time you view the form in the Web Form Designer. You must use the Web Form Designer to make any changes to this code.

Exercise 2
Executing a Query and Displaying the Results

In this exercise, you will add a button and a DataGrid to your form.

When the user clicks the button, you will query the Northwind database by using the **SqlConnection** and **SqlCommand** objects that you created in Exercise 1. You will use a **SqlDataReader** object to copy the retrieved data into the DataGrid.

▶ **Add a button and a DataGrid to the form**

1. In the Web Forms Designer, view your form.

2. In the **Toolbox**, select the **Web Forms** tab, and then drop a **Button** onto your form.

3. Set the following properties for the **Button** object.

Property	Value
(ID)	btnQuery
Text	Query

4. Drop a DataGrid object onto your form.

5. Set the following property for the DataGrid object.

Property	Value
(ID)	dgResult

▶ **Execute a query and display the results in the DataGrid**

1. In the Web Forms Designer, double-click the button. This adds a method named **btnQuery_Click**, to handle the **ButtonClick** event.

    Note All of the Visual Basic or Visual C# code in the following steps must be added to the **btnQuery_Click** method.
    ---

2. In the **btnQuery_Click** method, add the following Visual Basic or Visual C# code to open a connection to the Northwind database:

```
' Visual Basic
SqlConnection1.Open()
```

```
// Visual C#
sqlConnection1.Open();
```

3. Add the following code to query the database, and then create a **SqlDataReader** object to read the results:

```
' Visual Basic
Dim Reader As System.Data.SqlClient.SqlDataReader
Reader = SqlCommand1.ExecuteReader()
```

```
// Visual C#
System.Data.SqlClient.SqlDataReader Reader;
Reader = sqlCommand1.ExecuteReader();
```

4. Add the following code to bind the DataGrid to the **SqlDataReader** object. The **SqlDataReader** object will iterate through the data, and the DataGrid will display the data on the screen.

```
' Visual Basic
dgResult.DataSource = Reader
dgResult.DataBind()
```

```
// Visual C#
dgResult.DataSource = Reader;
dgResult.DataBind();
```

5. Add the following code to close the **SqlDataReader** and **SqlConnection** objects:

```
' Visual Basic
Reader.Close()
SqlConnection1.Close()
```

```
// Visual C#
Reader.Close();
sqlConnection1.Close();
```

6. On the **Build** menu, click **Rebuild Solution**, and fix any errors that are found.

7. On the **Debug** menu, click **Start** or press **F5** to run the project.

8. When your Web form appears in Internet Explorer, click the **Query** button. Notice that a security exception occurs, because the database connection is being opened by the ASPNET account, which does not have permissions to do so.

Note By default, ASP.NET applications run in the context of the ASPNET user account, which has minimal permissions. When using impersonation, ASP.NET applications can optionally execute with the identity of the client on whose behalf they are operating. Impersonation uses IIS to authenticate the user. Impersonation is disabled by default.

9. Close Internet Explorer.

10. In the **Solution Explorer**, double-click the **Web.config** file.

11. After the line that sets the authentication mode (<authentication mode="Windows" />), add a line to enable impersonation.

```
<identity impersonate="true" />
```

12. On the **Debug** menu, click **Start** or press **F5** to run the project.

13. When your Web form appears in Internet Explorer, click the **Query** button. Notice that a security exception occurs, because the database connection is being opened by the IUSR_*COMPUTERNAME* account, which does not have permissions to do so.

14. Close Internet Explorer.

15. Start the **Internet Services Manager**. It is one of the Administrative Tools installed with Windows 2000 Server.

16. Expand the **Default Web Site**.

17. Right-click the \2389\Labs\Lab01\Starter\MyWebApplication\ virtual directory and then click **Properties**.

18. Click the **Directory Security** tab.

19. In the **Anonymous access and authentication control** section, click **Edit**.

20. Unselect the **Anonymous access** check box. Click **OK**.

21. Click **OK**.

22. Close the **Internet Services Manager**.

23. In Microsoft Visual Studio .NET, on the **Debug** menu, click **Start** or press **F5** to run the project.

24. When your Web form appears in Internet Explorer, click the **Query** button.

25. A DataGrid appears in the Web form, showing the values of the ProductName and UnitPrice of every product in the Northwind database.

26. Close Internet Explorer and Visual Studio .NET.

msdn training

Module 2: Connecting to Data Sources

Contents

Microsoft

Overview

- **Choosing a .NET Data Provider**
- **Defining a Connection**
- **Managing a Connection**
- **Handling Connection Exceptions**
- **Connection Pooling**

Introduction	This module explains the concepts and procedures necessary to create and manage a Microsoft® ADO.NET connection to Microsoft SQL Server™ or other data sources.
Objectives	After completing this module, you will be able to:

- Choose a .NET data provider.
- Connect to SQL Server.
- Connect to OLE DB data sources.
- Manage a connection.
- Handle common connection exceptions.
- Implement and control connection pooling.

Lesson: Choosing a .NET Data Provider

- **What Are .NET Data Providers?**
- **The .NET Data Provider Classes**
- **Which .NET Data Provider Should You Use?**

Introduction

When connecting to a data source, you must first choose a .NET data provider. The data provider includes classes that enable you to connect to the data source, read data efficiently, modify and manipulate data, and update the data source.

This lesson explains the various types of data providers, and enables you to choose the appropriate provider for your application.

Lesson objectives

After completing this lesson, you will be able to:

- Describe the different .NET data providers.
- Choose a .NET data provider.

What Are .NET Data Providers?

■ **Definition**

  ● A .NET data provider is a set of classes that you use to connect to a data source, and retrieve and update data

■ **Types of .NET data providers**

  ● SQL Server .NET Data Provider

  ● OLE DB .NET Data Provider

  ● ODBC .NET Data Provider

  ● Others

Definition

The .NET data providers are a core component within the ADO.NET architecture that enables communication between a data source and a component, an XML Web service, or an application. A data provider allows you to connect to a data source, retrieve and manipulate data, and update the data source.

Types of .NET data providers

The following .NET data providers are included with the release of the Microsoft .NET Framework:

■ SQL Server .NET Data Provider

■ OLE DB .NET Data Provider

Other .NET data providers will be made available for other data sources. Microsoft will make the following provider available as a World Wide Web release download:

● Open Database Connectivity (ODBC) .NET Data Provider

Each of these data providers includes implementations of the generic ADO.NET classes so that you can programmatically communicate with different data sources in a similar way.

The .NET Data Provider Classes

- **XxxConnection – for example, SqlConnection**
  - XxxTransaction – for example, SqlTransaction
  - XxxException – for example, SqlException
  - XxxError – for example, SqlError
- **XxxCommand – for example, SqlCommand**
  - XxxParameter – for example, SqlParameter
- **XxxDataReader – for example, SqlDataReader**
- **XxxDataAdapter – for example, SqlDataAdapter**
- **XxxPermission – for example, SqlClientPermission**

Introduction

ADO.NET uses the .NET data providers to connect to a data source, retrieve data, manipulate data, and update the data source. The .NET data providers are designed to be lightweight. That is, they create a minimal layer between your code and the data source, to increase performance without sacrificing functionality.

Definition

The .NET Framework includes the following two data providers.

Data provider	Description
SQL Server .NET	Provides optimized access to SQL Server 2000 and SQL Server 7.0 databases.
OLE DB .NET	Provides access to SQL Server versions 6.5 and earlier. Also provides access to other databases, such as Oracle, Sybase, DB2/400, and Microsoft Access.

In addition, Microsoft will provide an ODBC .NET Data Provider for access to other data sources. This data provider will be available as a publicly accessible Web release download.

SQL Server .NET Data Provider

To use the SQL Server .NET Data Provider, you need to include the System.Data.SqlClient namespace in your applications. This provider is more efficient than using the OLE DB .NET Data Provider because it does not pass through an OLE DB or ODBC layer.

OLE DB .NET Data Provider

To use the OLE DB .NET Data Provider, you need to include the System.Data.OleDb namespace in your applications.

Data provider classes

ADO.NET exposes a common object model for .NET data providers. The following table describes the four core classes that make up a .NET data provider.

In the SQL Server .NET Data Provider, the class names begin with the prefix **Sql**. For example, the connection class is called **SqlConnection**.

In the OLE DB .NET Data Provider, the class names begin with the prefix **OleDb**. For example, the connection class is called **OleDbConnection**.

In the future, more .NET data providers will be written with other prefixes. In the following table, these different prefixes are indicated with Xxx.

Class	Description
XxxConnection	Establishes a connection to a specific data source. For example, the **SqlConnection** class connects to SQL Server data sources.
XxxCommand	Executes a command from a data source. For example, the **SqlCommand** class can execute stored procedures and SQL statements in a SQL Server data source.
XxxDataReader	Reads a forward-only, read-only stream of data from a data source. For example, the **SqlDataReader** class can read rows from tables in a SQL Server data source. It is returned by the **ExecuteReader** method of the **XxxCommand** class, typically as a result of a SELECT SQL statement.
XxxDataAdapter	Uses **XxxCommand** objects to populate a DataSet, and resolves updates with the data source. For example, the **SqlDataAdapter** class can manage the interaction between a DataSet and the underlying data in a SQL Server data source.

Which .NET Data Provider Should You Use?

- **SQL Server .NET Data Provider**
  - SQL Server version 7.0 or later
- **OLE DB .NET Data Provider**
  - SQL Server 6.5, Microsoft Access, Oracle, other data sources with OLE DB providers
- **ODBC .NET Data Provider**
  - Legacy data sources that only have ODBC drivers
- **Guidelines for choosing a .NET data provider**

Introduction

Choosing the appropriate .NET data provider for your application depends on the type of data source that is being accessed.

How to reference a .NET data provider

You use the Microsoft Visual Studio .NET Solution Explorer to manage references to assemblies that implement .NET data providers.

The System.Data.dll assembly (physically a single DLL file) implements the SQL Server .NET Data Provider and the OLE DB .NET Data Provider in the System.Data.SqlClient and System.Data.OleDb namespaces.

The System.Data.Odbc.dll assembly implements the ODBC .NET Data Provider. This assembly is not part of the Visual Studio .NET installation. To download the assembly from the Microsoft Web site, go to http://msdn.microsoft.com/downloads/, click **.NET Framework**, and then click **ODBC .NET Data Provider**. You can then manually reference the assembly in your project to use the ODBC .NET Data Provider.

SQL Server .NET Data Provider

The SQL Server .NET Data Provider establishes a thin layer of communication between an application and SQL Server. Because the SQL Server .NET Data Provider uses its own protocol, Tabular Data Stream (TDS), to communicate with SQL Server, it is lightweight and accesses SQL Server directly without any additional layers. This results in improved performance and scalability.

It is also recommended that you use the SQL Server .NET Data Provider for single-tier applications that use the Microsoft Data Engine (MSDE), because MSDE is based on the SQL Server engine.

OLE DB .NET Data Provider

The OLE DB .NET Data Provider uses native OLE DB and COM interoperability to connect to and communicate with a data source. Therefore, you must use an OLE DB provider to use the OLE DB .NET Data Provider.

To use the OLE DB .NET Data Provider, you must indicate the provider type in the connection string. The **Provider** keyword in a connection string indicates the type of OLE DB data source that you will connect to; for example, "Provider=MSDAORA" to connect to an Oracle database. You do not need to include a **Provider** keyword in a connection string when using the SQL Server .NET Data Provider because the data source is assumed to be Microsoft SQL Server version 7.0 or later.

Data source	Example connection string parameters
SQL Server 6.5	Provider=SQLOLEDB;Data Source=London;Initial Catalog=pubs;User ID=sa;Password=2389;
Oracle Server	Provider=MSDAORA;Data Source=ORACLE8I7;User ID=OLEDB;Password=OLEDB;
Microsoft Access database	Provider=Microsoft.Jet.OLEDB.4.0;Data Source=c:\bin\LocalAccess40.mdb;

Warning!

The OLE DB .NET Data Provider does not work with the OLE DB provider for ODBC, Microsoft OLE DB Provider for ODBC Data (MSDASQL). To access data sources by using ODBC, use the ODBC .NET Data Provider.

ODBC .NET Data Provider

The ODBC .NET Data Provider uses native ODBC application programming interface (API) calls to connect to and communicate with a data source.

The ODBC .NET Data Provider has been implemented as a separate assembly called System.Data.Odbc.dll. It is not selected by default in project templates, and must be manually referenced.

Data source	Provider/driver	Example connection string parameters
Oracle Server	ORA ODBC	Driver={Microsoft ODBC for Oracle}; Server=ORACLE8I7; UID=OLEDB; PWD=OLEDB;
Microsoft Access database	Jet ODBC	Driver={Microsoft Access Driver (*.mdb)}; DBQ=c:\bin\localaccess40.mdb;

Guidelines for choosing a .NET data provider

The following table lists general guidelines for choosing a .NET data provider.

If your data source is	Then choose
SQL Server 7.0 or SQL Server 2000	SQL Server .NET Data Provider
SQL Server version 6.5 or earlier	OLE DB .NET Data Provider
Any heterogeneous data source that can be accessed by using an OLE DB provider	OLE DB .NET Data Provider
Any heterogeneous data source that can be accessed by using an ODBC driver	ODBC .NET Data Provider

Lesson: Defining a Connection

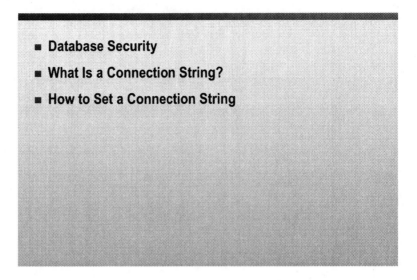

- Database Security
- What Is a Connection String?
- How to Set a Connection String

Introduction

A *connection string* is an essential part of connecting to a data source. The **ConnectionString** property of a connection object provides information for that connection object. This lesson describes what a connection string is and how to use one.

Lesson objectives

After completing this lesson, you will be able to:

- Set SQL Server database security options in a connection.
- Set a connection string property.

Database Security

> ## Using SQL Server security
>
> - ■ **Windows Authentication**
>   - ● Secure validation and encryption
>   - ● Auditing
>   - ● Password expiration and minimum length
>   - ● Account lockout
> - ■ **Mixed Mode (Windows Authentication and SQL Server authentication)**
>   - ● Primarily for backward compatibility

Introduction

When you build an application that accesses data by using ADO.NET, you will normally have to connect to secure databases. To do so, security information such as user name and password must be passed to the database before a connection can be made. The database security that is available depends on the database that is accessed.

Using SQL Server security

SQL Server can operate in one of two authentication modes: Microsoft Windows® Authentication and Mixed Mode (Windows Authentication and SQL Server authentication).

Using Windows Authentication

Windows Authentication allows a user to connect through a Windows user account. Network security attributes for the user are established at network login time, and are validated by a Windows domain controller.

When a network user tries to connect, SQL Server verifies that the user is who they say they are, and then permits or denies login access based on that network user name alone, without requiring a separate login name and password.

Benefits of using Windows Authentication

Windows Authentication provides:

- ■ Secure validation and encryption of passwords.
- ■ Auditing.
- ■ Password expiration.
- ■ Minimum password length.
- ■ Account lockout after multiple invalid login requests.

Warning!

Because Windows users and groups are maintained only by Windows, SQL Server reads information about a user's group membership when the user connects. If changes are made to the accessibility rights of a connected user, the changes become effective the next time the user connects to an instance of SQL Server or logs on to Windows (depending on the type of change).

Using Mixed Mode Authentication

Mixed Mode Authentication allows users to connect to an instance of SQL Server by using either Windows Authentication or SQL Server authentication. Users who connect through a Microsoft Windows NT® 4.0 or Windows 2000 user account can use trusted connections in either Windows Authentication mode or Mixed Mode Authentication.

When a user connects by using a specified login name and password from a non-trusted connection, SQL Server performs the authentication itself by checking to see if a SQL Server login account has been set up, and if the specified password matches the one that was previously recorded. If SQL Server does not have a login account set, authentication fails and the user receives an error message.

Warning! (SQL Server 7.0 only)

If a user attempts to connect to an instance of SQL Server 7.0 (not SQL Server 2000) by providing a blank login name, SQL Server 7.0 uses Windows Authentication. Additionally, if a user attempts to connect to an instance of SQL Server 7.0 configured for Windows Authentication Mode by using a specific login, the login is ignored and Windows Authentication is used.

Mixed Mode is primarily for backward compatibility

SQL Server authentication is provided primarily for backward compatibility because applications written for SQL Server version 7.0 or earlier might require the use of SQL Server logins and passwords. Additionally, SQL Server authentication is required when an instance of SQL Server is running on Microsoft Windows 98, because Windows Authentication Mode is not supported on Windows 98. Therefore, SQL Server uses Mixed Mode when running on Windows 98 (but supports only SQL Server authentication).

What Is a Connection String?

■ **A connection string defines the parameters required to make a connection to a data source**

■ **Connection string parameters**

- Provider (OLE DB only)

- Data Source

- Initial Catalog

- Integrated Security

- User ID/Password

- Persist Security Info

Introduction

To move data between a data store and your application, you must first have a connection to the data store.

Definition

The **ConnectionString** property provides the information that defines a connection to a data store by using a string of parameters.

Syntax

The following table describes several common parameters of connection strings. The table contains only a partial list of the values; not all of these are needed to establish a connection.

Parameter	Description
Provider	The property used to set or return the name of the provider for the connection, used only for **OleDbConnection** objects.
Connection Timeout or Connect Timeout	The length of time in seconds to wait for a connection to the server before terminating the attempt and generating an exception. **15** is the default.
Initial Catalog	The name of the database.
Data Source	The name of the SQL Server to be used when a connection is open, or the filename of a Microsoft Access database.
Password	The login password for the SQL Server account.
User ID	The SQL Server login account.
Integrated Security or Trusted Connection	The parameter that determines whether or not the connection is to be a secure connection. **True**, **False**, and **SSPI** are the possible values. (**SSPI** is the equivalent of **True**.)
Persist Security Info	When set to **False**, security-sensitive information, such as the password, is not returned as part of the connection if the connection is open or has ever been in an open state. Setting this property to **True** can be a security risk. **False** is the default.

How to Set a Connection String

- **You can set the ConnectionString property only when the connection is closed**

- **To reset a connection string, you must close and reopen the connection**

- **Microsoft Access connection**

```
Dim cnNorthwind As New _
    System.Data.OleDb.OleDbConnection()
cnNorthwind.ConnectionString = _
    "Provider=Microsoft.Jet.OLEDB.4.0;" & _
    "Data Source=\Samples\Northwind.mdb;"
```

- **Practice**

Visual Basic Example   C# Example

Introduction

You can create and manage a connection by using one of the connection objects that ADO.NET makes available, including the **SqlConnection** object and the **OleDbConnection** object.

Note

You can set the **ConnectionString** property only when the connection is closed. To reset a connection string, you must close and reopen the connection.

Examples

The following examples show connection strings that contain commonly used parameters. Note that not all connection strings contain the same parameters.

The following is an example of connecting to a SQL Server 2000 database by using a **SqlConnection** object and Microsoft Visual Basic®.

Product	Microsoft SQL Server 2000
Server name	London
Database name	Northwind
Security	Mixed mode
Username	sa
Password	2389
Timeout	1 minute

```
Dim cnNorthwind as New _
    System.Data.SqlClient.SqlConnection()

cnNorthwind.ConnectionString = _
    "User ID=sa;" & _
    "Password=2389;" & _
    "Initial Catalog=Northwind;" & _
    "Data Source=London;" & _
    "Connection TimeOut=60;"
```

The following is an example of connecting to a Microsoft Access database by using an **OleDbConnection** and Visual Basic.

Product	Microsoft Access 2000
Database location	\Samples\Northwind.mdb

```
Dim cnNorthwind as New _
    System.Data.OleDb.OleDbConnection()

cnNorthwind.ConnectionString = _
    "Provider=Microsoft.Jet.OLEDB.4.0;" & _
    "Data Source=\Samples\Northwind.mdb;"
```

The following is an example of connecting to a SQL Server 6.5 database by using an **OleDbConnection** object and Microsoft Visual C#™.

Product	Microsoft SQL Server 6.5
Server name	ProdServ01
Database name	Pubs
Security	Windows authentication

```
System.Data.OleDb.OleDbConnection cnNorthwind = new
    System.Data.OleDb.OleDbConnection();

cnNorthwind.ConnectionString =
    "Provider=SQLOLEDB;" +
    "Data Source=ProdServ01;" +
    "Initial Catalog=Pubs;" +
    "Integrated Security=SSPI;";
```
Security support
provider interface.

Demonstration

The easiest method of setting a connection string is to use the Visual Studio .NET development environment.

1. Start the Visual Studio .NET development environment.
2. Create a new Windows Application project by using Visual Basic.
3. Drag and drop a SqlConnection control from the Toolbox onto Form1.
4. In the Properties window, set the ConnectionString property.

Note The Properties window uses a version of the OLE DB provider connection string builder, so most developers will be familiar with this tool.

5. Open the Code Editor window and review the code that was automatically generated.

Practice

For each of the following examples, determine if the .NET data provider and connection string that follow each example are valid. If not, correct them.

Exercise 1

Product	Microsoft Access 2000
Database location	\MyDB\MyDB.mdb

```
Use OLE DB .NET Data Provider
Provider=Microsoft.Access;Initial Catalog=\MyDB\MyDB.mdb;
```
Jet

Data Source =\MyDB\MyDB.mdb.

Exercise 2

Product	Microsoft SQL Server 2000
Server name	ProdServ01
Database name	Pubs
Security	Windows authentication

Use SQL Server .NET Data Provider
Data Source=ProdServ01;Initial Catalog=Pubs;~~User
ID=JohnK;Password=JohnK~~;

windows auth.

Exercise 3

Product	Microsoft SQL Server 2000
Server name	ProdServ01
Database name	Pubs
Security	Mixed Mode
Username	JohnK
Password	JohnK

Use SQL Server .NET Data Provider
Data Source=Pubs;Initial Catalog=ProdServ01;User
ID=JohnK;Password=JohnK;

Exercise 4

Product	Microsoft SQL Server 6.5
Server name	ProdServ01
Database name	Pubs
Security	Windows authentication

Use SQL Server .NET Data Provider
Data Source=ProdServ01;Initial Catalog=Pubs;Integrated
Security=True;

Exercise 5

Product	Microsoft SQL Server 7.0
Server name	ProdServ02
Database name	Northwind
Security	Windows authentication

Use SQL Server .NET Data Provider
Data Source=ProdServ02;Initial Catalog=Northwind;Integrated
Security=SSPI;

Exercise 6

Product	Microsoft SQL Server 7.0
Server name	ProdServ02
Database Name	Pubs
Security	Windows authentication

Use SQL Server .NET Data Provider
DataSource=ProdServ02;Initial Catalog=Pubs;~~User
ID=AmyJ;Password=AmyJ~~;

Exercise 7

Product	Microsoft SQL Server 2000
Server name	ProdServ01
Database name	Pubs
Security	Windows authentication
Timeout	1 minute = 60 sec

Use SQL Server .NET Data Provider
Data Source=ProdServ01;Initial Catalog=Pubs;Integrated
Security=True;Connection Timeout=1;

Exercise 8

Product	Microsoft SQL Server 2000
Server name	ProdServ01
Database name	Pubs
Security	Windows authentication
Timeout	15 seconds

Use SQL Server .NET Data Provider
Data Source=ProdServ01;Initial Catalog=Pubs;Integrated
Security=True; Timeout default = 30sec, so specify.

Exercise 9

Product	Microsoft SQL Server 2000
Server name	ProdServ02
Database name	Pubs
Security	Mixed Mode
Username	JohnK
Password	JohnK (visible if connection string is read)

Use SQL Server .NET Data Provider
Data Source=ProdServ02;Initial Catalog=Pubs;User
ID=JohnK;Password=JohnK;

Lesson: Managing a Connection

- **Opening and Closing a Connection**
- **Handling Connection Events**

Introduction

After you have defined the **ConnectionString** property of a connection object, you use the **Open** and **Close** methods to manage the connection's current state. This lesson describes how to use these methods, and how to respond to connection events.

Lesson objectives

After completing this lesson, you will be able to:

- Open and close a connection.
- Handle connection events (such as **StateChange**, **InfoMessage**).

Opening and Closing a Connection

- **Opening and closing connections explicitly**
  - Open and Close methods
- **Opening and closing connections implicitly**
  - Data adapters can open and close connections automatically when needed
- **Using the Dispose method**
  - Removes the connection from the connection pool

Visual Basic Example

Introduction	You can open and close connections either implicitly, by calling methods on an object that uses the connection, or explicitly, by calling the **Open** and **Close** methods.

The two primary methods for connections are **Open** and **Close**.

- The Open method uses the information in the ConnectionString property to contact the data source and establish an open connection.
- The Close method shuts down the connection.

Closing connections is essential, because most data sources support only a limited number of open connections, and open connections take up valuable system resources.

Opening and closing connections explicitly	Opening and closing connections explicitly is the recommended approach, because it:

- Results in cleaner, more readable code.
- Helps you debug.
- Is more efficient.

You must always close the connection when you have finished using it. To do this, you can use either the **Close** or **Dispose** methods of the connection object. Connections are not closed implicitly when the connection object falls out of scope or is reclaimed by garbage collection.

The **Close** method rolls back any pending transaction. It then closes the connection, or releases the connection to the connection pool if pooling is enabled. An application can call the **Close** method more than one time.

Opening and closing connections implicitly

If you work with DataAdapters, you do not have to explicitly open and close a connection. When you call a method of these objects (for example, the SqlDataAdapter's **Fill** or **Update** method), the method checks whether the connection is already open. If not, the SqlDataAdapter opens the connection, performs its logic, and then closes the connection.

Best practice

If you are filling multiple tables in a DataSet from the same database, you will have multiple DataAdapters, one for each table, but only one connection. When filling, the connection will open and close multiple times if you use connections implicitly. It is better to explicitly open the connection, call the **Fill** methods of the multiple DataAdapters, and then explicitly close the connection.

Using the Dispose method

When you close a connection, the flow to and from the data source closes, but unmanaged resources used by the connection object have not been released. If connection pooling is enabled, the connection is released to the pool. Both the **SqlConnection** object and the **OleDbConnection** object have a **Dispose** method to release the unmanaged resources. Calling the **Dispose** method removes the connection from the connection pool.

Example of using the Dispose method

The following Visual Basic example shows how to create a **SqlConnection** object, open the connection with the **Open** method, and then close and release the resources used by the connection by calling the **Dispose** method and then setting the object to **Nothing**. (Use **null** in Visual C#.)

```
' Declare and instantiate a new SqlConnection object

Dim cnNorthwind As New _
    System.Data.SqlClient.SqlConnection()

' Set the ConnectionString property

cnNorthwind.ConnectionString = _
    "Data Source=(local);" & _
    "Initial Catalog=Northwind;" & _
    "Integrated Security=SSPI;"

' Open the connection

cnNorthwind.Open()

' perform some database task

' Close the connection, which releases the connection to
' the connection pool on the server

cnNorthwind.Close()

' Dispose the connection, which removes the connection from
' the connection pool on the server, saving server resources

cnNorthwind.Dispose()

' Release the memory taken by the SqlConnection object
' (the memory will not be reclaimed until the Garbage
' Collector next executes)

cnNorthwind = Nothing
```

Handling Connection Events

- **Connection events**
  - StateChange and InfoMessage
- **StateChangeEventArgs class**
  - Provides data for the state change event of a .NET data provider
  - CurrentState and OriginalState properties are read-only
- **Visual Basic code sample**

```
Private Sub cnNorthwind_StateChange( _
    ByVal sender As Object, _
    ByVal e As System.Data.StateChangeEventArgs _
    ) Handles cnNorthwind.StateChange
```

- **Practice**

Visual Basic Example   Visual C# Example

Introduction

The **StateChange** event occurs whenever the connection state changes, from closed to open or from open to closed. To handle any event, you must have an *event handler*, which is a method with a signature defined by the class that defines the event you want to handle. Different events have slightly different event handlers. The event handler for the **StateChange** event is a method that must have an argument of the type **StateChangeEventArgs**. This argument contains data related to this event.

The StateChange event

The type of .NET data provider that you use determines the specific arguments for the **StateChange** event.

- **SqlConnection.StateChange** event for a **SqlConnection** object
- **OleDbConnection.StateChange** event for an **OleDbConnection** object

Remember that all events in the .NET Framework have two parameters:

- sender (of type Object)
- e (of type XxxEventArgs)

For the **StateChange** event, e is of type **StateChangeEventArgs**.

Definition

The event handlers for the two events receive the same type of argument, **StateChangeEventArgs**, which contains data related to this event. The following table describes the properties of the **StateChangeEventArgs** class.

Property	Description
CurrentState	Gets the new state of the connection. The connection object will already be in the new state when the event is fired.
OriginalState	Gets the original state of the connection.

Example of a StateChange event handler

The following example shows code for creating a **StateChangeEventHandler** delegate by using both Visual Basic and Visual C#. Note the different ways of handling events in Visual Basic and Visual C#.

```vb
' Visual Basic

' The Handles keyword associates the procedure with the event

Private Sub cnNorthwind_StateChange( _
  ByVal sender As Object, _
  ByVal e As System.Data.StateChangeEventArgs _
  ) Handles cnNorthwind.StateChange

  ' Display current and original state
  ' in a message box whenever
  ' the connection state changes

  MessageBox.Show( _
    "CurrentState: " & e.CurrentState.ToString() & vbCrLf & _
    "OriginalState: " & e.OriginalState.ToString(), _
    "cnNorthwind.StateChange", _
    MessageBoxButtons.OK, _
    MessageBoxIcon.Information)

End Sub
```

```csharp
// Visual C#

// the following code is usually added to the constructor
// for the class so that the function is linked to the
// appropriate event

this.cnNorthwind.StateChange += new
  System.Data.StateChangeEventHandler(
  this.cnNorthwind_StateChange);


private void cnNorthwind_StateChange(
  object sender,
  System.Data.StateChangeEventArgs e)
{
  MessageBox.Show(
    "CurrentState: " + e.CurrentState.ToString() + "\n" +
    "OriginalState: " + e.OriginalState.ToString(),
    "cnNorthwind.StateChange",
    MessageBoxButtons.OK,
    MessageBoxIcon.Information);
}
```

Practice

▶ **Create a Windows Application that handles the StateChange event for a SqlConnection object by using Visual Basic**

1. Create a new Windows Application project by using Visual Basic named HandlingStateChange.

2. Add two buttons labeled **Open** and **Close** to **Form1**.

3. Name the buttons **btnOpen** and **btnClose**.

4. In the Properties window, disable the **Close** button.

5. Add a **SqlConnection** control to **Form1** named **cnNorthwind**.

6. Set the connection string for **cnNorthwind** to use the (local) SQL Server, the Northwind database, and integrated security.

7. Add code to the **Open** button to open the connection.

   ```
   cnNorthwind.Open()
   ```

8. Add code to the **Close** button to close the connection.

   ```
   cnNorthwind.Close()
   ```

9. Add code to handle the **StateChange** event for **cnNorthwind** by checking the current state, and enabling or disabling the two buttons appropriately.

   Note   The Visual Basic .NET development environment allows the object and event to be chosen from the drop-down lists at the top of the Code Editor.

   ```
   btnOpen.Enabled = (e.CurrentState = ConnectionState.Closed)
   btnClose.Enabled = (e.CurrentState = ConnectionState.Open)
   ```

10. Start the application and click the **Open** button.

    What happens? Why?

11. Click the **Close** button.

    What happens? Why?

12. Stop the application.

The solution for this practice is located in
<install folder>\Practices\Mod02\Lesson3\VB\HandlingStateChange\

▶ **Create a Windows Application that handles the StateChange event for a SqlConnection object by using Visual C#**

1. Create a new Windows Application project using Visual C# named HandlingStateChange.

2. Add two buttons labeled **Open** and **Close** to **Form1**.

3. Name the buttons **btnOpen** and **btnClose**.

4. In the **Properties** window, disable the **Close** button.

5. Add a **SqlConnection** control to **Form1** named **cnNorthwind**.

6. Set the connection string for **cnNorthwind** to use the local SQL Server, the Northwind database, and integrated security.

7. Add code to the **Open** button to open the connection.

```
cnNorthwind.Open();
```

8. Add code to the **Close** button to close the connection.

```
cnNorthwind.Close();
```

9. Add code to handle the **StateChange** event by checking the current state, and enabling or disabling the two buttons appropriately.

Note The Visual C# .NET development environment does NOT allow the object and event to be picked from the drop-down lists at the top of the Code Editor. You must handle this event manually by writing the following code.

```
// the following code must be added to the class constructor
// after the existing call to InitializeComponent

this.cnNorthwind.StateChange += new
  System.Data.StateChangeEventHandler(
  this.cnNorthwind_StateChange);

// the following code can be added anywhere in the class,
// but outside any other procedures

private void cnNorthwind_StateChange(
  object sender,
  System.Data.StateChangeEventArgs e)
{

  btnOpen.Enabled =
      (e.CurrentState == ConnectionState.Closed);

  btnClose.Enabled =
      (e.CurrentState == ConnectionState.Open);

}
```

10. Start the application and click the **Open** button.

   What happens? Why?

11. Click the **Close** button.

   What happens? Why?

12. Stop the application.

   The solution for this practice is located in
   <install folder>\Practices\Mod02\Lesson3\CS\HandlingStateChange\

Lesson: Handling Connection Exceptions

- **What Is Structured Exception Handling?**
- **How to Handle SqlExceptions**
- **How to Handle the InfoMessage Event**

Introduction

This lesson describes how to handle connection exceptions in a .NET environment. Visual Basic programmers will find that exception handling in the .NET environment is different from previous versions of Visual Basic. The familiar **On Error** style error handling is supported but not recommended for the .NET Framework.

Lesson objectives

After completing this lesson, you will be able to:

- Describe what structured exception handling is.
- Handle multiple types of exceptions.
- Handle connection exceptions.

What Is Structured Exception Handling?

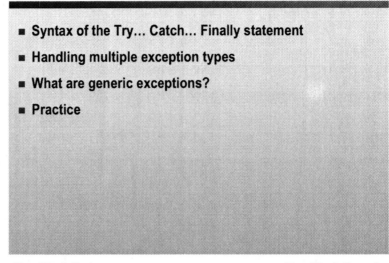

- ■ Syntax of the Try... Catch... Finally statement
- ■ Handling multiple exception types
- ■ What are generic exceptions?
- ■ Practice

Visual Basic Syntax   Visual Basic Example

Introduction

An exception is an error condition or unexpected behavior that is encountered by an executing program from the program itself or from the run-time environment.

Earlier versions of Visual Basic had only one error, with a limited amount of information about the error. Therefore, you had to check the number property on the **Err** object to determine what problem had occurred. You would typically write a **Select Case** statement to branch to different chunks of code to deal with those specific errors. Today, instead of having one error object, you have the option of handling more specific errors, now known as *exceptions*.

In the past, each language had a different method of handling errors. Today, all .NET languages use the Common Language Runtime (CLR), and must be able to interact closely with each other. This means that the languages that use the .NET Framework need to support the new, standardized style of error handling, called *structured exception handling*.

Structured exception handling provides more specific information when an error occurs. A class can define its own custom exceptions with additional information that is specific to the task the class was written to perform, such as the name of a stored procedure, a line number or an error, or a server name. You can create your own exception classes by deriving classes from the appropriate base exception.

Exception handling in ADO.NET is similar to a game of catch: code in the application throws an exception, and exception handling in your code catches it.

Definition of structured exception handling

Structured exception handling is code designed to detect and respond to errors during program execution by combining a control structure with exceptions, protected blocks of code, and filters. In the .NET Framework, the control structure is the **Try...Catch...Finally** statement. If an error occurs in the **Try** block, code in the **Catch** block handles the error.

Syntax for the Try...Catch...Finally statement

The following example shows the syntax for the **Try...Catch...Finally** statement in Visual Basic. One **Try** block can have many **Catch** blocks.

When you write an exception handler that uses a **Try...Catch...Finally** block, you can use as many **Catch** blocks as you feel are necessary. Write a **Finally** block to run the code unconditionally.

For multiple exceptions, you must start with the most specific exceptions and then proceed to the least specific, which is the **System.Exception** class, the generic exception.

```
Try
    [ tryStatements ]
[ Catch1 [ exception1 [ As type1 ] ] [ When expression1 ]
    catchStatements1
[ Exit Try ]
Catch2 [ exception2 [ As type2 ] ] [ When expression2 ]
    catchStatements2
[ Exit Try ]
...
Catchn [ exceptionn [ As typen ] ] [ When expressionn ]
    catchStatementsn ]
[ Exit Try ]
[ Finally
    [ finallyStatements ] ]
End Try
```

Visual Basic example

The following example shows how to use a **Try...Catch...Finally** statement to catch multiple types of exceptions. In this example, the code catches the **InvalidOperationException** type of exception, and any other types of exception using a generic exception handler.

```
Dim cnNorthwind As System.Data.SqlClient.SqlConnection

Try
  cnNorthwind = New System.Data.SqlClient.SqlConnection()

  cnNorthwind.ConnectionString = _
      "Data Source=(local);" & _
      "Initial Catalog=Northwind;" & _
      "Integrated Security=SSPI;"

  cnNorthwind.Open()

  ' perform some database task

Catch XcpInvOp As System.InvalidOperationException

  MessageBox.Show("You must close the connection first")

Catch Xcp As System.Exception

  MessageBox.Show(Xcp.ToString())

Finally

  cnNorthwind.Close()
  cnNorthwind.Dispose()
  cnNorthwind = Nothing

End Try
```

What are generic exceptions?

The **System.Exception** class applies to all exceptions in the .NET environment. All exceptions share the following properties:

- Message. This is a read-only property that you can use to display a description of the cause of the exception in a message box.

- InnerException. This read-only property refers to the cause of the current exception. When InnerException is a non-null value (non-Nothing value in Visual Basic), this property refers to the exception that ultimately caused the current exception.

- HelpLink. This property gets or sets a link to a Help file that you associate with the current exception. The return value is a Uniform Resource Name (URN) or Uniform Resource Locator (URL) that you associate with the Help file.

Practice

The Visual Studio .NET documentation lists the specific exceptions that can occur for a specific method call. Look up the exceptions that can occur when calling the **Open** and **ChangeDatabase** methods of the **System.Data.SqlClient.SqlConnection** class.

How to Handle SqlExceptions

- **Write the code to execute inside a Try block**
- **Write a Catch statement for each specific exception that you want to catch**
  - System.Data.SqlClient.SqlException
  - Errors collection
  - SqlError properties (Class, Number)
- **Write a generic Catch statement for all other exceptions**
- **Write a Finally statement to run the code no matter what happens**
- **End the exception handler with an End Try block**
- **Practice**

Visual Basic Example

Introduction

The **SqlException** class contains the exception that is thrown when SQL Server returns a warning or error. This class is created whenever the SQL Server .NET Data Provider encounters a situation that it cannot handle. The class always contains at least one instance of **SqlError**. You can use the severity level to help determine the content of a message that an exception displays.

The SqlException class and the Errors collection

To catch **SqlExceptions**, catch the **System.Data.SqlClient.SqlException** class. When a **SqlException** occurs, the exception object contains an **Errors** collection. You should loop through the **Errors** collection to discover details about the errors that occurred.

The SqlError class and common properties

Each **SqlError** object has the following common properties. For a complete list, see the VS.NET documentation.

Property	Description
Class	Gets the severity level of the error returned from SQL Server.
LineNumber	Gets the line number within the Transact-SQL command batch or stored procedure that contains the error.
Message	Gets the text describing the error.
Number	Gets a number that identifies the type of error.

SQL Server error numbers

The **Number** property allows you to determine the specific problem that occurred. For example, the following table lists some common SQL error numbers and their descriptions.

SQL Error Number	Description
17	Invalid server name
4060	Invalid database name
18456	Invalid user name or password

SQL Server severity levels

The following table describes severity levels, accessed through the **Class** property, of the **SqlError** class.

Severity	Description	Action
11-16	Generated by user	Can be corrected by user.
17-19	Software or hardware errors	You can continue working, but might not be able to execute a particular statement. SqlConnection remains open.
20-25	Software or hardware errors	Server closes SqlConnection. User can reopen connection.

Scenario

You want to call the **Open** method on one of your connections. Although opening a connection is one method call, multiple problems can occur when the call is made. You cannot assume that there will be only one problem. You must be able to handle multiple exceptions, and if a **SqlException** occurs, to loop through all of the SQL errors sent to your application.

Procedure

The exception handler in the following procedure handles a series of exceptions that might occur when code in an application tries to open a connection.

▶ **To handle SqlExceptions**

1. Write the code to execute inside a **Try** block.

```
Try
    Me.cnSQLNorthwind.ConnectionString = _
        "Data Source=London;" & _
        "Initial Catalog=Northwind;" & _
        "Integrated Security=SSPI;"

    Me.cnSQLNorthwind.Open()
```

2. Write a **Catch** statement for SqlExceptions.

```
Catch XcpSQL As System.Data.SqlClient.SqlException

  Dim sErrorMsg As String
  Dim se As System.Data.SqlClient.SqlError

  For Each se In XcpSQL.Errors

    Select Case se.Number
    Case 17
        sErrorMsg = "Wrong or missing server!"
    Case 4060
        sErrorMsg = "Wrong or missing database!"
    Case 18456
        sErrorMsg = _
            "Wrong or missing user name or password!"
    Case Else
        sErrorMsg = se.Message
    End Select

    MessageBox.Show(sErrorMsg, "SQL Server Error " & _
        se.Number, MessageBoxButtons.OK, _
        MessageBoxIcon.Error)

  Next
```

3. Write a handler for any other specific exceptions you want to catch.

```
Catch XcpInvOp As System.InvalidOperationException

    MessageBox.Show("Close the connection first!", _
        "Invalid Operation", _
        MessageBoxButtons.OK, MessageBoxIcon.Error)
```

4. Write a generic **Catch** statement for all other exceptions. If in a class that will be called, then throw the exception up to the calling code. Otherwise, if your code is part of the presentation tier, display a warning message to the end user.

```
Catch Xcp As System.Exception ' generic exception handler

    MessageBox.Show(Xcp.Message, "Unexpected Exception", _
        MessageBoxButtons.OK, MessageBoxIcon.Error)
```

5. Write a **Finally** block after the **Catch** blocks.

```
Finally ' run this code in every case

    ' write cleanup code here
```

6. End the **Try** block.

```
End Try
```

Practice

The solution for this practice is located in
<install folder>\Practices\Mod02\Lesson4\xx\CatchingSqlExceptions\ where xx
is either VB or CS.

In this example scenario, the Northwind Traders IT Director would like all
applications developed by his team to provide better feedback to enable the
Help Desk staff to track issues.

Add code to handle exceptions for the connection, and use a message box to
display a description and the class (severity level) of each **SqlError** contained
in the exception

1. Create a new Windows Application project named **CatchingSqlExceptions**.

2. Add two button controls from the Toolbox, labeled **Open** and **Close**, and
   name them **btnOpen** and **btnClose**.

3. Add a text box control named **txtServerName** to the form. Set the **Text**
   property to **(local)**.

4. Add a **SqlConnection** control from the Toolbox and name it **cnNorthwind**.

5. Add code to the **Open** button that tries to set the **ConnectionString**
   property of **cnNorthwind** to connect to the Northwind database on the
   computer running SQL Server specified in the text box. Use integrated
   security and a connection timeout of 5 seconds.

```
' Visual Basic
Try
  cnNorthwind.ConnectionString = _
      "Data Source=" & txtServerName.Text & ";" & _
      "Connect Timeout=5;" & _
      "Initial Catalog=Northwind;Integrated Security=SSPI;"
```

```
// Visual C#
try
{
  cnNorthwind.ConnectionString =
      "Data Source=" + txtServerName.Text + ";" +
      "Connect Timeout=5;" +
      "Initial Catalog=Northwind;Integrated Security=SSPI;";
```

6. Add code to the **Open** button that tries to open the connection.

```
' Visual Basic
  cnNorthwind.Open()
```

```
// Visual C#
  cnNorthwind.Open();
}
```

7. Add code to the **Open** button that catches the **SqlException** type of
   exception and loops through the **Errors** collection displaying a message
   containing details about the error, and the severity level of the error in the
   title bar of the message box.

```
' Visual Basic
Catch XcpSQL As System.Data.SqlClient.SqlException
    Dim se As SqlClient.SqlError
    For Each se In XcpSQL.Errors
        MessageBox.Show(se.Message, _
            "SQL Error Level " & se.Class, _
            MessageBoxButtons.OK, MessageBoxIcon.Information)
    Next
```

```
// Visual C#
catch (System.Data.SqlClient.SqlException XcpSQL)
{
    foreach (System.Data.SqlClient.SqlError se in
XcpSQL.Errors)
    {
        MessageBox.Show(se.Message,
            "SQL Error Level " + se.Class,
            MessageBoxButtons.OK,
MessageBoxIcon.Information);
    }
}
```

8. Add code to the **Open** button that catches all other exceptions and displays a
   generic message describing the exception.

```
' Visual Basic
Catch Xcp As System.Exception ' generic exception handler
    MessageBox.Show(Xcp.Message, "Unexpected Exception", _
        MessageBoxButtons.OK, MessageBoxIcon.Error)
End Try
```

```
// Visual C#
catch (System.Exception Xcp)
{
    MessageBox.Show(Xcp.Message, "Unexpected Exception",
        MessageBoxButtons.OK, MessageBoxIcon.Error);
}
```

9. Add code to the **Close** button that closes and disposes of the connection.

10. Run and test the application by changing the server name to **Manchester**.

How to Handle the InfoMessage Event

- **The InfoMessage event is triggered when a SQL Server raises an error of severity level 1 - 10**
  - These are not fatal errors
  - InfoMessageEventArgs
  - Errors collection
  - SqlError
- **Generated by the T-SQL Print statement**
  - Useful for debugging stored procedures
- **Practice**

Introduction

Many different problems can occur when you work with databases. Because some problems are more serious than others, you can apply severity levels to them. For less serious problems, exceptions might not even be thrown. Instead, an event might be triggered. For example, the **InfoMessage** event of the **SqlConnection** object is triggered when the database server needs to communicate potentially important information to the user.

The SqlException class

The **SqlException** class contains the exception that is thrown when SQL Server returns a warning or error. This class is created whenever the SQL Server .NET Data Provider encounters a situation that it cannot handle. The class always contains at least one instance of **SqlError**. You can use the severity level to help determine the content of a message that an exception displays.

The following table describes severity levels of the **SqlException** class.

Severity	Description	Action
1-10	Informational, indicating problems caused by mistakes in information that a user has entered	SqlConnection remains open, so you can continue working.

What is the InfoMessage event?

There are **InfoMessage** events for both the **SqlConnection** and **OleDbConnection** classes. These events occur when the provider sends a warning or an information message.

When do you use InfoMessage?

You use the **InfoMessage** event when you add an information message to an error-handling routine. When an **InfoMessage** event is triggered, an argument containing a **SqlErrorCollection** is passed to the event handler. The handler can then loop through all of the **SqlError** objects and retrieve detailed information about the messages.

Practice (optional)

The solution for this practice is located in
<install folder>\Practices\Mod02\Lesson4\xx\HandlingInfoMessage\ where xx
is either VB or CS.

In this example, the Northwind Traders IT Director would like all applications
developed by his team to provide better feedback to enable the Help Desk staff
to track issues. In a previous lesson you learned how to write code to handle the
StateChange event. In this practice, you will write code to handle the
InfoMessage event.

Add code to handle the **InfoMessage** event of the connection, and use a
message box to display a description and the class (severity level) of each
SqlError contained in the **InfoMessage**.

1. Use Visual Studio .NET to create a new Windows Application solution
   named **HandlingInfoMessage**.

2. Add two button controls from the Toolbox, with the captions **Open** and
   Close, and name them **btnOpen** and **btnClose**.

3. Add a **SqlConnection** control from the Toolbox and name it **cnNorthwind**.

4. Set the **ConnectionString** property of **cnNorthwind** to connect to the
   Northwind database in your local SQL Server by using integrated security.

5. Add code to the **Open** button that opens the connection. Then call the
   ChangeDatabase method, to change the current database to **"pubs"**.

6. Add code to the **Close** button that closes and disposes of the connection.

7. Add code to handle the **InfoMessage** event of the connection object by
   double-clicking the **cnNorthwind** control in the Forms Designer.

Note   This works in both Visual Basic and Visual C# because InfoMessage is
the default event for a **SqlConnection** object.

8. Add code to the **InfoMessage** event to loop through all of the **SqlError** objects in the **Errors** collection of the **SqlInfoMessageEventArgs** object named **e** and show the **Message** property in a message box. Include the severity level of the error in the title bar.

```vb
' Visual Basic
Dim se As SqlClient.SqlError
For Each se In e.Errors
        MessageBox.Show(se.Message, _
            "SQL Error Level " & se.Class, _
            MessageBoxButtons.OK, MessageBoxIcon.Information)
Next
```

```csharp
// Visual C#
foreach (System.Data.SqlClient.SqlError se in e.Errors)
{
        MessageBox.Show(se.Message,
            "SQL Error Level " + se.Class,
            MessageBoxButtons.OK,
MessageBoxIcon.Information);
}
```

9. Run and test the application.

   How many SqlErrors are generated when the database is changed to **"pubs"**?

Lesson: Connection Pooling

- **What Is Connection Pooling?**
- **Controlling OLE DB Connection Pooling**
- **Controlling SQL Server Connection Pooling**
- **Demonstration: Monitoring SQL Server Activity**

Introduction

Each time you establish a connection to a data source, cycles and memory are used. Because applications often require multiple connections with multiple users, connecting to a data source can be resource-intensive. By pooling connections, you can keep connections available for reuse, which enhances application performance and scalability.

This lesson describes how to implement connection pooling with SQL Server and OLE DB data sources in ADO.NET.

Lesson objectives

After completing this lesson, you will be able to:

- Describe what connection pooling is and how it works.
- Control OLE DB connection pooling.
- Control SQL Server connection pooling.

What Is Connection Pooling?

- **Connection pooling is the process of keeping connections active and pooled so that they can be efficiently reused.**

- **How connection pooling works**

- **Example of connection pooling**

Visual Basic Example

Definition

Connection pooling is the process of keeping connections active and pooled so that they can be efficiently reused. Connections with identical connection strings are pooled together and can be reused without reestablishing the connection.

A connection pool is created when one or more connections share a unique connection string, and connection-pooling functionality has been requested. If any one parameter of the new connection string is not identical to the first string, the new connection will be placed in its own pool.

Applications often require many of the same connections for different purposes. By pooling these connections and reusing them:

- Application performance is improved.

- Scalability is enhanced.

Why use connection pooling?

Connection pooling is especially important for Internet applications and other applications that are accessed by multiple users and multiple connection strings.

How connection pooling works

Connection pooling is the ability of SQL Server or an OLE DB data source to reuse connections for a particular user or security context.

Connection pooling occurs on the computer where the database is installed. When the database is installed, memory is allocated for its processes, including connections. The ADO.NET connection string specifies different parameters for connection pooling.

When the connection to the data source is attempted, the security context and the Pooling parameter are examined. If the Pooling parameter is set to 'false', connection pooling will not occur. However, if pooling is enabled (it is set to 'true' by default), connection pooling will occur.

A security context is a unique combination of parameter values in the connection string. The security context is checked to see if it is valid and if it is identical to other connection strings. If two connections have the same connection string parameters, those connections have the same security context. Connections that have the same security context are pooled together. If any part of a connection string is not identical to another connection string, a new pool is created.

When a connection is closed, the connection is returned to the pool and ready for reuse. When a connection is disposed, the connection is deleted from memory. It is not returned to the pool and is not available for reuse. When the last connection in a connection pool is deleted, the pool is also deleted from memory.

Example of connection pooling

Of the three connection strings below, the first two connection strings match exactly, and because connection pooling is enabled by default, they are pooled together. For the third connection string, the initial catalog (the default database that is accessed upon connection) is different than the initial catalog in the first two connection strings. A separate pool is created for the third connection, and any connections identical to it are added to that pool.

Connection 1

```
Dim myConnection as New SqlClient.SqlConnection()
myConnection.ConnectionString = "User ID=sa;" & _
   "Password=me2I81sour2;" & _
   "Initial Catalog=Northwind;" & _
   "Data Source=mySQLServer;" & _
   "Connection TimeOut=30;"
```

Connection 2

```
Dim myConnection as New SqlClient.SqlConnection()
myConnection.ConnectionString = "User ID=sa;" & _
   "Password=me2I81sour2;" & _
   "Initial Catalog=Northwind;" & _
   "Data Source=mySQLServer;" & _
   "Connection TimeOut=30;"
```

Connection 3

```
Dim myConnection as New SqlClient.SqlConnection()
myConnection.ConnectionString = "User ID=sa;" & _
   "Password=me2I81sour2;" & _
   "Initial Catalog=Pubs;" & _
   "Data Source=mySQLServer;" & _
   "Connection TimeOut=30;"
```

Multimedia: How SQL Server Connection Pooling Works

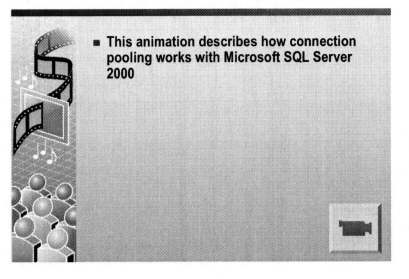

- This animation describes how connection pooling works with Microsoft SQL Server 2000

Introduction

This animation describes connection pooling and shows how connection pooling works with Microsoft SQL Server 2000. Understanding connection pooling will help you to plan, design, and deploy your ADO.NET applications for enhanced performance, security, and scalability.

Controlling OLE DB Connection Pooling

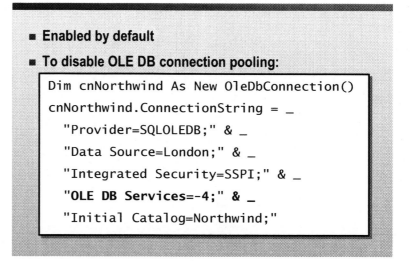

■ **Enabled by default**

■ **To disable OLE DB connection pooling:**

```
Dim cnNorthwind As New OleDbConnection()
cnNorthwind.ConnectionString = _
   "Provider=SQLOLEDB;" & _
   "Data Source=London;" & _
   "Integrated Security=SSPI;" & _
   "OLE DB Services=-4;" & _
   "Initial Catalog=Northwind;"
```

Introduction

When you connect to an OLE DB data source, connection pooling is automatic. The OLE DB .NET Data Provider uses OLE DB session pooling by default.

You can control OLE DB connection pooling from your application by:

■ Disabling pooling in individual connection strings.

■ If you write directly to the OLE DB API, controlling pooling through the properties you set when connecting to the database.

To disable pooling in a connection string that uses the OLE DB .NET Data Provider, specify "OLE DB Services=-4" in your connection string.

Controlling SQL Server Connection Pooling

■ **Connection string parameters for connection pooling**

- Connection Lifetime
- Connection Reset
- Enlist
- Max Pool Size
- Min Pool Size
- Pooling

Visual Basic Example

Introduction

You can control several elements of connection pooling when you connect to SQL Server by using the SQL Server .NET Data Provider. You can control how long the connection exists, whether the database connection is reset when the connection is removed from the pool, how many connections are allowed and maintained in the pool, and whether pooling is enabled.

Connection string parameters

The following parameters are specified in the connection string to control connection pooling.

Connection string parameter	Default	Description
Connection Lifetime	0	When a connection is returned to the pool, its creation time is compared with the current time, and the connection is destroyed if that time span (in seconds) exceeds the value specified by connection lifetime. This is useful in clustered configurations to force load balancing between a running server and a server that was just brought online.
Connection Reset	True	Determines whether the database connection is reset when the connection is removed from the pool. Setting this to **False** prevents an additional server round-trip when obtaining a connection, but you must be aware that the connection state, such as database context, is not being reset. This default option makes the connection change back to its original database context automatically when it is reused. This costs an extra (potentially unnecessary) call to the server. If database contexts will not be changed, set this parameter to **False**. Use the **ChangeDatabase** method rather than the SQL USE command to enable ADO.NET to automatically reset connections when they are returned to the pool.
Enlist	True	When set to True, the pooler automatically enlists the connection in the current transaction context of the creation thread if a transaction context exists.
Max Pool Size	100	The maximum number of connections allowed in the pool.
Min Pool Size	0	The minimum number of connections maintained in the pool.
Pooling	True	When set to **True**, the **SqlConnection** object is drawn from the appropriate pool, or if necessary, is created and added to the appropriate pool.

Examples of controlling SQL Server connection pooling

The following code samples show how you can control connection pooling by using the parameters of a SQL Server connection string.

To disable connection pooling:

```
Dim cnNorthwind as New SqlClient.SqlConnection()

cnNorthwind.ConnectionString = _
    "Integrated Security=True;" & _
    "Initial Catalog=Northwind;" & _
    "Data Source=London;" & _
    "Pooling=False;"
```

To specify the minimum pool size:

```
cnNorthwind.ConnectionString = _
    "Integrated Security=True;" & _
    "Initial Catalog=Northwind;" & _
    "Data Source=London;" & _
    "Min Pool Size=5;"
```

To specify the connection lifetime:

```
cnNorthwind.ConnectionString = _
    "Integrated Security=True;" & _
    "Initial Catalog=Northwind;" & _
    "Data Source=London;" & _
    "Connection Lifetime=120;"
```

Demonstration: Monitoring SQL Server Activity

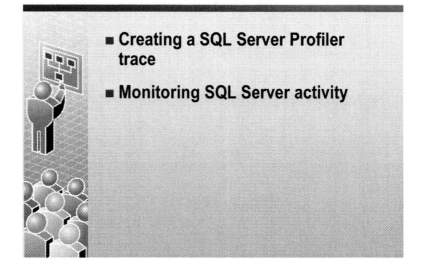

- Creating a SQL Server Profiler trace
- Monitoring SQL Server activity

In this demonstration, you will see how to configure a SQL Server Profiler trace to monitor SQL Server activity.

▶ **To monitor SQL Server activity**

1. Start SQL Server Profiler.

2. On the toolbar, click **New Trace**.

3. Use the information in the following table to connect to SQL Server.

Option	Value
SQL Server	(local)
Connect using	SQL Server authentication
User Name	sa
Password	2389

4. In the **Trace Properties** dialog box, click the **Events** tab.

5. Expand the **Security Audit** item in the Available event classes tree view control.

6. Double-click **Audit Login Failed** to add it to the Selected event classes tree view control.

7. Start the trace by clicking **Run**.

8. Start SQL Server Query Analyzer.

9. Use the information in the following table to connect to SQL Server.

Option	Value
SQL Server	(local)
Connect using	SQL Server authentication
User Name	sa
Password	2389

10. Switch to SQL Profiler and verify that a successful **Audit Login** occurred.

11. Switch to SQL Query Analyzer and execute the following query:

```
USE Northwind
SELECT * FROM CUSTOMERS
```

12. Switch to SQL Profiler and examine the trace.

    What is the SQL Server Process ID (SPID) of the process that executed the statement?

    What was the duration of the execution of the statement?

13. Start SQL Server Enterprise Manager.

14. Expand the (local) SQL Server.

15. In the **Security** folder, click **Logins**. You will see a list of the logins established for this SQL Server.

16. Switch to SQL Profiler and verify that the application named MS SQLEM successfully connected and executed a SQL statement that retrieved the **loginname** column from the **syslogins** table in the master database.

17. Stop SQL Server Enterprise Manager.

    Switch to SQL Query Analyzer, and on the **File** menu, click **Disconnect**. You do not need to save changes.

18. Switch to SQL Profiler and verify that two successful Audit Logouts occurred.

    What were the SPIDs of the processes that logged out?

19. Switch to SQL Query Analyzer, and on the **File** menu, click **Connect**.

20. Use the information in the following table to connect to SQL Server.

Option	Value
SQL Server	(local)
Connect using	SQL Server authentication
User Name	sa
Password	mypassword

21. Click **OK** to accept the error message, and then click **Cancel** to abandon connecting.

22. Stop the SQL Query Analyzer.

23. Switch to SQL Profiler and verify that an **Audit Login Failed** occurred for the user, but an **Audit Logout** occurred for the SQL Query Analyzer.

24. Stop the trace and exit from the SQL Profiler.

Review: Connecting to Data Sources

- Choosing a .NET Data Provider
- Defining a Connection
- Managing a Connection
- Handling Connection Exceptions
- Connection Pooling

1. What is a .NET data provider?

2. What are the two security modes in SQL Server 2000?

3. Which connection object methods do you use to manage a connection?

4. What is the difference between closing and disposing a connection?

5. How are exceptions handled in the .NET Framework?

6. What is connection pooling?

Lab 2.1: Connecting to Data Sources

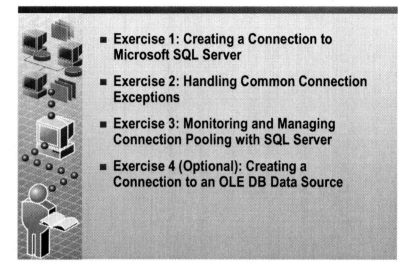

■ Exercise 1: Creating a Connection to Microsoft SQL Server

■ Exercise 2: Handling Common Connection Exceptions

■ Exercise 3: Monitoring and Managing Connection Pooling with SQL Server

■ Exercise 4 (Optional): Creating a Connection to an OLE DB Data Source

Objectives

After completing this lab, you will be able to:

■ Create a connection to SQL Server.

■ Handle common connection exceptions.

■ Monitor and manage connection pooling.

■ Create a connection to an OLE DB data source.

Scenario

Northwind Traders, an international company that imports and exports specialty food, stores data in many different locations and different data sources. To build needed applications, the company needs to establish connections to the different data sources.

This lab allows you to practice connecting to multiple types of data sources and practice handling common problems, by using the Northwind Traders sample databases that are included with Microsoft SQL Server 2000.

Estimated time to complete this lab: 90 minutes

Exercise 0
Lab Setup

To complete this lab, you must:

▶ **Create SQL Server login accounts**

1. Start Microsoft SQL Server Query Analyzer and connect to the (local) SQL Server using Windows authentication.

2. Open and execute the following script: <install folder>\Labs\Lab02\createusers.sqlStart Microsoft SQL Server Enterprise Manager.

3. Expand the connection to your (local) SQL Server.

4. Look in the **Security – Logins** folder to check that the accounts listed in the table below have been successfully created. You may need to refresh the folder by right-clicking the folder and then clicking **Refresh**.

Account name	Password	Default database
JohnK	JohnK	Northwind
AmyJ	AmyJ	Northwind

5. Close SQL Server Enterprise Manager and SQL Query Analyzer.

Exercise 1
Creating a Connection to Microsoft SQL Server

Microsoft Visual Studio .NET includes a native .NET data provider for Microsoft SQL Server versions 7.0 and later. This native provider gives better performance and functionality when connecting to SQL Server than using the OLE DB .NET Data Provider to connect to SQL Server.

Scenario

Northwind Traders needs to build an application that accesses customer and sales data. The company uses a variety of different data sources, including SQL Server 2000. When building a data-related application, you begin by connecting to the data source.

In this exercise, you will create a connection to read from a SQL Server 2000 database by using the SQL Server .NET Data Provider within a Windows application. The connections that you make will be used in future exercises.

▶ Open an existing Visual Studio .NET solution

1. Start the Visual Studio .NET development environment.

2. Open the starter solution for either Visual Basic or Visual C#.

The path is
<install folder>\Labs\Lab02\Starter\VB\ConnectingToDataSources.sln or
<install folder>\Labs\Lab02\Starter\CS\ConnectingToDataSources.sln

3. Open the class module **Form1** and review the code that is provided.

Note: The **Integrated Security** check box and the **Exit** button have existing code that handles their click events. You will write code to complete the rest of the functionality for this application.

▶ Declare a new connection object

1. Drag a **SqlConnection** control from the Toolbox onto **Form1**.

2. Change the **(Name)** property to **cnSQLNorthwind**.

▶ **Create a connection string**

1. In the **Exercises 1 and 2** group box, double-click **Open** to automatically add code to handle the **Click** event.

   Note: You will be adding exception handling in Exercise 2. It is not necessary to write any exception handling during this exercise.

2. Write some code to build a connection string by using the information provided in the controls in the **Exercises 1 and 2** group box. Use the information provided in the following table.

Connection parameter	Control and property
Data Source	txtServer.Text
Initial Catalog	txtSQLDatabase.Text
Connection Timeout	txtTimeout.Text
Integrated Security	chkIntegratedSecurity.Checked.ToString()
User ID	txtUsername.Text
Password	txtPassword.Text

```
' Visual Basic

Me.cnSQLNorthwind.ConnectionString = _
  "Data Source=" & Me.txtServer.Text & ";" & _
  "Initial Catalog=" & Me.txtSQLDatabase.Text & ";" & _
  "Integrated Security=" & _
      Me.chkIntegratedSecurity.Checked.ToString() & ";" & _
  "User ID=" & Me.txtUsername.Text & ";" & _
  "Password=" & Me.txtPassword.Text & ";" & _
  "Connection Timeout=" & Me.txtTimeout.Text & ";"

// Visual C#

this.cnSQLNorthwind.ConnectionString =
  "Data Source=" + this.txtServer.Text + ";" +
  "Initial Catalog=" + this.txtSQLDatabase.Text + ";" +
  "Integrated Security=" +
      this.chkIntegratedSecurity.Checked.ToString() + ";" +
  "User ID=" + this.txtUsername.Text + ";" +
  "Password=" + this.txtPassword.Text + ";" +
  "Connection Timeout=" + this.txtTimeout.Text + ";";
```

3. Write code to open the connection.

```
' Visual Basic

Me.cnSQLNorthwind.Open()

// Visual C#

this.cnSQLNorthwind.Open();
```

▶ **Close the connection**

1. Double-click **Close** to automatically add code to handle the **Click** event.

2. Write code to close and dispose of the connection.

```
' Visual Basic

Me.cnSQLNorthwind.Close()
Me.cnSQLNorthwind.Dispose()

// Visual C#

this.cnSQLNorthwind.Close();
this.cnSQLNorthwind.Dispose();
```

▶ **Trace the application events**

1. Start the SQL Server Profiler.

2. Create a new trace by clicking the **File** menu, clicking the **New** menu, and then clicking **Trace**.

3. Connect to the (local) server by using Windows Authentication.

4. Complete the **Trace Properties** dialog box by using the information in the following tables.

Events	Values
Security Audit	Audit Login
	Audit Logout
	Audit Login Failed
Sessions	Existing Connection

Data Columns	Values
Columns	EventClass
	TextData
	ApplicationName
	LoginName
	LoginSid
	SPID
	StartTime

5. In the **Trace Properties** dialog box, click **Run** to run the trace.

6. Leave the trace running, and switch to the Visual Studio .NET development environment.

7. Run the **ConnectingToDataSources** solution.

8. When the solution starts, use the information in the following table to complete the text boxes on the form, and then click **Open** in the **Exercises 1 and 2** group box.

Text box	Value
User Name	sa
Password	2389

9. Switch to SQL Profiler and verify that a successful **Audit Login** occurred.

10. Switch to the running solution and click **Exit**, to terminate the application

11. Switch to SQL Profiler and verify that a successful **Audit Logout** occurred.

12. Run the **ConnectingToDataSources** solution again.

13. When the solution starts, use the information in the following table to complete the text boxes on the form, and then click **Open** in the **Exercises 1 and 2** group box (notice that the password is deliberately invalid):

Text box	Value
User Name	sa
Password	12345

Note: you will get an exception. You will add exception handling in the next lab exercise.

14. Click **Continue** to end the application.

15. Switch to SQL Profiler and verify that an **Audit Login Failed** occurred.

16. Close the SQL Profiler.

▶ **Explore connection timeouts**

1. Run the **ConnectingToDataSources** solution.

2. When the **ConnectingToDataSources** solution starts, change the server name to **Alpha** by typing **Alpha** in the **Server** text box, and then click **Open** in the **Exercises 1 and 2** group box.

   How long do you have to wait before an error is displayed?

   _____

3. Click **Continue** to end the application.

4. Run the solution again.

5. Modify the connection string to time out after 5 seconds, and change the server name to **Alpha**.

6. Click **Open**.

   How long do you have to wait before an error is displayed?

   _____

7. Optional: Test the application's ability to log on to a SQL Server by using Integrated Security.

Exercise 2
Handling Common Connection Exceptions

There are many situations in which errors can occur, including:

- An invalid connection string; for example:
- Wrong or missing database name or location
- Wrong or missing security information
- Network problems (for example, slow or down)
- Server problems (for example, overloaded, over license limit, or unavailable)

Scenario

Although Northwind Traders uses a robust Windows networking environment, there could be situations where unexpected errors occur. Northwind Traders is a rapidly growing company, and increased network usage can impact network latency. To handle these and other situations, you must implement exception handling in the Northwind Traders data application.

In this exercise, you will handle common errors that can occur when connecting to a data source.

▶ **Open an existing Visual Studio .NET solution**

- Open the solution you created during Exercise 1, or open the provided solution in one of the paths below.

<install folder>\Labs\Lab02\Solution\Ex1\VB\ConnectingToDataSources.sln
<install folder>\Labs\Lab02\Solution\Ex1\CS\ConnectingToDataSources.sln

▶ **Code the Open and Close buttons**

1. In the Exercises **1 and 2** group box, add code to the **Open** button to handle the following common exceptions.

Action	Exception	Result
Attempt to open connection with an invalid connection string	System. Data. SqlClient. SqlException	Check the exception number and show a message as follows: 17: invalid server name 4060: invalid database 18456: invalid user name or password
Attempt to open connection before the connection has been closed	System. InvalidOperationException	Show a message box that explains that the connection must be closed first.
Unexpected problem when attempting to open or close the connection	System. Exception	Show a message box that includes a description of the exception.

2. In the **Finally** statement, display a message box that shows the connection string used by the connection.

3. In the **Exercises 1 and 2** group box, add code to the **Close** button to handle any System.Exceptions that occurs.

Note For help, see the topic How To Handle SqlExceptions in this module.

▶ **Test the exception handling code**

1. Run the **ConnectingToDataSources** solution.

2. Enter valid connection information and attempt to open the connection.

   Do you receive any exceptions?

   _____

3. Close the connection.

4. Change the server name to **Alpha** and the connection timeout to 5 seconds.

5. In the **Exercises 1 and 2** group box, click **Open**.

   Does your code handle the error caused by the invalid server name?

   _____

6. Enter other invalid connection information such as an invalid user name or password.

   Does your exception handling code differentiate between exception types and error numbers?

   _____

Exercise 3
Monitoring and Managing Connection Pooling with SQL Server

Because applications often require multiple connections with multiple users, connecting to a data source can be resource-intensive. By pooling connections, you can keep connections available for reuse, which will enhance application performance and scalability.

Scenario

The number of employees at Northwind Traders is rapidly growing, and as a result more applications are connecting to data sources. The company needs to optimize server resources by pooling connections.

In this exercise, you will monitor SQL Server connection pooling and modify connections based on the connection string settings and security context.

▶ **Examine the Pooling Monitor application**

1. Open <install folder>\Labs\Lab02\Pooling Monitor\PoolingMonitor.sln.

2. Examine **LaunchConnection.vb**. Note that the **btnNew_Click** procedure creates a new instance of the **OpenNewConnection** class, and sets the title bar of the new form with a supplied string before showing the form.

3. Examine **OpenNewConnection.vb**. Note the following points:

   a. The **btnOpenSQL_Click** procedure builds a connection string and attempts to connect to SQL Server.

   b. The **btnCloseSQL_Click** procedure closes the current connection but does not release resources.

   c. The **btnRelease_Click** procedure releases connection resources and closes the current window.

4. Compile the application. Note the path of the executable; for example: <install folder>\Labs\Lab02\PoolingMonitor\bin\PoolingMonitor.exe

5. Close Visual Studio .NET.

6. Create a shortcut to the executable on the desktop.

▶ **Create a SQL Profiler trace to monitor connection activity**

1. Start SQL Server Profiler.

2. Create a new trace by using the following information.

Connect to SQL Server	Values
SQL Server	. *(Local)*
Authentication	Windows

Events	Values
Security Audit	Audit Login
	Audit Logout
Sessions	Existing Connection

Data Columns	Values
Columns	EventClass
	TextData
	ApplicationName
	LoginName
	ClientProcessID
	SPID
	Start Time

3. Save the trace so that you can run it again later.

4. Run the trace.

▶ **Examine non-pooled connections**

In this procedure, you will examine connection activity by using SQL Profiler.

Important You must run the PoolingMonitor.exe program executable rather than running the program from within Visual Studio .NET.

---

1. Run **PoolingMonitor.exe** by using the desktop shortcut you created previously.

2. Create a connection by using the following information. Use the default value for any unspecified information. Enter the connection name on the **Launch Connection** form, click **Open**, and then enter the other parameters on the second form.

Parameter	Value
Connection Name	JohnK1
Database	Northwind
User Name	JohnK
Password	JohnK
Enable Pooling	Cleared

3. Examine the activity in SQL Profiler.

   What is the SPID (server process identifier) of this connection?

   _____

4. Leave the **JohnK1** connection form running, and switch back to the **Launch Connection** form.

5. Create another connection by using the following information.

Parameter	Value
Connection Name	JohnK2
User Name	JohnK
Password	JohnK

6. Examine the activity in SQL Profiler.

    What is the SPID of this connection?

    _____

7. Leave the **JohnK2** connection form running, and switch back to the **Launch Connection** form.

8. Create another connection by using the following information.

Parameter	Value
Connection Name	AmyJ1
User Name	AmyJ
Password	AmyJ

9. Examine the activity in SQL Profiler.

    What is the SPID of this connection?

    _____

    How is SQL Server responding to requests for new connections? Why?

    _____

    _____

10. Close and release the **JohnK1**, **JohnK2**, and **AmyJ1** connections.

11. Examine the trace.

12. Close PoolingMonitor.exe and stop the trace.

▶ **Examine pooling by setting the Pooling parameter**

In this procedure, you will examine pooling behavior when specifying **Pooling** in the connection string. Examine the trace after each step.

1. Start the trace. If prompted, do not save the output from the last trace.

2. Run **PoolingMonitor.exe** by using the desktop shortcut you created previously.

3. Create a connection by using the following information.

Parameter	Value
Connection Name	JohnK1
User Name	JohnK
Password	JohnK
Enable Pooling	Checked

How many connections are created for this user? Why?

_____

_____

_____

4. Close and release the **JohnK1** connection.

5. Create a new connection named **JohnK2** by using the same set of information.

    How many connections are created for this user? Why?

_____

_____

6. Close and release the **JohnK2** connection.

    What activity does the trace show? Why?

_____

7. Close the Pooling Monitor application.

    What activity does the trace show? Why?

_____

8. Stop the trace.

▶ **Manage pooling by using security context**

In this procedure, you will examine pooling behavior when specifying various security contexts in the connection string. Examine the trace after each step.

1. Start the trace.

2. Run **PoolingMonitor.exe** by using the desktop shortcut you created previously.

3. Create a connection by using the following information.

Parameter	Value
Connection Name	JohnK1
Database	Pubs
User Name	JohnK
Password	JohnK
Enable Pooling	Checked

How many connections are created for this user? Why?

_____

4. Create a connection by using the following information.

Parameter	Value
Connection Name	JohnK2
Database	Northwind
User Name	JohnK
Password	JohnK
Enable Pooling	Checked

How many connections are created for this user? Why?

_____

_____

_____

5. Close and release the **JohnK1** and **JohnK2** connections.

6. Close the Pooling Monitor application.

7. Stop the trace.

▶ **Manage the pool size**

In this procedure, you will examine pooling behavior when specifying **Pool Size** in the connection string. Examine the trace after each step.

1. Start the trace.

2. Run **PoolingMonitor.exe** by using the desktop shortcut you created previously.

3. Create a connection by using the following information.

Parameter	Value
Connection Name	JohnK1
User Name	JohnK
Password	JohnK
Enable Pooling	Checked
Min Pool Size	5

How many connections are created for this user? Why?

_____

4. Create a connection named **JohnK2** by using the same set of information.

How many connections are created for this user? Why?

_____

5. Close and release the **JohnK1** and **JohnK2** connections.

What activity does the trace show? Why?

_____

6. Close the Pooling Monitor application.

What activity does the trace show? Why?

_____

7. Restart the Pooling Monitor application.

8. Create a connection by using the following information.

Parameter	Value
Connection Name	JohnK1
User Name	JohnK
Password	JohnK
Enable Pooling	Checked
Max Pool Size	3

9. Create three more connections named **JohnK2**, **JohnK3**, and **JohnK4** by using the same set of information.

   What happens when the fourth connection is attempted? Why?

10. Close the Pooling Monitor application.

11. Stop the trace.

12. Close SQL Profiler.

If Time Permits
Creating a Connection to an OLE DB Data Source

Scenario

Northwind Traders uses a variety of different data sources, including SQL Server 6.5, Microsoft Access, and Microsoft Excel.

In this exercise, you will create an OLE DB connection to read from an Access database by using the OLE DB .NET Data Provider within a Microsoft Windows application.

▶ Open an existing Microsoft Visual Studio .NET solution

1. Start the Microsoft Visual Studio .NET development environment.

2. Open the solution you created in the Exercise 2, or open the solution provided for you in the following location.

The path is
<install folder>\Labs\Lab02\Solution\Ex2\VB\ConnectingToDataSources.sln or
<install folder>\Labs\Lab02\Solution\Ex2\CS\ConnectingToDataSources.sln

▶ Declare a new connection object

1. Drag an **OleDbConnection** control from the Toolbox onto **Form1**.

2. Change the **(Name)** property to **cnOleDbNorthwind**.

▶ Create a connection string

1. In the **Exercise 4** group box, double-click **Open** to automatically add code to handle the **Click** event.

2. Write code to build a connection string by using the information provided in the controls in the Exercise 4 group box. Use the information provided in the following table.

Connection parameter	Text box
Provider	txtProvider.Text
Data Source	txtOleDbDatabase.Text

```
' Visual Basic

Me.cnOleDbNorthwind.ConnectionString = _
   "Provider=" & Me.txtProvider.Text & ";" & _
   "Data Source=" & Me.txtOleDbDatabase.Text & ";"

// Visual C#

this.cnOleDbNorthwind.ConnectionString =
   "Provider=" + this.txtProvider.Text + ";" +
   "Data Source=" + this.txtOleDbDatabase.Text + ";";
```

3. Write code to open the connection.

```
' Visual Basic

Me.cnOleDbNorthwind.Open()

// Visual C#

this.cnOleDbNorthwind.Open();
```

▶ **Close the connection**

1. In the **Exercise 4** group box, double-click **Close** to automatically add code to handle the **Click** event.

2. Write code to close and dispose of the connection.

```
' Visual Basic

Me.cnOleDbNorthwind.Close()
Me.cnOleDbNorthwind.Dispose()

// Visual C#

this.cnOleDbNorthwind.Close();
this.cnOleDbNorthwind.Dispose();
```

▶ **Handle the StateChange event for the connection**

1. Add an event handler for the **StateChange** event for the **cnOleDbNorthwind** connection object.

```
' Visual Basic

Private Sub cnOleDbNorthwind_StateChange( _
   ByVal sender As System.Object, _
   ByVal e As System.Data.StateChangeEventArgs) _
   Handles cnOleDbNorthwind.StateChange

End Sub
```

```csharp
// Visual C#

// add the following to the Form1_Load event
// (hint: double-click the form's title bar)

this.cnOleDbNorthwind.StateChange += new
    System.Data.StateChangeEventHandler(
    this.cnOleDbNorthwind_StateChange);

// add the following as a new function

private void cnOleDbNorthwind_StateChange(
    object sender, System.Data.StateChangeEventArgs e)
{

}
```

2. Use a message box to show the current and original state of the connection.

```vbnet
' Visual Basic

MessageBox.Show( _
    "CurrentState: " & e.CurrentState.ToString() & ", " & _
    "OriginalState: " & e.OriginalState.ToString(), _
    "cnOleDbNorthwind.State", _
    MessageBoxButtons.OK, MessageBoxIcon.Information)
```

```csharp
// Visual C#

MessageBox.Show(
    "CurrentState: " + e.CurrentState.ToString() + ", " +
    "OriginalState: " + e.OriginalState.ToString(),
    "cnOleDbNorthwind.State",
    MessageBoxButtons.OK, MessageBoxIcon.Information);
```

▶ **Run and test the connection**

1. Run the **ConnectingToDataSources** solution.

2. Click **Open**.

   Is a successful connection made?

   _____

3. Click **Close**.

   Is the connection closed?

   _____

▶ **Add exception handling**

- In the **Exercise 4** group box, add exception handling to the **Open** and **Close** buttons (for example, for the OLE DB .NET Data Provider).

Note: Use the .NET Framework documentation to find the list of exceptions that occur for the OLE DB .NET Data Provider. You can search for "OLE DB Errors".

► **Test for exceptions**

1. In Windows Explorer, move the database file to a different location (the initial database path is \Program Files\Microsoft Office\Office10\Samples\Northwind.mdb). Or, to save time, change the path specified in the text box on the form of the solution.

2. Run the **ConnectingToDataSources** solution.

3. Click **Open**.

   Does an exception occur?

   _____

   Why?

   _____

4. In Windows Explorer, move the database file back to its original location, or correct the path.

5. Use Microsoft Access to open the database file exclusively.

   Note: The **Open** dialog box in Microsoft Access has an **Open** button that gives you multiple options if you click its drop-down arrow.

6. Run the **ConnectingToDataSources** solution.

7. Click **Open**.

   Does an exception occur?

   _____

   Why?

   _____

8. Close Microsoft Access and close your application.

msdn training

Module 3: Performing Connected Database Operations

Contents

Microsoft

Overview

- **Working in a Connected Environment**
- **Building Command Objects**
- **Executing Command Objects That Return a Single Value**
- **Executing Commands That Return Rows**
- **Executing Commands That Do Not Return Rows**
- **Using Transactions**

Introduction

In many situations, you will design your data access strategy around the use of a DataSet. However, in other situations you might find it useful or necessary to bypass DataSets and use data commands to communicate directly with the data source (typically, a database). These situations include:

- Performing queries on data intended to be read-only in your application. This might include executing a command that performs a database lookup.

- Designing data access in a Microsoft® ASP.NET Web application that only requires a single pass through data, such as displaying the results of a search.

- Executing a query that returns a single value, such as a calculation or the result of an aggregate function.

- Creating and modifying database structures, such as tables and stored procedures.

When you create tables and stored procedures, or otherwise execute logic that does not return a result set, you cannot use a DataSet and must use data commands.

Objectives

After completing this module, you will be able to:

- Build a command object.

- Execute command objects that return a single value.

- Execute a command that returns a set of rows, and process the result.

- Execute a command that defines database structure and permissions by using the data definition language (DDL) and data control language (DCL).

- Execute a command that modifies data.

- Use transactions.

Lesson: Working in a Connected Environment

- **Object Model for Connected Applications**
  - Typical scenarios for a connected environment
  - .NET Framework classes used in a connected environment application

Introduction

This lesson explains typical disconnected data access scenarios that will be examined in more detail during the rest of this course.

Lesson objectives

After completing this lesson, you will be able to:

- Describe typical connected data access scenarios.
- Describe the ADO.NET classes that are used in those scenarios.

Object Model for Connected Applications

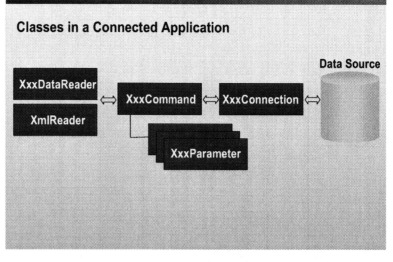

Classes in a Connected Application

XxxDataReader			Data Source
XmlReader	XxxCommand	XxxConnection	
	XxxParameter		

Typical scenarios for a connected application

You might need to build a connected application whenever your application must have a direct and continuous connection to the data source. Some examples of connected applications include:

- A factory that requires a real-time connection to monitor production output and storage
- A brokerage house that requires a constant connection to stock quotes

Classes used in a connected environment

The following table describes the core classes that are used in a connected environment.

Class	Description
XxxConnection	Establishes a connection to a specific data source. For example, the **SqlConnection** class connects to Microsoft SQL Server™ data sources.
XxxCommand	Executes a command from a data source. For example, the **SqlCommand** class can execute stored procedures or SQL statements in a SQL Server data source.
XxxDataReader	Reads a forward-only, read-only stream of data from a data source. For example, the **SqlDataReader** class can read rows from tables in a SQL Server data source. It is returned by the **ExecuteReader** method of the **XxxCommand** class, typically as a result of a **SELECT** SQL statement.
XxxXMLReader	Provides fast, non-cached, forward-only access to XML data.

Lesson: Building Command Objects

- **What Is a Command Object?**
- **How to Create a Stored Procedure**
- **How to Create a Command Object**
- **Demonstration: Creating a Command Object Graphically**
- **What Are Command Parameters?**
- **How to Create Parameters for a Command Object**

Introduction

Command objects allow you to access data directly in the database in a connected environment.

You can use a command object to perform the following tasks:

- Execute **SELECT** statements that return a single value, such as a row count, the results of a credit-card authentication lookup, or a calculated value.

- Execute **SELECT** statements that return rows. This is an efficient way to load large volumes of read-only data into a control such as a Web Forms DataList or DataGrid.

- Execute **DDL** statements to create, edit, and remove tables, stored procedures, and other database structures. You need the required permissions to perform these actions.

- Execute **DCL** statements to grant or deny permissions.

- Execute statements to get database catalog information.

- Execute commands that return data from a Microsoft SQL Server (version 7.0 or later) database in XML format. A typical use is to execute a query and get back data in XML format, apply an Extensible Stylesheet Language for Transformations (XSLT) transformation to convert the data to HTML format, and then send the results to a browser such as Microsoft Internet Explorer.

Lesson objectives

After completing this lesson, you will be able to:

- Create a command object.
- Configure the properties in a command object.
- Set parameters in a command object.

What Is a Command Object?

- **A command object is a reference to a SQL statement or stored procedure**
- **Properties**
  - (Name), Connection, CommandType, CommandText, Parameters
- **Methods**
  - ExecuteScalar, ExecuteReader, ExecuteNonQuery
  - ExecuteXmlReader (SqlCommand only)

Introduction

A command object contains a reference to a SQL statement or stored procedure that you can execute directly. The two command classes are described in the following table.

Command class	Description
System.Data.SqlClient.SqlCommand	SQL Server .NET Data Provider command
System.Data.OleDb.OleDbCommand	OLE DB .NET Data Provider command

Properties of a command object

The properties of a command object contain all of the information necessary to execute a statement against a database. This information includes:

- **(Name)**. The programmatic name of the command object. Use this name in your code, to refer to the command object.
- **Connection**. The command object references a connection object, which it uses to communicate with the database.
- **CommandType**. One of: Text, StoredProcedure, TableDirect.
- **CommandText**. The command object includes the text of a SQL statement or the name of a stored procedure to execute.
- **Parameters**. The command object may include zero or more parameters.

Methods of a command object

After configuring the properties for a command object, you call one of the following methods to execute the command. The method you call depends on the statement or procedure being executed, and the results that you expect to be returned.

Method in XxxCommand class	Description
ExecuteScalar	Executes a command that returns a single value.
ExecuteReader	Executes a command that returns a set of rows.
ExecuteNonQuery	Executes a command that updates the database or changes the database structure. This method returns the number of rows affected.
ExecuteXmlReader (SqlCommand only)	Executes a command that returns an XML result. Capability supported by SQL Server version 7.0 or later.

How to Create a Stored Procedure

- ■ **Server Explorer**
  - On the View menu, click Server Explorer, or press Ctrl+Alt+S
  - Create a data connection
  - Click New Stored Procedure
  - Insert SQL
- ■ **Demonstration**
  - Creating a stored procedure
  - Testing a stored procedure

Introduction

Microsoft Visual Studio® .NET includes tools to help you create a stored procedure.

Creating a stored procedure

▶ **To use the Server Explorer to create a stored procedure**

1. On the **View** menu, click **Server Explorer**, or press **Ctrl+Alt+S**.

2. To create a connection to the database in which you wish to create the stored procedure, right-click the **Data Connections** folder and then click **Add Connection**.

3. Expand the new connection and the **Stored Procedures** folder.

4. Right-click the **Stored Procedures** folder and then click **New Stored Procedure**.

5. Enter the SQL script. You can right-click anywhere on the script and then click **Insert SQL** to use the graphical Query Editor.

6. Close and save the stored procedure.

Demonstration

▶ **To use the Server Explorer to create a stored procedure**

In this demonstration, you will see how to create a project and a stored procedure in the SQL Server Northwind database. The stored procedure will return all products that have not been discontinued.

1. Start the Visual Studio .NET development environment.

2. Open the Server Explorer.

3. Expand your data connections, or create a new connection to the local computer running SQL Server and the Northwind sample database.

4. Expand the Northwind database.

5. Right-click the **Stored Procedures** folder and then click **New Stored Procedure**.

6. Change the name of the stored procedure to **dbo.GetCurrentProducts**.

7. Insert a new blank line before the **RETURN** statement. Right-click before the **RETURN** statement, and then click **Insert SQL**.

8. Add the **Products** table.

9. In the **Products** table, select the ProductID, ProductName, and Discontinued fields.

10. Set the **Discontinued Criteria** column to **=0**.

11. Clear the **Discontinued Output** column.

12. Close the Query Builder and click **Yes** to save changes.

13. Save the stored procedure.

How to Create a Command Object

- **Programmatically**

- **Server Explorer**
  - On the View menu, click Server Explorer, or press Ctrl+Alt+S
  - Drag stored procedure onto form or component
- **Toolbox**
  - Use SqlConnection or OleDbConnection
  - Use SqlCommand or OleDbCommand

Introduction

You can build a command object programmatically. Alternatively, you can use the tools in Visual Studio .NET to help you create a command object in your form or component. You can create a **SqlCommand** object or an **OleDbCommand** object, depending on the type of your data source.

Creating a command programmatically

To create a command programmatically, create a new **SqlCommand** or **OleDbCommand** object. In the constructor, specify the command text for the command. Also specify a **Connection** object, which will be used when the command is executed.

Examples

The following example creates a **SqlCommand** object. The **SqlCommand** object specifies a query that returns a list of categories from the Northwind database, assuming an existing connection object named **cnNorthwind**.

```
Dim cmCategories As New SqlCommand( _
   "SELECT * FROM Categories", cnNorthwind)
```

The following example creates an **OleDbCommand** object. The **OleDbCommand** object specifies a stored procedure that returns a list of all categories from the Northwind database.

```
Dim cmCategories As New OleDbCommand( _
   "dbo.AllCategories", cnNorthwind)

cmCategories.CommandType = CommandType.StoredProcedure
```

Creating a command object graphically

▶ **To add a command object to a form or component by using the Toolbox**

1. If you do not already have a connection object available on the form or component, add one.

2. From the **Data** tab of the Toolbox, drag a **SqlCommand** or **OleDbCommand** onto your form or component.

3. Set the following properties for the command object.

Property	Description
(Name)	The name by which you want to refer to the command object in your code.
Connection	A reference to a connection object that the command will use to communicate with the database. You can select an existing connection from the drop-down list or create a new connection.
CommandType	A value specified by the **CommandType** enumeration, indicating what type of command you want to execute: **Text**. A SQL statement. **StoredProcedure**. A stored procedure. **TableDirect**. A way of fetching the entire contents of a table. (This option is available only for **OleDbCommand** objects.)
CommandText	The command to execute. The command text you specify depends on the value of the **CommandType** property: **Text**. Enter the SQL statement to execute. **StoredProcedure**. Enter the name of the stored procedure. **TableDirect**. Enter the name of the table to fetch.
Parameters	A collection of objects of the type **SqlParameter** or **OleDbParameter**. You use this collection to pass parameters into the command, and to retrieve output parameters from the command. You will learn more about parameters later in this lesson.

Note   The SQL Server .NET Data Provider does not support the question mark (?) placeholder for parameters in a SQL statement. Instead, you must use a named parameter. For example, SELECT * FROM Products WHERE ProductID = @ProdID

Demonstration: Creating a Command Object Graphically

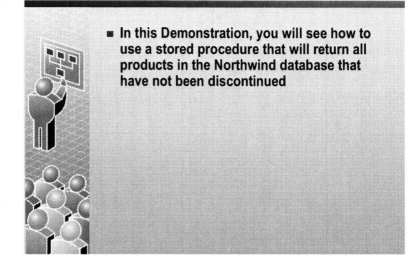

- In this Demonstration, you will see how to use a stored procedure that will return all products in the Northwind database that have not been discontinued

Introduction

In this demonstration, you will see how to use a stored procedure that will return all products in the Northwind database that have not been discontinued.

Demonstration

▶ **To use the Server Explorer to create a command object**

1. Start the Visual Studio .NET development environment.

2. Create a new Windows Application project.

3. Open the Server Explorer.

4. Expand your data connections.

5. Expand the **Northwind** database and the **Stored Procedures** folder.

6. Drag the stored procedure named **GetCurrentProducts** onto the form.

7. View the code written by the designer.

What Are Command Parameters?

- ■ **Introduction**
  - SQL statements and stored procedures can have input and output parameters, and a return value
  - Command parameters allow these parameters to be set and retrieved
  - SqlParameter, OleDbParameter
- ■ **Properties**
  - ParameterName, DbType, Size, Direction

Visual Basic Example

Introduction

SQL statements and stored procedures can specify both input parameters and output parameters. A stored procedure can also specify a separate return value.

You must configure your command object so that it deals correctly with these input parameters, output parameters, and the return value.

Configuring these parameters at development time ensures that the commands will execute efficiently at run time. There is no need for an extra round trip to the server, to determine the data types of the parameters.

Definition

SqlCommand and **OleDbCommand** have a Parameters collection. This collection specifies a set of **SqlParameter** or **OleDbParameter** objects, which represent the input parameters, output parameters, and return value for the command.

Before you execute a command, you must set a value for every input parameter in the command. After execution, you can retrieve the output parameters and the return value from the command.

Example

The following stored procedure returns information about a particular category of products in the Northwind database.

The @CatID input parameter specifies the required category. The stored procedure assigns the name of the category to the @CatName output parameter, and returns the number of products in the category.

```
/* Stored procedure with an input parameter named @CatID,
   an output parameter named @CatName, and a return value */

CREATE PROCEDURE dbo.CountProductsInCategory
  (
    @CatID int,
    @CatName nvarchar(15) OUTPUT
  )
AS
  SET NOCOUNT ON
  DECLARE @ProdCount int

  SELECT @CatName = Categories.CategoryName,
         @ProdCount = COUNT(Products.ProductID)
  FROM Categories INNER JOIN Products
    ON Categories.CategoryID = Products.CategoryID
  WHERE (Categories.CategoryID = @CatID)
  GROUP BY Categories.CategoryName

  RETURN @ProdCount
```

How to Create Parameters for a Command Object

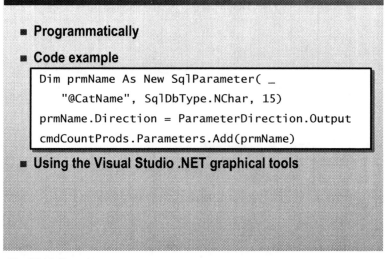

- **Programmatically**
- **Code example**

```
Dim prmName As New SqlParameter( _
    "@CatName", SqlDbType.NChar, 15)
prmName.Direction = ParameterDirection.Output
cmdCountProds.Parameters.Add(prmName)
```

- **Using the Visual Studio .NET graphical tools**

Visual Basic Example

Introduction

There are two ways to create parameters for a command object:

- Programmatically create **XxxParameter** objects, and then add these objects to the Parameters collection in the command object.
- Set the **Parameters** property automatically, by using the Properties window.

How to define a parameter programmatically

▶ **To define a parameter programmatically**

1. Create a new **SqlParameter** object or **OleDbParameter** object.
2. Set the properties for the parameter object. The following table describes the most commonly used properties.

Property	Description
ParameterName	The name of the parameter, such as "@CatID".
DbType, SqlDbType, or OleDbType	The data type of the parameter. The **DbType** property is linked to the **SqlDbType** or **OleDbType** property, depending on which data provider you are using.
Size	The maximum size, in bytes, of the data in the parameter.
Direction	A value specified by the ParameterDirection enumeration. Use one of the following values: • ParameterDirection.Input (default value) • ParameterDirection.InputOutput • ParameterDirection.Output • ParameterDirection.ReturnValue

3. Call the **Add** method on the Parameters collection for the command object. If the command calls a stored procedure that returns a result, you must add the ParameterDirection.ReturnValue parameter before any other parameters. The order of the other parameters is insignificant.

Note   If you declare an Output parameter in a SQL Server stored procedure, SQL Server treats it as an InputOutput parameter. This means you can pass an initial value into the parameter when you call the stored procedure.

Example

The following example creates three parameters for the **CountProductsInCategory** stored procedure, which was introduced in the previous topic. The parameters are added to a **SqlCommand** object named **cmCountProductsInCategory**.

```
Dim prmRet As New SqlParameter( _
  "@RETURN_VALUE", SqlDbType.Int, 4)
prmRet.Direction = ParameterDirection.ReturnValue

Dim prmID As New SqlParameter( _
  "@CatID", SqlDbType.Int, 4)
prmID.Direction = ParameterDirection.Input

Dim prmName As New SqlParameter( _
  "@CatName", SqlDbType.NChar, 15)
prmName.Direction = ParameterDirection.Output

cmCountProductsInCategory.Parameters.Add(prmRet)
cmCountProductsInCategory.Parameters.Add(prmID)
cmCountProductsInCategory.Parameters.Add(prmName)
```

How to define parameters by using the Visual Studio .NET graphical tools

▶ **To define parameters automatically by using the Visual Studio .NET developer environment**

1. Drag a **SqlCommand** or **OleDbCommand** object from the Toolbox onto your form or component.

2. In the Properties window, set the **Connection**, **CommandType**, and **CommandText** properties for the command object.

3. When you set the **CommandText** property, you are asked if you want to regenerate the parameters for the command. Click **Yes**.

4. The Visual Studio .NET developer environment generates the code to create the parameters for your command object.

▶ **PracticeBuild command objects and parameters**

1. Create a new Windows® Application project named **BuildingCommandObjects**.

2. Create a stored procedure in the Northwind database named **CountOrders**.

   The required code for this stored procedure is provided in the file CountOrders.sql in the following location:

   <install folder>\Practices\Mod03\Lesson2

   Copy this code into the stored procedure in the Visual Studio .NET code editor. The stored procedure should appear as follows:

   ```
   CREATE PROCEDURE dbo.CountOrders
     (
       @CustomerID nchar(5),
       @CompanyName nvarchar(40) OUTPUT
     )
   AS
     SET NOCOUNT ON
     DECLARE @OrdersCount int
     SELECT @CompanyName = Customers.CompanyName,
       @OrdersCount = COUNT(Orders.OrderID)
     FROM Customers INNER JOIN Orders
       ON Customers.CustomerID = Orders.CustomerID
     WHERE (Customers.CustomerID = @CustomerID)
       GROUP BY Customers.CompanyName
     RETURN @OrdersCount
   ```

3. Save the stored procedure.

4. Drag **CountOrders** from the Server Explorer onto **Form1**.

5. Right-click the form and then click **View Code**. Expand and examine the code generated by the Windows Form Designer that creates the connection and command objects and initializes the command parameters.

The solution for this practice is available in
<install folder>\Practices\Mod03\Lesson2\BuildingCommandObjects\

Lesson: Executing Command Objects That Return a Single Value

- Why Return a Single Value in a Command?
- How to Execute a Command That Returns a Single Value
- How to Retrieve Output and Return Values

Introduction

After you have built a command object, you are ready to execute the command against the database. The **SqlCommand** and **OleDbCommand** classes provide four different ways to execute a command, depending on the nature of the SQL statement or stored procedure.

In this lesson, you will learn how to execute a command that returns a single value. You will also learn how to set input parameters before you execute the command, and how to retrieve output parameters and the return value after execution.

Lesson objectives

After completing this lesson, you will be able to:

- Execute a command that returns a single value.
- Pass input parameters into a command.
- Retrieve output parameters and a return value from the command.

Why Return a Single Value in a Command?

- **ADO.NET is more efficient than ADO, where a complete record set is returned**
- **Examples**
  - Units in stock for a particular product
  - How many products?
  - COUNT, MAX, MIN, AVERAGE

Introduction

Occasionally, you might want to execute a database command or function that returns a single value, that is, a *scalar value*. Because you are returning only one value, this type of command is typically not performed by using DataSets. Instead, you execute the statement by using a command object.

Examples

The following are example scenarios of situations where you might want to return a single value in a command:

- You want to find the units in stock for a particular product. To do this, write a SQL statement that returns the UnitsInStock field for the product.

- You want to find out how many products are in the Northwind database. To do this, you write a SQL statement that uses the **COUNT()** function to count the products.

- You want to find out how many products there are in a particular category, and also obtain the name of that category. To do this, you can write a stored procedure that uses the category ID as an input parameter, and sets the category name as an output parameter. The stored procedure can also return the product count.

Note   Some developers prefer to use output parameters for all values passed back from a command, and use the return value only for error conditions and row counts.

Definition

The **SqlCommand** and **OleDbCommand** classes provide the **ExecuteScalar** method, to execute a command and obtain a scalar result. The method returns the value of the first column of the first row in the recordset.

If the SQL statement or stored procedure returns a complete recordset, the extra columns or rows are ignored. This behavior in ADO.NET is more efficient than in ADO, where the complete recordset is returned.

How to Execute a Command That Returns a Single Value

- **Call the ExecuteScalar method**
  - ExecuteScalar returns a value of the type Object
  - Use CType or a cast, to convert into appropriate type
- **Microsoft Visual Basic® code example:**

```
cmProducts.Parameters("@ProdID").Value = 42
cnNorthwind.Open()
Dim qty As Integer = _
    CType(cmProducts.ExecuteScalar(), Integer)
cnNorthwind.Close()
```

Visual Basic Example

Introduction

The **ExecuteScalar** method allows you to execute a SQL statement or stored procedure that returns a scalar result. The **ExecuteScalar** method returns a value by using the **Object** data type, so you will usually want to convert the value to a more efficient data type.

Using the ExecuteScalar method

▶ **To use the ExecuteScalar method**

1. Add a command object to your form or component and set the properties and parameters if necessary.

2. Write code to open the database connection.

3. Write code to call the **ExecuteScalar** method of the command. Assign the return value to a variable of the appropriate data type.

4. Write code to close the database connection.

Example

The following example uses a command object to execute a SQL statement that returns a scalar value. The statement queries the Products table. It takes the product ID as a parameter, and returns an integer value indicating the quantity in stock for that product. In this example, there is no aggregate function (for example, SUM), because the quantity in stock is stored as a column value in the Products table.

```
Dim sql As String = "SELECT UnitsInStock FROM Products " & _
                    "WHERE ProductID = @ProdID"

Dim cmProducts As New SqlCommand(sql, cnNorthwind)

Dim prmID As SqlParameter = cmProducts.Parameters.Add( _
    New SqlParameter("@ProdID", SqlDbType.Int, 4))

cmProducts.Parameters("@ProdID").Value = 42

cnNorthwind.Open()

Dim qty As Integer = _
  CType(cmProducts.ExecuteScalar(), Integer)

cnNorthwind.Close()

MessageBox.Show("Quantity in stock: " & qty.ToString())
```

Practice

▶ **Use the ExecuteScalar method**

1. Start the Visual Studio .NET development environment.

2. Create a new Windows Application project named **ScalarValues**.

3. Use the Server Explorer to create a new stored procedure in the Northwind database named **CountCustomers** with the following statement:

    ```
    SELECT COUNT(*) from Customers
    ```

4. Drag the **CountCustomers** stored procedure onto **Form1**.

5. Add a label and a button to the form.

6. Define a click event handler for the button, and write some code to perform the following tasks:

    a. Open the connection.

        ```
        Me.SqlConnection1.Open()
        ```

    b. Execute the command, and display the result in the label.

        ```
        Me.Label1.Text = _
            Me.SqlCommand1.ExecuteScalar() & _
            " customers"
        ```

    c. Close the connection.

        ```
        Me.SqlConnection1.Close()
        ```

7. Run and test the program.

The solution for this practice is available in
<install folder>\Practices\Mod03\Lesson3\ScalarValues\

How to Retrieve Output and Return Values

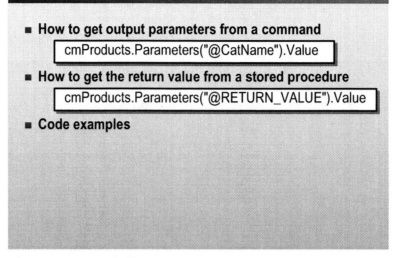

- ■ **How to get output parameters from a command**

  > cmProducts.Parameters("@CatName").Value

- ■ **How to get the return value from a stored procedure**

  > cmProducts.Parameters("@RETURN_VALUE").Value

- ■ **Code examples**

Stored Procedure and Visual Basic Example

Introduction

SQL statements and stored procedures often pass values back to the application that called them. They can do so by assigning a value to an output parameter. In addition, stored procedures can also specify a distinct return value.

How to get output parameters from a command

▶ **To get output parameters from a command**

To get an output parameter from a command object, follow these steps:

1. Configure the Parameters collection in the command object. For each output parameter, define a **Parameter** object with the **Direction** property set to **ParameterDirection.Output**. If a parameter is used to both receive and send values, set the **Direction** property to **ParameterDirection.InputOutput**.

2. Ensure that the data type of each parameter matches the expected data type in the stored procedure.

3. After executing the procedure, read the **Value** property of the parameter that is being passed back.

Note If you use the Designer to create the connection and command objects, the parameters are configured automatically. You only need to write code to retrieve the parameter values after executing the command.

How to get the return value from a stored procedure

▶ **To get the return value of a stored procedure**

1. Configure the Parameters collection for the stored procedure. The first parameter in the collection must have a **Direction** property set to **ParameterDirection.ReturnValue**.

2. Ensure that the data type of this parameter matches the data type that is returned from the stored procedure. Note that **INSERT**, **UPDATE**, and **DELETE** statements return an integer value, which indicates the number of records affected by the statement.

3. After executing the procedure, read the **Value** property of the parameter that is being passed back.

Note If you use the Designer to create the connection and command objects, the parameters are configured automatically. The default name of the return parameter is @RETURN_VALUE.

Example

The following example uses the **CountProductsInCategory** stored procedure:

```
/* Stored procedure with an input parameter named @CatID,
   an output parameter named @CatName, and a return value */

CREATE PROCEDURE dbo.CountProductsInCategory
  (
    @CatID int,
    @CatName nvarchar(15) OUTPUT
  )
AS
  SET NOCOUNT ON
  DECLARE @ProdCount int

  SELECT @CatName = Categories.CategoryName,
         @ProdCount = COUNT(Products.ProductID)
  FROM Categories INNER JOIN Products
    ON Categories.CategoryID = Products.CategoryID
  WHERE (Categories.CategoryID = @CatID)
  GROUP BY Categories.CategoryName

  RETURN @ProdCount
```

The stored procedure receives an input parameter named @CatID, and assigns an output parameter named @CatName. The stored procedure also returns a count of the products in this category.

This example assumes that the connection, command, and parameter objects have already been configured. The following code shows how to set and retrieve parameter values when you execute the stored procedure:

```
' Set input parameters, and execute the stored procedure
' Note: We use ExecuteScalar in this example. A more efficient
'       approach would be to use ExecuteNonQuery

cmProducts.Parameters("@CatID").Value = 1
cnNorthwind.Open()
cmProducts.ExecuteScalar()
cnNorthwind.Close()

MessageBox.Show("Category name: " & _
                cmProducts.Parameters("@CatName").Value & _
                "Number of products in category: " & _
                cmProducts.Parameters("@RETURN_VALUE").Value)
```

Lesson: Executing Commands That Return Rows

- **Returning Rows**
- **DataReader Properties and Methods**
- **How to Use a DataReader to Process Rows**
- **How to Execute Multiple SQL Statements**

Introduction

In this lesson, you will learn how to execute a command that returns a result set. This is a common requirement for applications that need to query a database, to obtain data that matches specific criteria.

You will also learn how to iterate efficiently through the result set, by using a DataReader object.

Lesson objectives

After completing this lesson, you will be able to:

- Execute a command that returns rows.
- Use a DataReader object to iterate through the rows.
- Access the fields in a row by using strongly typed methods in the DataReader object.
- Describe scenarios where it is appropriate to use a DataReader object.
- Execute a command that contains multiple SQL statements.

Returning Rows

- **DataReader**
  - Read-only, forward-only, stream of rows
- **The ExecuteReader method**
  - Returns a DataReader
  - For example, SqlDataReader, OleDbDataReader

Introduction

The DataReader is a fast, forward-only cursor that loops through a stream of rows. When you execute an XxxCommand that returns a set of rows, you use a DataReader to loop through the set of rows.

The ExecuteReader method

You can use a command object and the **ExecuteReader** method to return a DataReader. You can execute any **SELECT** statement or a stored procedure that contains a **SELECT** statement.

The DataReader provides strongly typed methods, to get the value of a specific column in the current row. You can also obtain metadata about the rows, such as the column name and the column data type.

When you process a result set with a DataReader, the associated connection is kept busy until you close the DataReader. For this reason, you should close the DataReader as soon as you finish processing the result set.

Example

The following are examples of situations where you might want to use a command object to return a DataReader:

- You want to obtain a single record from a table, such as the details for a particular customer. To do this, you specify the customer ID, and get back a single record containing the details for that customer.

- You want to obtain a set of records that you insert into a control on a form. This is especially useful in Web Forms, which often display read-only information such as search results or inventory lists.

DataReader Properties and Methods

- **Read method**
  - Loads the next row
  - Returns true if a row exists, false if at end of rows
- **Item property**
- **GetXxx methods – for example, GetString, GetInt32**
- **GetValues method**
- **IsDbNull method**
- **Close method**

Introduction

SqlDataReader and **OleDbDataReader** contain properties and methods for processing a result set retrieved by a command object. These properties and methods enable you to:

- Iterate through the result set, one row at a time.
- Get the value of a specific column, or all columns, in the current row.
- Check whether a column contains a missing or nonexistent value.
- Get metadata for a column, such as its name, ordinal position, and data type.

Guidelines for iterating through a result set

To iterate through a result set, call the **Read** method on the DataReader object. The **Read** method moves to the next row in the result set, by using the associated connection object.

The **Read** method returns **false** when there are no more records to read. At this point, you should call the **Close** method to close the DataReader and release the connection object.

Guidelines for getting column values

The following are various ways to get values for columns in the current row:

- The **Item** property gets the value of a column with a specified name or ordinal position. Because the value is returned in its native format, you might need to cast the value before you can use it in your code.

  Note In Microsoft Visual C#™, **Item** is the indexer for the DataReader object. Use the syntax **aReader["aColumnName"]** or **aReader[columnPosition]** to access the required column value.

- The DataReader has strongly typed methods, such as **GetDateTime**, **GetDouble**, **GetGuid**, and **GetInt32**. These methods return Common Language Specification (CLS) data types, such as **DateTime**, **GUID**, and **Int32**. Use these methods when you know the data types in the record set, to minimize the amount of type conversion required in your code.

  Note The SQL Server .NET Data Provider also has methods such as **GetSqlDateTime**, **GetSqlDouble**, and so on. These methods return SQL Server data types such as **SqlDateTime** and **SqlDouble**. These types are located in the **System.Data.SqlTypes** namespace.

- The **GetValues** method returns an array of objects containing all of the column values for the current row. This can be more efficient than retrieving each column individually.

Guidelines for checking for missing column values

When you design a database, you can specify whether a column is allowed to contain a null value. You can also specify a default value for a column, if appropriate.

To test whether a column value is null, use the **IsDbNull** method in the DataReader object. **IsDbNull** returns **true** if the column value is null and there is no default value for the column.

Guidelines for getting result set metadata

The following are various ways to get metadata for the result set:

- The **GetName** method returns the name of the column with a specified ordinal position.
- The **GetOrdinal** method returns the ordinal position of the column with a specified name.
- The **GetSchemaTable** method returns detailed schema information about the current result set. **GetSchemaTable** returns a DataTable object, which contains one row for each column in the result set. Each column of the DataTable maps to a property of the column returned in the result set.

How to Use a DataReader to Process Rows

- **Using a DataReader object to process a result set**
- **Code example**

```
Dim cmProducts As New SqlCommand( _
   "SELECT ProductName, UnitsInStock " & _
   "FROM Products", cnNorthwind)
cnNorthwind.Open()
Dim rdrProducts As SqlDataReader
rdrProducts = cmProducts.ExecuteReader()
Do While rdrProducts.Read()
   ListBox1.Items.Add(rdrProducts.GetString(0))
Loop
rdrProducts.Close()
```

Visual Basic Example

Introduction

You use a DataReader object to process the result set returned by the **ExecuteReader** method in a command object.

Using a DataReader object to process rows

▶ **To use a DataReader object to process rows**

1. Add a command object to your form or component and set the properties and parameters if necessary.

2. Declare a **SqlDataReader** or **OleDbDataReader** variable, depending on which data provider you are using.

3. Write code to open the database connection.

4. Call the **ExecuteReader** method on the command object, including the option to close the connection immediately after the DataReader is closed. Assign the return value to the DataReader variable.

5. Loop through the DataReader by using its **Read** method, until the method returns **false**.

6. Close the DataReader.

Example

The following example executes a **SELECT** statement to get product details from the Northwind database. The example iterates through the rows by using a **SqlDataReader**, and gets the ProductName and UnitsInStock for each product.

```
Dim cmProducts As New SqlCommand( _
  "SELECT ProductName, UnitsInStock " & _
  "FROM Products", cnNorthwind)

cnNorthwind.Open()

Dim rdrProducts As SqlDataReader

rdrProducts = cmProducts.ExecuteReader( _
  CommandBehavior.CloseConnection)

Do While rdrProducts.Read()

  ListBox1.Items.Add(rdrProducts.GetString(0) & _
      vbTab & rdrProducts.GetInt16(1))

Loop
rdrProducts.Close()
```

Practice

▶ **Call the ExecuteReader method**

1. Start the Visual Studio .NET development environment.

2. Create a new Windows Application project named **ProcessingMultipleRows**.

3. In the Northwind database, create a stored procedure named **AllCustomers** that returns all of the data in the **Customers** table, sorted by company name.

4. Drag the **AllCustomers** stored procedure onto **Form1**.

5. Add a list box and button to **Form1**.

6. Define a click event handler for the button, and write some code to perform the following tasks:

   a. Declare a **SqlDataReader** variable.

   b. Open the connection.

   c. Call the **ExecuteReader** method of the command object.

   d. Loop through the rows in the result set.

   e. Inside the loop, add items to the list box by using the **GetString** method.

   f. Outside the loop, close the DataReader.

```
Dim rdrCustomers As SqlClient.SqlDataReader
Me.SqlConnection1.Open()
rdrCustomers = Me.SqlCommand1.ExecuteReader( _
    CommandBehavior.CloseConnection)
Do While rdrCustomers.Read()
    Me.ListBox1.Items.Add(rdrCustomers.GetString(1))
Loop
rdrCustomers.Close()
```

7. Build and run the application.

8. Click the button.

The solution for this practice is available in
<install folder>\Practices\Mod03\Lesson4\ProcessingMultipleRows\

How to Execute Multiple SQL Statements

> - **A stored procedure can contain multiple SQL statements**
>   - Group-related tasks
>   - Encapsulate business rules
> - **If the stored procedure returns multiple result sets**
>   - Call NextResult to move to the next result set
> - **To determine how many rows were affected by the stored procedure**
>   - Use the RecordsAffected property

Introduction

A stored procedure can contain any number of SQL statements. This enables you to group related tasks into the same stored procedure, to encapsulate business rules and improve run-time performance.

When you execute the stored procedure, you can use a DataReader to retrieve the following two pieces of information:

- The result set returned by each **SELECT** statement in the stored procedure
- The total number of records affected by the stored procedure

Example of executing multiple SQL statements

A retailer decides to discontinue all products that cost more than $50. All other products will continue to be available.

To do this, the retailer uses a stored procedure that has two **UPDATE** statements. The first **UPDATE** statement discontinues products costing more than $50. The second **UPDATE** statement ensures that all other products are still available.

The stored procedure returns two result sets. The first result set contains the discontinued products. The second result set contains the available products:

```
CREATE PROCEDURE dbo.AdjustProductAvailability
AS
  UPDATE Products SET Discontinued=1 WHERE UnitPrice > 50
  SELECT ProductName FROM Products WHERE Discontinued = 1
  UPDATE Products SET Discontinued=0 WHERE UnitPrice <= 50
  SELECT ProductName FROM Products WHERE Discontinued = 0
  RETURN
```

To process a command that contains multiple statements

▶ **To process a command that contains multiple SQL statements**

1. Create a connection object and a command object, and configure these objects for the command that you wish to execute.

2. Open the database connection.

3. Call **ExecuteReader** on the command, and assign the return value to a DataReader variable.

4. Use the DataReader to loop through the rows in the first result set.

5. If there are multiple **SELECT** statements, call the **NextResult** method on the DataReader, to advance to the next result set, and then repeat step 4.

6. Close the DataReader and the database connection.

7. Use the **RecordsAffected** property in the DataReader, to find the total number of records changed, inserted, or deleted during execution of the command object.

Example of processing a command that contains multiple statements

The following example uses a **SqlDataReader** to execute the **AdjustProductAvailability** stored procedure.

The example has a **Do...While** loop, to iterate through all of the result sets returned by the stored procedure. The **NextResult** method is used to move through the result sets. **NextResult** returns **false** when there are no more result sets.

For each result set, the example creates a form named FormResult. The example fills a list box with the rows in the result set. The example then uses the **RecordsAffected** property to find out how many records have been affected in the stored procedure so far:

```
Dim cmProducts As New SqlCommand( _
  "dbo.AdjustProductAvailability", cnNorthwind)
cmProducts.CommandType = CommandType.StoredProcedure

cnNorthwind.Open()

Dim rdrProducts As SqlDataReader
rdrProducts = cmProducts.ExecuteReader( _
  CommandBehavior.CloseConnection)

Do
  Dim frmResult As New ResultForm()
  frmResult.Show()
  frmResult.Text = "Total rows affected so far: " & _
                    rdrProducts.RecordsAffected
  Do While rdrProducts.Read()
    frmResult.ListBox1.Items.Add(rdrProducts.GetString(0))
  Loop
Loop While rdrProducts.NextResult()
rdrProducts.Close()
```

Practice

▶ **Retrieve Multiple Result Sets**

1. Start the Visual Studio .NET development environment.

2. Create a new Windows Application project called **ExecutingMultipleStatements**.

3. Create a stored procedure called **CategoriesAndProducts**. Define a **SELECT** statement to return all the Categories, sorted by name. Define another **SELECT** statement to return all the Products, sorted by name.

4. Add two list boxes and a button to Form1.

5. Drag the **CategoriesAndProducts** stored procedure onto Form1.

6. Define a click event handler for the button, and add code for the following tasks:

    a. Open the database connection.

    b. Call the **ExecuteReader** method, and assign the return value to a **SqlDataReader** variable.

    c. Use a loop to read the rows. Inside the loop, add items to the first list box by using the **GetString** method of the **SqlDataReader**.

    d. Outside the loop, call the **NextResult** method of the **SqlDataReader**.

    e. Use another loop to read the rows in the second result set. Add items to the second list box, using the **GetString** method of the **SqlDataReader**.

f. Outside the loop, close the **SqlDataReader**.

```vbnet
' Visual Basic

Dim dr As SqlClient.SqlDataReader
Me.SqlConnection1.Open()
dr = Me.SqlCommand1.ExecuteReader( _
        CommandBehavior.CloseConnection)
Do While dr.Read()
  Me.ListBox1.Items.Add(dr.GetString(1))
Loop
dr.NextResult()
Do While dr.Read()
  Me.ListBox2.Items.Add(dr.GetString(1))
Loop
dr.Close()
```

```csharp
// C#

System.Data.SqlClient.SqlDataReader dr;
this.sqlConnection1.Open();
dr = this.sqlCommand1.ExecuteReader(
        CommandBehavior.CloseConnection);
while (dr.Read())
{
   this.listBox1.Items.Add(dr.GetString(1));
}
dr.NextResult();
while (dr.Read())
{
   this.listBox2.Items.Add(dr.GetString(1));
}
dr.Close();
```

The solution for this practice is available in
<install folder>\Practices\Mod03\Lesson4\ExecutingMultipleStatements\

Lesson: Executing Commands That Do Not Return Rows

- **What Are DDL and DCL Statements?**
- **How to Execute DDL and DCL Statements**
- **What Are DML Modification Statements?**
- **How to Execute DML Modification Statements**
- **Troubleshooting Data Modification**

Introduction

In this lesson, you will learn how to execute commands that do not return rows.

You will see how to use the Data Definition Language (DDL) to create and manage database structures, such as tables, views, and triggers. You will also see how to use the Data Control Language (DCL) to specify security settings for a database. Finally, you will see how to use the Data Manipulation Language (DML) to modify data in a database.

Lesson objectives

After completing this lesson, you will be able to:

- Describe scenarios where DDL and DCL statements are used.
- Use a command object to execute DDL and DCL statements.
- Describe scenarios where DML modification statements are used.
- Use a command object to execute a DML modification statement.
- Test whether the DML statement has executed successfully.

What Are DDL and DCL Statements?

- **Definition**
  - Automate database administration tasks
- **DDL and DCL statements**
  - CREATE, ALTER, DROP, GRANT, DENY, REVOKE
- **Code example**

```
CREATE PROCEDURE dbo.SummarizeProducts AS
  CREATE TABLE ProductSummary
  ( ProductName nvarchar(40),
    CategoryName nvarchar(15) )
```

Introduction

DDL enables you to automate database administration tasks in your application. You can programmatically execute DDL statements to manage the structure of the database.

DCL enables you to grant or deny permissions for user accounts, to control who can do what in the database.

Definition

The following table describes the DDL and DCL statements.

DDL or DCL statement	Description
CREATE	Create a new database object such as a table, view, index, stored procedure, or trigger.
ALTER	Alter an existing database object.
DROP	Drop an existing database object.
GRANT	Grant permissions to a user account, to allow the user to perform specific actions on the current database.
DENY	Deny permissions to a user account, to prevent the user from performing specific actions on the current database.
REVOKE	Revoke a previously granted or denied permission.

Examples

The following DDL example shows a stored procedure that creates a new table named ProductSummary. The table contains product and category names:

```
/* Stored procedure to create a new table */
CREATE PROCEDURE dbo.SummarizeProducts
AS
  CREATE TABLE ProductSummary
  (
    ProductName nvarchar(40),
    CategoryName nvarchar(15)
  )
```

The following DCL example shows a stored procedure that grants or denies permissions for all users to query the ProductSummary table:

```
/* Stored procedure to grant or deny permission to query
   the ProductSummary table */
CREATE PROCEDURE dbo.ManagePermission
  (
    @Allow int
  )
AS
  IF @Allow = 1
    GRANT SELECT ON ProductSummary TO PUBLIC
  ELSE
    DENY SELECT ON ProductSummary TO PUBLIC
```

How to Execute DDL and DCL Statements

- **ExecuteNonQuery method**
  - Returns count of rows affected
- **Code example**

```
cnNorthwind.Open()
Dim affected As Integer = _
  cmSummarizeProducts.ExecuteNonQuery()
cnNorthwind.Close()
MessageBox.Show("Records affected: " & _
  affected)
```

Visual Basic Example

Introduction

To execute a DDL or DCL statement in ADO.NET, you call the **ExecuteNonQuery** method on a **SqlCommand** or **OleDbCommand** object.

When you use the **ExecuteNonQuery** method to execute DDL, the method returns the number of rows affected.

To execute a DDL or DCL command

▶ **To execute a DDL or DCL command**

1. Create a connection object and a command object, and configure these objects for the statement you wish to execute.
2. Open the database connection.
3. Call the **ExecuteNonQuery** method on the command.
4. Close the database connection.

Example

The following stored procedure uses DDL to create a new table named **ProductSummary**:

```
CREATE PROCEDURE dbo.SummarizeProducts
AS
  CREATE TABLE ProductSummary
  (
    ProductName nvarchar(40),
    CategoryName nvarchar(15)
  )
```

The following ADO.NET code calls the **SummarizeProducts** stored procedure:

```
Dim cmSummarizeProducts As New SqlCommand( _
  "dbo.SummarizeProducts", cnNorthwind)

cmSummarizeProducts.CommandType = CommandType.StoredProcedure

cnNorthwind.Open()

Dim affected As Integer = _
  cmSummarizeProducts.ExecuteNonQuery()

cnNorthwind.Close()

MessageBox.Show("Records affected: " & affected)
```

Practice

► **Execute DDL statements**

1. Start the Visual Studio .NET development environment.

2. Create a new Windows Application project named **ExecutingDDL**.

3. Create a stored procedure named **CreateContactsTable** in the Northwind database.

4. The required code for this stored procedure is provided in the file CreateContactsTable.sql in the following location:

   <install folder>\Practices\Mod03\Lesson5\

5. Copy this code into the stored procedure in the Visual Studio .NET code editor. The stored procedure should appear as follows:

```
CREATE PROCEDURE dbo.CreateContactsTable
AS
  CREATE TABLE Contacts
  (
    CustomerID nvarchar(5),
    EmployeeID int,
    Started datetime
  )
```

6. Drag the **CreateContactsTable** stored procedure onto **Form1**.

7. Add a button to **Form1**.

8. Define a click event handler for the button, and add the code that will:

   a. Open the database connection.

   b. Call the **ExecuteNonQuery** method on the command object.

   c. Close the database connection.

9. Run the application, click the button on the form, and then close the application.

10. Use the Server Explorer to verify that the Contacts table has been created in the database.

The solution for this practice is available in
<install folder>\Practices\Mod03\Lesson5\ExecutingDDL\

What Are DML Modification Statements?

- **Definition**
  - Modify data in the database
- **DML Statements**
  - INSERT, UPDATE, DELETE
- **Code example**

```
CREATE PROCEDURE dbo.InsertRegion
  ( @RegID int,
    @RegName nchar(50) )
AS
    INSERT INTO Region VALUES (@RegID, @RegName)
```

Introduction

DML includes statements that insert new rows, update existing rows, or delete rows in a database.

DML statements

The following table describes the DML statements that modify data in a database.

DML statement	Description
INSERT	Insert a new row into a table or view. To insert multiple rows from another table or view, use the **INSERT...SELECT** statement.
UPDATE	Update existing rows in a table or view. Use this statement to set specific columns or parameter values.
DELETE	Delete existing rows from a table or view.

Note For more information about DML modification statements, see Appendix A, "Overview of SQL Statements and Stored Procedures," in Course 2389B, *Programming with Microsoft ADO.NET*.

Examples

The following stored procedure inserts a new row into the Region table in the Northwind database. The stored procedure takes two input parameters, to specify the values for the new row:

```
/* Insert a row into the Region table */
CREATE PROCEDURE dbo.InsertRegion
  (
    @RegID int,
    @RegName nchar(50)
  )
AS
  INSERT INTO Region VALUES (@RegID, @RegName)
```

The following stored procedure increases the unit price for all products in the Products table. Each unit price is increased by 2 percent:

```
/* Update the UnitPrice for all products */
CREATE PROCEDURE dbo.IncreaseProductPrices
AS
  UPDATE Products SET UnitPrice = UnitPrice * 1.02
```

The following stored procedure deletes discontinued items from the Products table:

```
/* Delete discontinued items from the Products table */
CREATE PROCEDURE dbo.DeleteDiscontinuedProducts
AS
  DELETE FROM Products WHERE Discontinued = 1
```

How to Execute DML Modification Statements

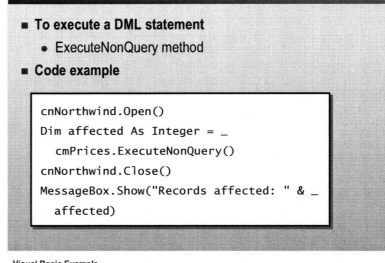

- **To execute a DML statement**
  - ExecuteNonQuery method
- **Code example**

```
cnNorthwind.Open()
Dim affected As Integer = _
    cmPrices.ExecuteNonQuery()
cnNorthwind.Close()
MessageBox.Show("Records affected: " & _
    affected)
```

<u>Visual Basic Example</u>

Introduction

To execute a DML statement to modify data, call the **ExecuteNonQuery** method on a command object. The method returns an integer, to indicate the number of rows affected.

To execute a DML statement

▶ **To execute a DML statement to modify data**

1. Create a connection object and a command object, and configure these objects for the DML statement that you wish to call.

2. Open the database connection.

3. Call **ExecuteNonQuery** on the command. Assign the return value to an integer variable, to indicate the number of rows affected by the DML statement.

4. Close the database connection.

Example

The following example calls the **IncreaseProductPrices** stored procedure, which was introduced in the previous topic. The stored procedure increases the unit price of all products by 2 percent:

```
Dim cmPrices As New SqlCommand( _
    "dbo.IncreaseProductPrices", cnNorthwind)

cmPrices.CommandType = CommandType.StoredProcedure

cnNorthwind.Open()

Dim affected As Integer = cmPrices.ExecuteNonQuery()

cnNorthwind.Close()

MessageBox.Show("Records affected: " & affected)
```

Practice

▶ **Execute a DML statement to insert a record into a table**

1. Start the Visual Studio .NET development environment.

2. Create a new Windows Application project named **ExecutingDML**.

3. Create a stored procedure named **InsertProduct** in the Northwind database.

   The required code for this stored procedure is provided in the file **InsertProduct.sql** in the following location:

   <install folder>\Practices\Mod03\Lesson5\

   Copy this code into the stored procedure in the Visual Studio .NET code editor. The stored procedure should appear as follows:

   ```
   CREATE PROCEDURE dbo.InsertProduct
     (
       @ProductName nvarchar(40),
       @CategoryID int,
       @SupplierID int
     )
   AS
     INSERT INTO Products(ProductName, CategoryID, SupplierID)
           VALUES(@ProductName, @CategoryID, @SupplierID)
     RETURN @@IDENTITY
   ```

4. Drag the **InsertProduct** stored procedure onto **Form1**.

5. Add a text box and a button to **Form1**.

6. Define a click event handler for the button, and add the following code:

   a. Set the @ProductName parameter in the command object, by using the value in the text box.

   b. Set the @CategoryID and @SupplierID parameters to the value **1**.

   c. Open the database connection.

   d. Call the **ExecuteNonQuery** method on the command object. Assign the return value to an integer variable.

   e. Close the database connection.

   f. Display the return value from the **ExecuteNonQuery** method.

   g. Also display the @RETURN_VALUE parameter of the data command object. The stored procedure assigns the generated ProductID to this parameter.

   ```
   Me.SqlCommand1.Parameters("@ProductName").Value = _
       Me.TextBox1.Text
   Me.SqlCommand1.Parameters("@CategoryID").Value = 1
   Me.SqlCommand1.Parameters("@SupplierID").Value = 1
   Me.SqlConnection1.Open()
   Dim iAffected As Integer =
   Me.SqlCommand1.ExecuteNonQuery()
   Me.SqlConnection1.Close()
   MessageBox.Show(iAffected & " rows were affected." & _
       vbCrLf & "Assigned Product ID " & _
       Me.SqlCommand1.Parameters("@RETURN_VALUE").Value)
   ```

7. Run and test the application.

8. Type any product name in the text field, for example, John Smith's Apples, and then click the button on the form. A message box should appear, indicating that one row has been affected. The message box should also display the auto-generated ProductID for the inserted product.

9. Close the application.

10. Using the Server Explorer, verify that a new record has been inserted into the Products table.

The solution for this practice is available in
<install folder>\Practices\Mod03\Lesson5\ExecutingDML\

Troubleshooting Data Modification

- **Common errors**
  - Incorrect object names
  - Server unavailability
  - Data integrity issues
  - Using connection before it is open
  - Invalid data types

Introduction

When you execute a SQL statement against a database, many different types of errors can occur, including the following:

- Errors due to programmer fault, such as a spelling mistake
- Errors due to run-time conditions, such as server unavailability
- Errors due to data integrity issues, such as inserting a record with a duplicate primary key

Common programming errors

The following are some of the common programming errors that can occur. To resolve these errors, fix the code and rebuild the application.

- Forgetting to open a database connection before you execute the data command
- Specifying invalid SQL syntax in the command text
- Specifying an invalid name for a stored procedure
- Forgetting to set an input parameter in a data command
- Setting an inappropriate value or data type for an input parameter
- Forgetting to set a required column when you insert a new record into a table

Common run-time errors

The following are some errors that can occur because of run-time conditions. To deal with these errors, catch a **SqlException** in your code and handle the error as appropriate.

- Unable to open a database connection
- Database connection broken during execution of the statement

Common data integrity errors

The following are some data integrity errors that can occur. To deal with these errors, catch a **SqlException** in your code.

- Inserting duplicate records into a table

- Inserting a record into a secondary table, but specifying a nonexistent record in the primary table

- Deleting a record from a primary table, where the record is still referenced in a secondary table

- Attempting to create a table that already exists

- Attempting to drop a table that is referenced by a secondary table

- Attempting to execute a statement without sufficient user privileges

---

Note Even if a DML statement executes without any exceptions, this does not necessarily mean that the DML statement had the desired effect. For example, if you try to delete a nonexistent record, the statement succeeds but returns 0 to indicate that no records were deleted.

Practice

▶ **Troubleshoot data modification errors**

1. Open the project named **ExecutingDML**, which you created earlier in this lesson, or open the solution provided in the folder.

   <install folder>\Practices\Mod03\Lesson5\ExecutingDML\

2. Create a stored procedure named **DeleteProduct** in the Northwind database.

   The required code for this stored procedure is provided in the file DeleteProduct.sql in the following location:

   <install folder>\Practices\Mod03\Lesson5\

3. Copy this code into the stored procedure in the Visual Studio .NET code editor. The stored procedure should appear as follows:

```
CREATE PROCEDURE dbo.DeleteProduct
  (
    @ProductID int
  )
AS
    DELETE FROM Products WHERE ProductID = @ProductID
```

4. Drag the **DeleteProduct** stored procedure onto **Form1**.

5. Add another text box and a button to **Form1**.

6. Define a click event handler for the button, and add code that will:

   a. Set the @ProductID parameter in the command object, by using the value in the text box.

   b. Open the database connection.

   c. Call the **ExecuteNonQuery** method on the new command object. Assign the return value to an integer variable.

   d. Close the database connection.

   e. Display the return value from the **ExecuteNonQuery** method.

```
Me.SqlCommand2.Parameters("@ProductID").Value = _
    Me.TextBox2.Text
Me.SqlConnection1.Open()
Dim iAffected As Integer = Me.SqlCommand2.ExecuteNonQuery()
Me.SqlConnection1.Close()
MessageBox.Show("Records affected: " & iAffected)
```

7. Run and test the application.

8. Try to delete one of the products you added in the previous lesson (ProductID > 77). You will be able to delete this product. 1 row will be affected.

9. Try to delete the same product ID again, or delete another product that does not exist, for example ProductID = 999. You will not get an error, but no records will be deleted.

10. Try to delete an original product, such as ProductID = 1. You will get an exception, because the record is referenced elsewhere in the database.

11. If time permits, modify the code in your application so that it catches any exceptions that might occur.

The solution for this practice is available in
<install folder>\Practices\Mod03\Lesson5\Troubleshooting\

Lesson: Using Transactions

- **What Is a Transaction?**
- **How to Manage Transactions Using SQL Statements**
- **How to Manage Transactions Using ADO.NET**
- **What Are Isolation Levels?**

Introduction

A *transaction* is a single unit of work. If a transaction is successful, all of the data modifications made during the transaction are committed and become a permanent part of the database. If a transaction encounters errors and must be canceled or rolled back, then all of the data modifications are erased.

You can use transactions in ADO.NET, to ensure the consistency and integrity of the database.

Lesson objectives

After completing this lesson, you will be able to:

- Describe why transactions are important.
- Begin a transaction.
- Specify an appropriate isolation level for a transaction.
- Commit or roll back a transaction.

What Is a Transaction?

- **A transaction is a set of related tasks that either succeed or fail as a unit**
- **Two types of transactions**
  - Local transactions
  - Distributed transactions

Definition

A transaction is a set of related tasks that either succeed or fail as a unit. In transaction processing terminology, the transaction either *commits* or *rolls back*. For a transaction to commit, all participants must guarantee that any change to data will be permanent. Changes must persist despite system failures or other unforeseen events.

If even a single participant fails to make this guarantee, the entire transaction fails. All changes to data within the scope of the transaction are rolled back to a specific set point.

For an example of using transactions, consider the following scenario: An ASP.NET page performs two tasks. First, it creates a new table in a database. Next, it calls a specialized object to collect, format, and insert data into the new table. These two tasks are related and even interdependent, in such a way that you want to avoid creating a new table unless you can fill it with data. Executing both tasks within the scope of a single transaction enforces the connection between them. If the second task fails, the first task is rolled back to a point before the new table was created.

Local and distributed transactions

You can create local or distributed transactions, described as follows:

- Local transactions

  A local transaction is confined to a single data resource, such as a database or message queue. It is common for these data resources to provide local transaction capabilities. Controlled by the data resource, these transactions are efficient and easy to manage.

- Distributed transactions

  Transactions can also span multiple data resources. Distributed transactions enable you to coordinate distinct operations on different systems, so that they all succeed or they all fail.

ACID properties

The term ACID refers to the role transactions play in an application. Coined by transaction-processing pioneers, ACID stands for atomicity, consistency, isolation, and durability.

These properties ensure predictable behavior, reinforcing the role of transactions as all-or-none propositions designed to reduce the management load when there are many variables.

- Atomicity

  A transaction is a unit of work in which a series of operations occur between the **BEGIN TRANS** and **END TRANS** statements of an application. A transaction executes exactly once and is atomic; that is, all of the work is done or none of it is.

- Consistency

  A transaction is a unit of integrity because it preserves the consistency of data, transforming one consistent state of data into another consistent state of data.

  Consistency requires that data bound by a transaction be semantically preserved. Some of the responsibility for maintaining consistency falls to the application developer, who must make sure that all known integrity constraints are enforced by the application.

- Isolation

  A transaction is a unit of isolation. It allows concurrent transactions to behave as though each were the only transaction running in the system.

  Isolation requires that each transaction appears to be the only transaction manipulating the data store, even though other transactions may be running at the same time. A transaction should never see the intermediate stages of another transaction.

- Durability

  If a transaction succeeds, the system guarantees that its updates will persist, even if the computer crashes immediately after the commit. Specialized logging allows the system restart procedure to complete unfinished operations, making the transaction durable.

How to Manage Transactions Using SQL Statements

- **SQL transaction statements**
  - BEGIN TRANS, COMMIT TRANS, ROLLBACK TRANS
- **Code example**

```
BEGIN TRANS
DECLARE @orderDetailsError int, @productError int
DELETE FROM "Order Details" WHERE ProductID=42
SELECT @orderDetailsError = @@ERROR
DELETE FROM Products WHERE ProductID=42
SELECT @productError = @@ERROR
IF @orderDetailsError = 0 AND @productError = 0
    COMMIT TRANS
ELSE
    ROLLBACK TRANS
```

Introduction

Transactions can be managed at the database tier by using SQL statements.

SQL transaction statements

The following table describes some of the SQL statements for managing transactions. You can use these statements in stored procedures, to control transactional behavior in the data tier.

Transaction statement	Description
BEGIN TRANS	Marks the beginning of the transaction. All statements executed after the **BEGIN TRANS** statement are considered to be part of the transaction.
COMMIT TRANS	Marks the end of a successful transaction, and commits all changes made since the **BEGIN TRANS** statement.
ROLLBACK TRANS	Rolls back a transaction to the beginning of the transaction.

Example

The following example shows how to manage transactions by using Transact-SQL. The example deletes all order details for a particular product, and then deletes the product itself. If any errors occur, the entire transaction is rolled back to ensure consistency.

```
BEGIN TRANS
DECLARE @orderDetailsError int, @productError int
DELETE FROM "Order Details" WHERE ProductID=42
SELECT @orderDetailsError = @@ERROR
DELETE FROM Products WHERE ProductID=42
SELECT @productError = @@ERROR
IF @orderDetailsError = 0 AND @productError = 0
  COMMIT TRANS
ELSE
  ROLLBACK TRANS
```

How to Manage Transactions Using ADO.NET

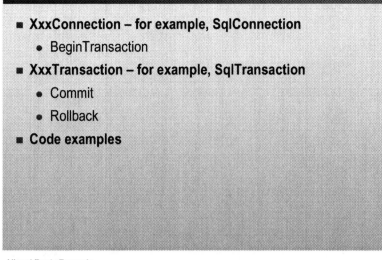

- **XxxConnection – for example, SqlConnection**
  - BeginTransaction
- **XxxTransaction – for example, SqlTransaction**
  - Commit
  - Rollback
- **Code examples**

Visual Basic Example

Introduction

ADO.NET enables you to manage transactions in a .NET Framework application at the middle tier. This is an alternative to performing transactions in the data tier.

The **SqlConnection** and **OleDbConnection** objects have a **BeginTransaction** method, which returns a **SqlTransaction** or **OleDbTransaction** object. The transaction object has methods named **Commit** and **Rollback** to manage the transaction in your application.

To perform a transaction

► **To perform a transaction by using ADO.NET**

1. Call the **BeginTransaction** method of the connection object. Assign the return value to a **SqlTransaction** or **OleDbTransaction** variable.

2. For all commands that you want to execute within this transaction, set the **Transaction** property to refer to the transaction object.

3. Execute the required command objects.

4. If the commands complete satisfactorily, call the **Commit** method on the transaction object. If any problems occur, call the **Rollback** method to roll back to the original conditions.

Example

The following example uses a transaction to coordinate multiple **DELETE** statements in the Northwind database. The first **DELETE** statement deletes all items in the Order Details table, for the ProductID 42. The second **DELETE** statement deletes the product with ProductID 42 in the Products table. If any errors occur, the transaction is rolled back and all deletions are canceled.

```
' Open the database connection, and begin a transaction.
' Execute two DELETE statements within the transaction.
' Commit or rollback the transaction, as appropriate

cnNorthwind.Open()

Dim trans As SqlTransaction = cnNorthwind.BeginTransaction()

Dim cmDel As New SqlCommand()
cmDel.Connection = cnNorthwind
cmDel.Transaction = trans

Try

    cmDel.CommandText = _
        "DELETE [Order Details] WHERE ProductID = 42"

    cmDel.ExecuteNonQuery()

    cmDel.CommandText = "DELETE Products WHERE ProductID = 42"

    cmDel.ExecuteNonQuery()

    trans.Commit()

Catch Xcp As Exception

    trans.Rollback()

Finally

    cnNorthwind.Close()

End Try
```

What Are Isolation Levels?

■ **Examples of concurrency problems**
■ **Guidelines for setting the isolation level**
■ **Code example**

```
trans = cnNorthwind.BeginTransaction( _
    IsolationLevel.Serializable)
```

■ **Support for isolation levels is dependent on which database you use**

Introduction

Isolation levels specify the transaction locking behavior for a connection. You choose an appropriate isolation level as follows to prevent concurrency problems when multiple transactions access the same data:

■ At one extreme, you can allow transactions to have unimpeded access to the database. This minimizes the wait time for statements in the transactions, but increases the risk of data corruption due to concurrent access.

■ At the other extreme, you can specify that transactions are completely isolated from each other. The transactions are executed serially, one after the other.

Examples of concurrency problems

If several transactions access the same data at the same time, the following concurrency errors may occur:

■ Dirty reads

A *dirty read* occurs when a transaction selects a row that is currently being updated by another transaction. The original transaction is reading data that has not yet been committed, and the data may be changed by the other transaction.

■ Non-repeatable reads

A *non-repeatable read* occurs when a transaction reads committed data once, then reads it again later and gets a different value. This happens if another transaction has updated the data between the two read operations.

■ Phantom reads

A *phantom read* occurs when a transaction reads data that is currently being deleted by another transaction. If the original transaction reads the data again, it will not see the deleted rows.

Guidelines for setting the isolation level

The **SqlTransaction** and **OleDbTransaction** objects have a property named **IsolationLevel**. You set this property when you call **BeginTransaction** on the connection object.

The following table describes the allowable isolation levels, in order of increasing isolation. These values are defined in the IsolationLevel enumeration.

Isolation level	Description
ReadUncommitted	Transaction isolation is only sufficient to prevent corrupt data from being read.
	Dirty reads, non-repeatable reads, and phantom reads can occur.
ReadCommitted	Shared locks are held while the data is being read, to prevent dirty reads. However, the data can be changed before the end of the transaction, causing non-repeatable reads or phantom reads.
	This is the default isolation level.
RepeatableRead	All data used in a query is locked. This prevents other users from updating the data, and therefore prevents non-repeatable reads. However, phantom reads can still occur.
Serializable	Transactions are completely isolated from each other. This prevents dirty reads, non-repeatable reads, and phantom reads.
Unspecified	A different isolation level than the one specified is being used, but the level cannot be determined

Example

The following example shows how to begin a transaction by using the Serializable isolation level. This ensures maximum protection against concurrency errors, at the expense of run-time performance.

```
trans = cnNorthwind.BeginTransaction( _
  IsolationLevel.Serializable)
```

Practice

▶ **Perform a transaction**

1. Start the Visual Studio .NET development environment.
2. Create a new Windows Application project named **ExecutingTransactions**.
3. Add two text boxes and a button to **Form1**
4. Drag the **InsertProduct** stored procedure in the Northwind database onto **Form1**.

5. Define a click event handler for the new button, and add the following code:

   a. Open the database connection.

   b. Create and assign a transaction to the command.

   c. Set the @ProductName parameter of the command, to the value in the first text box. Set the @CategoryID and @SupplierID parameters to **1**.

   d. Execute the command.

   e. Set the @ProductName parameter to the value of the second text box.

   f. Execute the command again.

   g. Display a message box asking if the user wants to save the changes. If the user selects **Yes**, commit the transaction. Otherwise, roll back the transaction.

   h. Close the database connection.

6. Run and test the application.

7. Type two product names in the text boxes, and then click the button. When you are prompted to save changes, click **Yes**. Use Server Explorer to verify that two new records have been added to the Products table.

8. Type two different product names in the text boxes, and then click the button. When you are prompted to save changes, click **No**. Verify that neither record has been added to the Products table.

The solution for this practice is available in
<install folder>\Practices\Mod03\Lesson6\ExecutingTransactions\

Review

- Working in a Connected Environment
- Building Command Objects
- Executing Commands That Return a Single Value
- Executing Commands That Return Rows
- Executing Commands That Do Not Return Rows
- Using Transactions

1. In what situations would you use the connected environment? What classes would you use for a connected application?

2. For what tasks can you use the command object?

3. How does the DataReader class work? When do you use the DataReader class?

4. What types of statements do you use when you do not want rows returned?

5. What is a transaction?

Lab 3.1: Performing Connected Database Operations

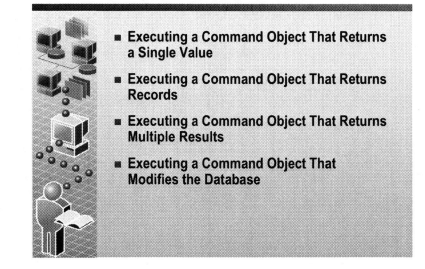

- Executing a Command Object That Returns a Single Value
- Executing a Command Object That Returns Records
- Executing a Command Object That Returns Multiple Results
- Executing a Command Object That Modifies the Database

Objectives

After completing this lab, you will be able to:

- Build a command object.
- Execute a command object that returns a single value.
- Execute a command object that returns records.
- Execute a command object that returns multiple results.
- Execute a command object that modifies the database.

Prerequisites

Before working on this lab, you must have:

- Microsoft Visual Basic® or Visual C# programming skills.
- Familiarity with the Visual Studio .NET development environment.

For more information

Search online Help for the topic "Databases in Server Explorer." Hint: Use quotation marks (" ") around the topic titles when searching the Visual Studio .NET online documentation.

Scenario

Northwind Traders has a corporate local area network (LAN) that provides employees with easy access to the Northwind database. Employees need to access the information in this database, to make business decisions about which products to stock and the pricing policy for these products. These tasks are performed only by office workers. Mobile workers do not perform these tasks. A connected Windows Application satisfies these requirements.

Solution Files

Before running the solution files you must create the stored procedures they use in Microsoft SQL Server.

▶ **To create the stored procedures**

1. Start the Microsoft SQL Server Query Analyzer.

2. Switch to the Northwind database.

3. Open and run the scripts named **CountProducts.sql**, **GetMultipleResults.sql**, **GetOrderSummary.sql**, and **SummarizeOrders.sql** in the folder

   <install path>\2389\Labs\Lab03\Starter\

4. Close the SQL Server Query Analyzer.

Estimated time to complete this lab: 60 minutes

Exercise 1
Executing a Command Object That Returns a Single Value

In this exercise, you will create a new stored procedure in the Northwind database. The stored procedure will return the number of products in the database.

You will then open an existing Windows Application and add a **SqlConnection** object to connect to the Northwind database. You will also add a **SqlCommand** object to represent the new stored procedure. You will execute the stored procedure by using the **ExecuteScalar** method and display the result in a message box.

Scenario

The Northwind database contains information about all products stocked by Northwind Traders. Employees at Northwind Traders need to know how many products are in a specified price range. Employees can access the database over the corporate LAN.

▶ **Add a stored procedure to get the number of products**

1. Start the Visual Studio .NET development environment.

2. In the Server Explorer, select the Northwind database on your local computer.

3. Add a new stored procedure to the Northwind database.

   The required code for this stored procedure is provided in the file CountProducts.sql in the following location:

   <install folder>\Labs\Lab03\Starter

4. Copy this code into the stored procedure in the Visual Studio .NET code editor.

5. Save the stored procedure.

▶ **Add data objects to a Windows Application**

1. In Visual Studio .NET, open one of the following starter solutions:

   - If you wish to use Visual Basic, open the starter solution provided in <install folder>\Labs\Lab03\Starter\VB.

   - If you wish to use Visual C#, open the starter solution provided in <install folder>\Labs\Lab03\Starter\CS.

2. Open the form named **FormConnectedApp**.

3. View the Server Explorer, and find the **CountProducts** stored procedure in the Northwind database. Drag this stored procedure onto your form. Visual Studio .NET creates a **SqlConnection** object and a **SqlCommand** object.

4. In the Properties window for the **SqlConnection** object, set the following property.

Property	Value
(Name)	cnNorthwind

5. In the Properties window for the **SqlCommand** object, set the following property.

Property	Value
(Name)	cmCountProducts

6. Review the code for your application. Notice the code that creates the parameters for the command.

► **Execute the stored procedure**

1. Add an event handler method for the **Click** event on the **Count Products** button.

2. In the event handler method, get the text in the **txtMinimumPrice** and **txtMaximumPrice** text boxes. Use the **double.Parse** method to convert these strings to the **double** data type. Assign the **double** values to two local **double** variables.

3. Use these values to set the **@Min** and **@Max** parameters in the **cmCountProducts** stored procedure command.

4. Open a connection to the database.

5. Use the **ExecuteScalar** method to execute the **cmCountProducts** stored procedure command. Convert the return value into an integer, and assign it to a local integer variable.

6. Close the database connection.

7. Display a message box, to show the return value from the **cmCountProducts** stored procedure command.

► **Build and test the Windows Application**

1. Build the application, and correct any build errors.

2. Run the application.

3. Enter values such as **10** and **100** for the minimum and maximum prices.

4. Click **Count Products**, and observe the result displayed in the message box.

Exercise 2
Executing a Command Object That Returns Records

In this exercise, you will create another stored procedure in the Northwind database. The stored procedure will execute a SQL query, to obtain all products in stock within a specified price range.

You will extend the Windows Application from Exercise 1, to call the stored procedure by using the **ExecuteReader** method. You will loop through the records by using a **SqlDataReader**, and display the product details in a list box.

Note: You will extend the stored procedure in Exercise 3, to return the out-of-stock records as well.

Scenario

Employees at Northwind Traders need to obtain information about all products currently in stock, within a specified price range.

▶ **Add a stored procedure to return products in stock**

1. In the Server Explorer, select the Northwind database on your local computer.

2. Add a new stored procedure to the Northwind database.

   The required code for this stored procedure is provided in the file GetProductsInRange.sql in the following location:

   <install folder>\Labs\Lab03\Starter

   Copy this code into the new stored procedure in the Visual Studio .NET code editor.

3. Save the stored procedure.

▶ **Add a SqlCommand object to represent the new stored procedure**

1. Open the solution you completed in the previous exercise.

2. In the Server Explorer, find the **GetProductsInRange** stored procedure in the Northwind database. Drag this stored procedure onto your form. Visual Studio .NET creates a new **SqlCommand** object.

3. In the Properties window for the new **SqlCommand** object, set the following property.

Property	Value
(Name)	cmGetProductsInRange

▶ **Execute the stored procedure**

1. Add an event handler method for the Click event on the **Display Products** button.

2. Clear the contents of the **lstInStock** list box.

3. Using the values in **txtMinimumPrice** and **txtMaximumPrice**, set the **@Min** and **@Max** parameters in the **cmGetProductsInRange** stored procedure command.

4. Open a connection to the database.

5. Declare a local variable named drProducts, of the type System.Data.SqlClient.SqlDataReader.

6. Call the ExecuteReader method on the cmGetProductsInRange command. Assign the result to the drProducts variable.

7. Use **drProducts** to loop through the product records. For each product record, get the following column values.

Column	Code to get this column value
ProductID	drProducts.GetInt32(0)
ProductName	drProducts.GetString(1)
UnitPrice	drProducts.GetSqlMoney(2).ToDouble()

For each product, add an item containing this information to the **lstInStock** list box.

8. Close **drProducts**.

9. Close the database connection.

▶ **Build and test the Windows Application**

1. Build the application, and correct any build errors.

2. Run the application.

3. Enter values such as 10 and 100 for the minimum and maximum prices.

4. Click **Display Products**.

5. Observe the information displayed in the in-stock list box. Note that the out-of-stock list box is still empty at this stage.

Exercise 3
Executing a Command Object That Returns Multiple Results

In this exercise, you will extend the stored procedure from Exercise 2. The stored procedure will now return two results: the products that are in stock, and the products that are out of stock.

You will also extend the Windows Application from Exercise 2, to process the multiple results. You will use the **SqlDataReader** to display the in-stock products first. You will then call the **NextResult** method in **SqlDataReader** to advance the data reader to the second result. You will loop through this result, to display the out-of-stock products.

Scenario

Employees at Northwind Traders need to know which products are in stock, and which products are out of stock. This enables employees to make business decisions based on current stock levels.

▶ **Return multiple results from a stored procedure**

1. In the Server Explorer, select the Northwind database on your local computer.

2. Open the **dbo.GetProductsInRange** stored procedure in the code editor.

3. Modify the stored procedure, so that it returns two results:

   • The in-stock products (within the specified price range). Note: the SELECT statement to do this already exists in the stored procedure.

   • The out-of-stock products (within the specified price range).

   The complete code for this stored procedure is provided in the file GetMultipleResults.sql in the following location:

   <install folder>\Labs\Lab03\Starter

4. Save the stored procedure.

▶ **Process multiple results**

1. Open the solution you completed in the previous exercise.

2. Find the event handler method for the **Click** event on the **Display Products** button.

3. After the **lstInStock** list box has been populated with the first result, but before closing **drProducts**, call the **NextResult** method on **drProducts**.

4. Clear the contents of the **lstOutOfStock** list box.

5. Use **drProducts** to loop through the out-of-stock products. For each record, get the following column values.

Column	Code to get this column value
ProductID	drProducts.GetInt32(0)
ProductName	drProducts.GetString(1)
UnitPrice	drProducts.GetSqlMoney(2).ToDouble()

For each product, add an item containing this information to the **lstOutOfStock** list box.

▶ **Build and test the Windows Application**

1. Build the application, and correct any build errors.

2. Run the application.

3. Enter values such as 10 and 100 for the minimum and maximum prices.

4. Click **Display Products**.

5. Observe which products are in stock, and which products are out of stock.

Exercise 4
Executing a Command Object That Modifies the Database

In this exercise, you will write a stored procedure to create an OrderSummary table in the Northwind database. The stored procedure will populate the table with the total number of orders for each product.

You will also write a stored procedure to query the data in the OrderSummary table.

In your Windows Application, you will use the **ExecuteNonQuery** method to execute the first stored procedure. You will use the **ExecuteQuery** method to execute the second stored procedure, and create a **SqlDataReader** to loop through the result.

Scenario

The Orders table in the Northwind database contains information for each customer order. The details of each order are in the Order Details table. The Order Details table indicates the quantity required for each product in the order.

Employees at Northwind Traders need a summary of the total number of orders for each product. This information will help Northwind Traders identify its most popular products, so that the company can offer the best possible service to its customers.

▶ **Add a stored procedure to create and fill the OrderSummary table**

1. In the Server Explorer, select the Northwind database on your local computer.

2. Add a new stored procedure to the Northwind database.

   The required code for this stored procedure is provided in the file SummarizeOrders.sql in the following location:

   <install folder>\Labs\Lab03\Starter

   Copy this code into the new stored procedure in the Visual Studio .NET code editor.

3. Save the stored procedure.

▶ **Add a stored procedure to query the OrderSummary table**

1. Add another new stored procedure to the Northwind database.

   The required code for this stored procedure is provided in the file GetOrderSummary.sql in the following location:

   <install folder>\Labs\Lab03\Starter

   Copy this code into the new stored procedure in the Visual Studio .NET code editor.

2. Save the stored procedure.

▶ **Add SqlCommand objects to represent the new stored procedures**

1. Open the solution you completed in the previous exercise.

2. In the Server Explorer, find the **SummarizeOrders** stored procedure in the Northwind database. Drag this stored procedure onto your form. Visual Studio .NET creates a new **SqlCommand** object.

3. In the Properties window for this **SqlCommand** object, set the following property.

Property	Value
(Name)	cmSummarizeOrders

4. Drag the **GetOrderSummary** stored procedure onto your form. Visual Studio .NET creates another new **SqlCommand** object.

5. In the Properties window for this **SqlCommand** object, set the following property.

Property	Value
(Name)	cmGetOrderSummary

▶ **Execute the stored procedures**

1. In the Windows Form Designer, click the **Product Orders** tab on your form.

2. Add an event handler method for the click event on the **Summarize Orders** button.

3. In the event handler method, clear the contents of the **lstOrderSummary** list box.

4. Open a connection to the database.

5. Call the **ExecuteNonQuery** method on the **cmSummarizeOrders** command.

6. Declare a local variable named drProducts, of the type System.Data.SqlClient.SqlDataReader.

7. Call the **ExecuteReader** method on the **cmGetOrderSummary** command. Assign the result to the drProducts variable.

8. Use **drProducts** to loop through the records. For each record, get the following column values.

Column	Code to get this column value
Orders	drProducts.GetInt32(0)
ProductName	drProducts.GetString(1)

For each record, add an item containing this information to the **lstOrderSummary** list box.

9. Close **drProducts**.

10. Close the database connection.

▶ **Build and test the Windows Application**

1. Build the application, and correct any build errors.

2. Run the application.

3. Click the **Product Orders** tab on the form.

4. Click **Summarize Orders**.

5. Observe the total number of orders for each product.

msdn training

Module 4: Building DataSets

Contents

Microsoft

Overview

- **Working in a Disconnected Environment**
- **Building DataSets and DataTables**
- **Binding and Saving a DataSet**
- **Defining Data Relationships**
- **Modifying Data in a DataTable**
- **Sorting and Filtering**

Introduction

This module presents the concepts and procedures you need to create and use DataSets and related objects. DataSets enable you to store, manipulate, and modify data in a local cache while disconnected from the data source.

Objectives

After completing this module, you will be able to:

- Describe the disconnected environment.
- Build a DataSet and a DataTable.
- Bind a DataSet to a DataGrid.
- Open and save a DataSet.
- Define a data relationship.
- Modify data in a DataTable.
- Find and select rows in a DataTable.
- Sort and filter a DataTable by using a DataView.

Lesson: Working in a Disconnected Environment

- **Typically disconnected scenarios**
- **.NET Framework classes used in scenarios**

Introduction

This lesson explains typical disconnected data access scenarios that will be examined in more detail during the rest of this course.

Lesson objectives

After completing this lesson, you will be able to:

- Describe some typical disconnected data access applications.
- Describe the Microsoft® ADO.NET classes that are used in disconnected applications.

Disconnected Applications

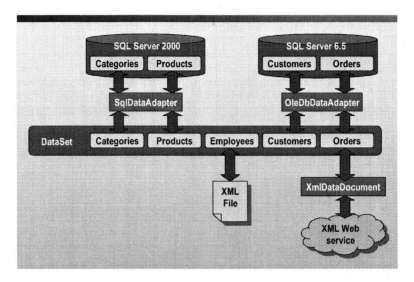

Introduction

When you build disconnected database applications that use ADO.NET, there are many sources for data, and methods for interacting with that data.

Relational databases

In today's business environment, most corporate data is stored in relational databases. DataAdapters are designed to allow subsets of data to be pulled from these databases and stored in a disconnected way in a DataSet.

XML Web services and files

As XML becomes more prevalent, corporate data is increasingly stored in XML format. DataSets can be saved as a combination of XSD (for the structure) and XML (for the data). You might need to convert other data sources into a schema that the DataSet object recognizes by using an intermediate XmlDataDocument object.

BizTalk and electronic data interchange

Microsoft BizTalk™ Server uses XML-Data Reduced (XDR), an early form of XSD, to send and receive messages.

Data provider classes

The .NET data providers and the System.Data namespace provide the ADO.NET classes that you will use in a disconnected scenario. ADO.NET exposes a common object model for .NET data providers. The following table describes the core classes that make up a .NET data provider, which are used in a disconnected scenario.

Class	Description
XxxDataAdapter	Uses the **Connection**, **Command**, and **DataReader** classes implicitly to populate a DataSet, and to update the central data source with any changes made to the DataSet. For example, the **SqlDataAdapter** class can manage the interaction between a DataSet and a Microsoft SQL Server™ 7 database.
XxxConnection	Establishes a connection to a specific data source. For example, the **SqlConnection** class connects to SQL Server data sources.
XxxCommand	Executes a command from a data source. For example, the **SqlCommand** class can execute stored procedures or SQL statements in a SQL Server data source.
XxxDataReader	Reads a forward-only, read-only stream of data from a data source. For example, the **SqlDataReader** class can read rows from tables in a SQL Server data source. It is returned by the **ExecuteReader** method of the **XxxCommand** class, typically as a result of a SELECT SQL statement.

Lesson: Building DataSets and DataTables

- **What Are DataSets, DataTables, and DataColumns?**
- **The DataSet Object Model**
- **How to Create a DataSet, a DataTable, and a DataColumn**
- **How to Create a Primary Key Constraint**
- **Using Unique Constraints**
- **Creating Custom Expressions**

Introduction

This lesson explains what DataSets, DataTables, and DataColumns are, how to create them programmatically, and how to include exception handling, constraints, AutoIncrement columns, and custom expressions in your ADO.NET DataSet.

Lesson objectives

After completing this lesson, you will be able to:

- Explain what DataSets, DataTables, and DataColumns are.
- Create a DataSet and a DataTable.
- Create a primary key.
- Use unique constraints.
- Create custom expressions.

What Are DataSets, DataTables, and DataColumns?

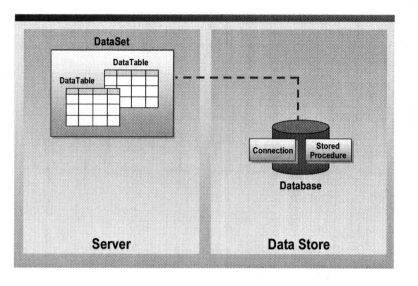

Introduction

In ADO.NET, DataSets, DataTables, and DataColumns enable you to represent data in a local cache and provide a relational programming model for the data regardless of its source.

Definitions

The ADO.NET DataSet is an in-memory cache of data, and functions as a disconnected relational view of the data. The connection to the data source does not need to be active for an application to view and manipulate data in a DataSet. This disconnected architecture enables greater scalability by using database server resources only when reading from or writing to the data source.

DataSets store data similarly to the way data is stored in a relational database with a hierarchical object model of tables, rows, and columns. Additionally, you can define constraints and relationships for the data in the DataSet.

DataTable objects are used to represent the tables in a DataSet. A DataTable represents one table of in-memory relational data. The data is local to the .NET application in which it resides, but it can be populated from an existing data source. A DataTable is composed of DataColumns.

A DataColumn is the building block for creating the schema of a DataTable. Each DataColumn has a DataType property that determines the kind of data that each DataColumn contains. For example, you can restrict the data type to integers, strings, or decimals. Because data contained in the DataTable is typically merged back into the original data source, you must match the data types to those in the data source.

DataSets and XML

DataSets represent data in a relational view regardless of its source. However, data in a DataSet can be represented in XML format. The integration of DataSets with XML enables you to define the structure of a DataSet schema. For more information, see Module 5, "Reading and Writing XML With ADO.NET," in Course 2389B, *Programming with Microsoft ADO.NET*.

The DataSet Object Model

dS. tablename . Constraints

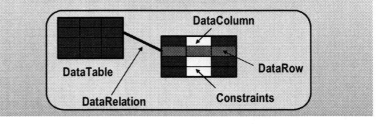

- ■ **Common collections**
  - ● Tables (collection of DataTable objects)
  - ● Relations (collection of DataRelation objects)
- ■ **Data binding to Web and Windows controls supported**
- ■ **Schema can be defined programmatically or using XSD**

Tables in a DataSet

The DataSet class has a **Tables** property that gets a collection of DataTable objects in the DataSet, and a **Relations** property that gets a collection of the DataRelation objects in the DataSet.

A DataTable object contains several collections that describe the data in the table and cache the data in memory. The following table describes the most important collections.

Collection name	Type of object in collection	Description of object in collection
Columns	DataColumn	Contains metadata about a column in the table, such as the column name, data type, and whether rows can contain a NULL value in this column.
Rows	DataRow	Contains a row of data in the table. A DataRow object also maintains the original data in the row, before any changes were made by the application.
Constraints	Constraint	Represents a constraint on one or more DataColumn objects. Constraint is an abstract class. There are two concrete subclasses: **UniqueConstraint** and **ForeignKeyConstraint**.
ChildRelations	DataRelation	Represents a relationship to a column in another table in the DataSet. You use **DataRelation** objects to create links between primary keys and foreign keys in your tables.

Relations between tables in a DataSet

If a DataSet has multiple tables, some of the tables might contain related data. You create DataRelation objects to describe these relationships. A DataSet can contain a collection of DataRelation objects.

You can use DataRelation objects to programmatically fetch related child records for a parent record, or a parent record from a child record.

Example of using the DataSet object model

The Northwind database in SQL Server contains a Products table. This table contains information for each product, including its product ID, product name, and supplier ID. The following table shows some data in the Products table.

ProductID	ProductName	SupplierID
1	Chai	1
2	Chang	1
3	Aniseed Syrup	1
4	Chef Anton's Cajun Seasoning	2

The Northwind database also contains a Suppliers table. This table contains information about companies that supply products to Northwind Traders. The following table shows some data in the Suppliers table.

SupplierID	CompanyName	City
1	Exotic Liquids	London
2	New Orleans Cajun Delights	New Orleans
3	Grandma Kelly's Homestead	Ann Arbor

You can create a DataSet object that contains copies of both of these tables, including both structure and data. You can also create a DataRelation object, to describe the relationship between the tables through the SupplierID column. This enables you to get the supplier details for a particular product. You can also get a list of all products supplied by a particular supplier.

How to Create a DataSet, a DataTable, and a DataColumn

- ■ **Creating a DataSet**
  - Drag and drop a DataSet control from the Toolbox
- ■ **Creating a DataTable**
  - Edit the Tables collection of a DataSet by using the Properties window
- ■ **Creating a DataColumn and adding it to a DataTable**
  - Edit the Columns collection of a DataTable by using the Properties window

---

Introduction

You can create DataSets and DataTables in the following ways:

- ■ Programmatically
- ■ By using the graphical tools in the Microsoft Visual Studio .NET development environment
- ■ By using a DataAdapter and filling the DataSet with data from a relational data source
- ■ By loading and persisting DataSet contents by using XML

In this topic, you will learn how to create a DataSet and a DataTable both programmatically and by using the graphical tools in the Visual Studio .NET development environment.

Note   Defining the structure or schema of a DataSet programmatically is rare. A common scenario is to define the structure by using an XML schema (XSD file). There will be situations in which programmatically defining a DataSet structure is necessary; for example, if the schema is not known at design time.

For information about defining the structure of a DataSet by using a DataAdapter, see Module 6, "Building DataSets From Existing Sources," in Course 2389B, *Programming with Microsoft ADO.NET.* For information about loading and persisting data in a DataSet by using XML, see Module 5, "Reading and Writing XML with ADO.NET," in Course 2389B, *Programming with Microsoft ADO.NET.*

The DataSet and DataTable constructors

To create a DataSet and a DataTable programmatically, you use the DataSet constructor to initialize a new instance of the DataSet class, and use the DataTable constructor to initialize a new instance of the DataTable class. You can name the DataSet or, if the name is omitted, the name is set by default to **NewDataSet**.

The DataSet must have a name to ensure that its XML representation always has a name for the document element, which is the highest-level element in an XML Schema definition.

You can create a DataTable object by using the DataTable constructor, or by passing constructor arguments to the **Add** method of the DataSet object's **Tables** property, which is a **DataTableCollection**.

You can set parameters for a DataTable or a DataColumn constructor at the time that the DataTable or DataColumn is created. This is recommended because you can create the DataTable and define parameters for it by using only one line of code.

After you have added a DataTable as a member of the Tables collection of one DataSet, you cannot add it to the collection of tables of any other DataSet. You can use the **Clone** method of a DataTable to create a new DataTable with the same structure (but no data), or you can use the **Copy** method to create a new DataTable with the same structure and data.

Example

The following example programmatically creates a DataSet named Northwind with a variable called dsNorthwind that can be used to reference it:

```
Dim dsNorthwind As DataSet
dsNorthwind = New DataSet("Northwind")
```

Example

The following example creates an instance of a DataTable object and assigns it the name Customers:

```
Dim dtCustomers As New DataTable("Customers")
```

When creating most ADO.NET objects, you can separate the declaration statement from the instantiation statement (as shown in the preceding DataSet example) or combine the statements (as shown in the preceding DataTable example).

Note that the DataTables created in the preceding examples are not yet associated with a DataSet.

Creating a DataTable programmatically

▶ **To add a DataTable to a DataSet programmatically**

Use the Add method of the Tables collection to add a DataTable object to a DataSet.

```
dsNorthwind.Tables.Add(dtCustomers)
```

The following example is the simplest way to create both a DataSet and an associated DataTable. The code creates an instance of a DataTable by adding it to the Tables collection of a newly created DataSet.

```
Dim dsNorthwind As New DataSet("Northwind")
Dim dtCustomers As DataTable = _
  dsNorthwind.Tables.Add("Customer")
```

You are not required to supply a value for the **TableName** property when you create a DataTable. You can specify the **TableName** property at another time, or you can leave it empty. However, when you add a table without a **TableName** value to a DataSet, the table is given an incremental default name of Table*N*, starting with "Table1" for the first unnamed table.

Creating DataColumns programmatically

When you first create a DataTable, it does not have a schema. To define the table's schema, you must create and add DataColumn objects to its Columns collection.

You create DataColumn objects within a table by using the DataColumn constructor, or by calling the **Add** method of the table's **Columns** property. The **Add** method will either accept optional **ColumnName**, **DataType**, and **Expression** arguments and create a new DataColumn as a member of the collection, or it will accept an existing DataColumn object and add it to the collection.

Example

The following examples add a column to a DataTable by using Microsoft Visual Basic® and Microsoft Visual C#™. Notice the use of the **typeof** statement in Visual C# and the **GetType** statement in Visual Basic.

```
' Visual Basic
Dim colCustomerID As DataColumn = _
  dtCustomers.Columns.Add("CustomerID", _
  GetType(System.Int32))

colCustomerID.AllowDBNull = False
colCustomerID.Unique = True


// Visual C#
DataColumn colCustomerID =
  dtCustomers.Columns.Add("CustomerID",
  typeof(Int32));

colCustomerID.AllowDBNull = false;
colCustomerID.Unique = true;
```

Handling exceptions

You will need to programmatically control any exceptions that occur when creating a DataSet and a DataTable. DataTable names must be unique, so that an exception will be thrown when duplicate table names are used.
The following example shows how to handle duplicate name exceptions programmatically:

```
Try
  dtCustomers = dsNorthwind.Tables.Add("Customers")

Catch DupXcp As System.Data.DuplicateNameException

  MessageBox.Show("A table named Customers already exists!")

...

End Try
```

Practice

Northwind Traders needs to build an application that includes data related to its products. You will use the Visual Studio .NET development environment graphical tools to build a Microsoft Windows® Application solution.

The solution for this practice is at the following location:

<install folder>\Practices\Mod04_1\Lesson2\CreateDataSets\

1. Create a new Windows Application solution named **CreateDataSets** in the following location:

   <install folder>\Practices\Mod04_1\

2. From the **Data** section of the **Toolbox**, drag and drop a **DataSet** control onto the form. For the type of DataSet, choose **Untyped**.

3. Change the **(Name)** property to **dsNorthwind**. This is how you will refer to the DataSet in code.

4. Select the **Tables** property for the DataSet, and click the ellipses (**...**) button for this property.

5. In the **Tables Collection Editor**, click **Add** to insert a new DataTable.

6. Change the **(Name)** property to **dtProducts**.

7. Change the **TableName** property to **Products**.

8. Select the **Columns** property, and then click the ellipses (**...**) button for this property.

9. In the **Columns Collection Editor**, click **Add** to insert a new DataColumn.

10. Change the **(Name)** property to **dcProductID**.

11. Change the **ColumnName** property to **ProductID**.

12. Change the **DataType** property to **System.Int32**.

13. Add two more columns named **ProductName** and **UnitPrice** and give them appropriate DataTypes.

14. Open the form in Code view and find the code that was written for you by the design tools.

15. Use the automatically generated code as a guide to write some new code that programmatically creates a fourth column named **UnitsInStock**.

16. Add a reference to your new column to the end of the call to the **AddRange** method of **dtProducts**. This will allow the design tools to recognize your new column.

    ```
    Me.dtProducts.Columns.AddRange(...
    ```

17. Return the form to Designer view and use the Properties window to see that the code you have written manually is recognized by the design tools.

How to Create a Primary Key Constraint

- **Set the PrimaryKey property of the DataTable**
  - Select the columns in order
  - Does not allow the naming of the constraint
- **Edit the Constraints collection of the DataTable**
  - Add a UniqueConstraint
  - Name the constraint
  - Select the columns
  - Check the primary key box

Introduction

A database table commonly has a column, or group of columns, that uniquely identifies each row in the table. This identifying column, or group of columns, is called the *primary key*.

Using the PrimaryKey property of a DataTable

The **PrimaryKey** property of a DataTable receives as its value an array of one or more DataColumn objects, as shown in the following example:

```
dtCustomers.PrimaryKey = New DataColumn() _
   {dtCustomers.Columns("CustomerID")}
```

Defining multiple columns as a primary key

The following example defines two columns as a primary key:

```
dtEmployees.PrimaryKey = New DataColumn() _
   {dtEmployees.Columns("LastName"), _
   dtEmployees.Columns("FirstName")}
```

Using a constraint to create a primary key

A better way to create a primary key is to add a unique constraint. When doing so, the last parameter, True, can be used to indicate that a primary key should be created instead of an ordinary unique constraint. This technique is better because it allows the naming of the constraint.

```
Dim pkCustomers As Constraint = dtCustomers.Constraints.Add( _
   "PK_Customers", dtCustomers.Columns("CustomerID"), True)
```

The AllowDBNull property

When you identify a single DataColumn as the primary key for a DataTable, the table automatically sets the **AllowDBNull** property of the column to **false** and the **Unique** property to **true**. For multiple-column primary keys, only the **AllowDBNull** property is automatically set to **false**.

Using Unique Constraints

- **Two types of constraints**
  - UniqueConstraint
  - ForeignKeyConstraint
- **Creating a constraint**
  - Edit the Constraints collection of a DataTable
- **UniqueConstraint**
  - Array of DataColumns
  - Can be the primary key for the DataTable

Introduction

A relational database must enforce data integrity to ensure the quality of the data in the database. One way to maintain integrity in ADO.NET is by adding constraints to the tables within a DataSet. A *constraint* is an automatic rule applied to a column, or to related columns, that determines what actions should take place when the value of a row is modified.

There are two kinds of constraints in ADO.NET: the ForeignKeyConstraint and the UniqueConstraint. When you add a DataRelation object, which creates a relationship between two or more tables, both constraints can be created automatically. Constraints are not enforced unless the **EnforceConstraints** property of the DataSet is set to **true**. Foreign key constraints are primarily intended for use with relationships to primary key columns, and will be discussed later in this module.

Unique constraints

The **UniqueConstraint** object, which can be assigned to either a single column or an array of columns in a DataTable, ensures that all data in the specified column(s) is unique per row. You can create a unique constraint for a single column by setting the **Unique** property of the column to **true**.

You can also create a unique constraint for a column or array of columns by using the UniqueConstraint constructor and passing the **UniqueConstraint** object to the **Add** method of the table's **Constraints** property (which is a **ConstraintCollection**). You also use the **Add** method to add *existing* constraint objects to the **Constraints** collection.

Additionally, defining a column or columns as the primary key for a table will automatically create a unique constraint for the specified column(s).

A **UniqueConstraint** object triggers an exception when attempting to set a value in a column to a non-unique value.

Examples

The following examples create a **UniqueConstraint** object for an existing column by using two different techniques. In the first example, setting the **Unique** property for a column creates a constraint automatically, but it will be assigned a default name such as Constraint1. In the second example, the name of the constraint can be specified as the first parameter of the **Add** method.

```
' Visual Basic

ds.Tables("Product").Columns("ProductName").Unique = True
```

```
// Visual C#

ds.Tables["Product"].Columns["ProductName"].Unique = true;
```

```
' Visual Basic

ds.Tables("Product").Constraints.Add( _
  New UniqueConstraint("UC_ProductName", _
  ds.Tables("Product").Columns("ProductName")))
```

```
// Visual C#

ds.Tables["Product"].Constraints.Add(
  new UniqueConstraint("UC_ProductName",
  ds.Tables["Product"].Columns["ProductName"]));
```

Practice

Northwind Traders needs product names in its online catalog to be unique.

1. Open the solution you built for the previous practice, or open the solution at the following location:

   <install folder>\Practices\Mod04_1\Lesson2\CreateDataSets\

2. Open the form in Designer view and double-click the form to create a handler for the **Form1_Load** event.

3. Write code to add a **UniqueConstraint** object to the **Products** DataTable that prevents duplicate product names. Or switch the form back to Designer view and use the Properties window.

The solution for this practice is at the following location:

<install folder>\Practices\Mod04_1\Lesson2\UsingUniqueConstraints\

Creating Custom Expressions

- ■ **Definition**
  - Custom expressions are columns derived from calculations, rather than stored values
- ■ **Using the DataColumn** Expression **property**
  - Sum([Unit Price] * [Quantity])
- ■ **Aggregate functions can use parent/child relationships**
  - Avg, Count, Sum, Max, Min

Definition

Custom expressions are column values derived from calculations, rather than values retrieved directly from the data source. A custom expression can be a calculation on one column or on multiple columns.

Syntax for a custom expression consists of standard arithmetic, Boolean, and string operators and literal values. You can reference a data value by using its column name (as you would in a SQL statement) and include aggregate functions (such as **Sum**, **Count**, **Min**, **Max**, and others).

Example

The Order Details table in the Northwind Traders database contains a column called UnitPrice that tracks the price of each product that is sold, and a column called Quantity that tracks the number of items that are sold. If you need to see the total cost for the purchase of a particular product, multiply the UnitPrice and the Quantity and then display the resulting value in its own column (UnitPrice*Quantity) and name the new column TotalCost.

Aggregate functions

Calculated columns can also include aggregate functions such as **Sum**, **Count**, **Min**, **Max**, and other functions available with the data source. Use aggregate functions when creating an expression based on data that is related to data in another table.

For example, suppose that you want to find the average unit price of products per category. To do this, you need to access two DataTables: Categories and Products. These tables are related because the CategoryID column of the Products table is the child of the Categories table. Programmatically, the new column that computes the average price of products per category would be:

```
Avg(Child.UnitPrice)
```

Using the DataColumn Expression property

The DataColumn **Expression** property gets or sets the expression that is used to calculate values in a column or create an aggregate. The DataType of the column determines the return type of an expression.

You can use the **Expression** property to:

- Create a calculated column.
- Create an aggregate column.
- Create expressions that include user-defined values.
- Concatenate a string.
- Reference parent and child tables in an expression.

Syntax

The syntax for the **Expression** property of the DataColumn object is:

```
DataColumn.Expression = "Expression"
```

Example

The following example creates three columns in a DataTable: a price column, a tax column, and a total column. The second and third columns contain expressions. The second column calculates tax by using a variable tax rate, and the third column is the result of adding the tax amount to the price.

```
Dim colPrice As New _
  DataColumn("Price", GetType(System.Decimal))

Dim colTax As New _
  DataColumn("Tax", GetType(System.Decimal))

colTax.Expression = "Price * 0.0862"

Dim colTotal As New _
  DataColumn("Total", GetType(System.Decimal))

colTotal.Expression = "Price + Tax"
```

Practice

The Northwind Traders Sales Director would like to know the value of stock being held for each product.

1. Open the solution you built for the previous practice, or open the solution at the following location:

   <install folder>\Practices\Mod04_1\Lesson2\UsingUniqueConstraints\

2. Use the Properties window to add a fifth column to the Products table named **StockValue** that is the result of the **UnitPrice** column multiplied by the **UnitsInStock** column.

3. Use the Code editor to view the changes you have made to the dsNorthwind DataSet.

The solution for this practice is at the following location:

<install folder>\Practices\Mod04_1\Lesson2\CreatingCustomExpressions\

Lesson: Binding and Saving a DataSet

- How to Bind Data to a Windows Control
- How to Bind a DataSet to a DataGrid
- How to Save and Open a DataSet

Introduction

After you have data cached in a DataSet, you must bind that DataSet to a Windows Form DataGrid control to display and manipulate or modify the data.

Lesson objectives

After completing this lesson, you will be able to:

- Bind data to a Windows control.
- Bind a DataTable to a DataGrid.
- Save and open a DataSet.

How to Bind Data to a Windows Control

- ■ **Simple data binding**
  - ● Binding to a simple control that can only display a single value – for example, a text box
- ■ **Complex data binding**
  - ● Binding to a more complex control that can display multiple values – for example, a data grid
- ■ **All controls have a (DataBindings) collection**
  - ● Use the Properties window to edit data bindings
- ■ **Best practice: use an intermediate DataView**

Introduction

Although an ADO.NET DataSet enables you to store data in a disconnected cache, the DataGrid and other Windows controls visually display data in a Windows Form and support selecting, sorting, and editing the data.

In Windows Forms, you can bind any property of any control to a data source. In addition to binding the display property (such as the **Text** property of a **TextBox** control) to the data source, you can also bind other properties. For example, you might need to bind the graphic of an image control or set the size or color properties of a control based on binding to the data source.

Types of data binding

There are two ways to bind data to a Windows control: simple data binding and complex data binding.

Simple data binding is the ability of a control to bind to a single data element, such as a value in a column in a DataSet table. This is typical for binding **TextBox** or **Label** controls, or any control that displays a single value.

Complex data binding is the ability of a control to bind to more than one data element, typically more than one record in a data source. Complex data binding typically uses a **DataGrid**, **ListBox**, or **ErrorProvider** control. Binding a DataSet to a **DataGrid** control will be covered later in this module.

DataViews

Although it is possible to bind directly to a DataTable in a DataSet, you will typically create an intermediate DataView object based on the DataTable and then bind to the DataView. This allows more flexibility.

To use a DataView, in the Visual Studio .NET development environment, drag a **DataView** control from the **Toolbox** onto a form and set the DataTable property of the DataView, or use the following code:

```
' Visual Basic

Dim dvEmployees As New DataView( _
    dsNorthwind.Tables("Employees"))

// Visual C#

DataView dvEmployees = new DataView(
    dsNorthwind.Tables["Employees"]);
```

Procedure

▶ **To bind data to a Windows control graphically**

1. In Visual Studio .NET, open a project form, select a control, and then display the Properties window.

2. Expand the **(DataBindings)** property.

3. If the property you want to bind is not one of the commonly bound properties, click the ellipsis (**...**) button in the **(Advanced)** box to display the **Advanced Data Binding** dialog box with a complete list of properties for that control.

4. Click the arrow next to the property you want to bind.

5. Expand the data source to which you want to bind, until you find the single data element that you want. For example, if you are binding to a column value in a table in a DataSet, expand the name of the DataSet, and then expand the table name to display column names.

6. Click the name of the element to which you want to bind.

7. If you were working in the **Advanced Data Binding** dialog box, click **Close** to return to the Properties window.

▶ **To bind a control programmatically**

- Call the Add method of the DataBindings collection for a control:

```
txtProductID.DataBindings.Add( _
    "Text", dsNorthwind, "Products.ProductID")
```

How to Bind a DataSet to a DataGrid

- **DataSource property**
  - Can be a DataSet, DataTable, or DataView
- **DataMember**
  - Can be a DataTable if the DataSource is a DataSet
- **Or, use the (DataBindings) collection**
- **Best practice: Use an intermediate DataView**

Definition

The Windows Forms **DataGrid** control displays data in a series of rows and columns. The simplest use of this control is when the grid is bound to a data source with a single table containing no relationships. In such a case, the data appears in simple rows and columns, as in a spreadsheet.

If the DataGrid is bound to data with multiple related tables, and if navigation is enabled on the grid, the grid will display expanders in each row. An *expander* allows navigation from a parent table to a child table. Clicking a node displays the child table, and clicking **Back** displays the original parent table. In this way, the grid displays the hierarchical relationships between tables.

If the DataSet contains a series of related tables, you can use two **DataGrid** controls to display the data in a relational format.

Binding a DataSet to a DataGrid

▶ **To bind a DataSet to a DataGrid graphically**

1. In a Visual Basic .NET project, drag a **DataGrid** control from the **Windows Forms** tab of the **Toolbox** onto your form.

2. Select the **DataGrid** control and set its **DataSource** property to a previously created DataSet.

3. Set the **DataMember** property to the name of one of the tables. For example, set the property to **Suppliers**.

▶ **To bind a DataSet to a DataGrid programmatically**

```
' Visual Basic
grdSuppliers.DataSource = dsNorthwind.Tables("Suppliers")
```

```
// Visual C#
grdSuppliers.DataSource = dsNorthwind.Tables["Suppliers"];
```

DataViews

When binding to a data grid, it is good practice to use an intermediate DataView.

```
' Visual Basic

grdSuppliers.DataSource = New DataView( _
  dsNorthwind.Tables("Suppliers"))

// Visual C#

grdSuppliers.DataSource = new DataView(
  dsNorthwind.Tables["Suppliers"]);
```

Practice

Northwind Traders needs an application allowing easy editing of product information.

1. Open the solution you built for the previous practice, or open the solution at:

   <install folder>\Practices\Mod04_1\Lesson2\CreatingCustomExpressions\

2. Open the form in Designer view.

3. Add five **TextBox** controls and a **DataGrid** control to the form.

4. Use the **Property** window to set the **(DataBindings)** for the **TextBox** controls. Bind the **Text** property of each box to the five columns in the **Products** table in the **dsNorthwind** DataSet.

   Caution   Do not bind to the dtProducts variable. If you do, you will only see the first record.

   ---

5. Set the **DataSource** for the DataGrid to the **dsNorthwind** DataSet.

6. Set the **DataMember** of the DataGrid to the DataTable.

7. Run the application.

8. Enter several products into the **DataGrid**. Enter any values you want for the columns.

9. Notice that the StockValue column is read-only and is calculated automatically.

10. Notice that the numeric fields do not accept alphabetic values.

11. Notice that you cannot have two records with the same ProductName, but that you can have two records with the same ProductID.

12. Select the first product row by using the mouse pointer. Notice that the **TextBox** controls display the same information as the currently selected row in the DataGrid.

    The solution for this practice is at the following location:

    <install folder>\Practices\Mod04_1\Lesson3\DataBinding\

How to Save and Open a DataSet

- ■ **Two DataSet methods**
  - ● ReadXml
  - ● WriteXml
    - ● Pass the path and filename as a string parameter
- ■ **ReadXml raises an exception if the file does not exist**
- ■ **WriteXml overwrites existing files**

Introduction

The DataSet has two methods that can be used to write the contents of a DataSet to disk and then retrieve the data later: the **WriteXml** method and the **ReadXml** method.

Saving a DataSet

▶ **To save a DataSet**

The **WriteXml** method requires the path to a file to which you want to write. A new file will be created if one does not exist. Existing files will be overwritten.

```
' Visual Basic

dsNorthwind.WriteXml("\My Documents\Northwind.ds")

// Visual C#

dsNorthwind.WriteXml(@"\My Documents\Northwind.ds");
```

▶ **To open a DataSet**

The **ReadXml** method requires the path to a file from which you want to read. If the file does not exist, an exception will be raised.

```
' Visual Basic

dsNorthwind.ReadXml("\My Documents\Northwind.ds")

// Visual C#

dsNorthwind.ReadXml(@"\My Documents\Northwind.ds");
```

Practice

Northwind Traders needs an application that allows the easy editing of product information and persists that data to disk.

1. Open the solution you built for the previous practice, or open the solution at the following location:

   <install folder>\Practices\Mod04_1\Lesson3\DataBinding\

2. Open the form in Code view.

3. Add code to handle the **Load** event for the form by reading the DataSet from a file named **Northwind.ds**.

```
' Visual Basic

Try
    dsNorthwind.ReadXml("Northwind.ds")
Catch
End Try

// Visual C#

try
{
    dsNorthwind.ReadXml("Northwind.ds");
}
catch {}
```

4. Add code to handle the **Closing** event for the form by writing the DataSet to a file named **Northwind.ds**.

```
' Visual Basic

dsNorthwind.WriteXml("Northwind.ds")

// Visual C#

dsNorthwind.WriteXml("Northwind.ds");
```

5. Run the application.

6. Enter several products into the **DataGrid**. Enter any values you want for the columns.

7. Stop and restart your application.

8. Notice that DataSet is automatically saved and reopened.

The solution for this practice is at the following location:

<install folder>\Practices\Mod04_1\Lesson3\PersistingDataSets\

Lab 4.1: Building, Binding, Opening, and Saving DataSets

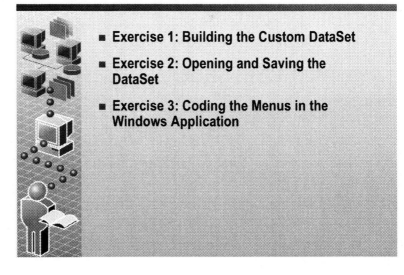

- ■ **Exercise 1: Building the Custom DataSet**
- ■ **Exercise 2: Opening and Saving the DataSet**
- ■ **Exercise 3: Coding the Menus in the Windows Application**

Objectives

After completing this lab, you will be able to:

- ■ Build a DataSet that contains multiple DataTables.
- ■ Bind DataSets to DataGrids.
- ■ Save a DataSet as a file.
- ■ Load a DataSet from an existing file.

Prerequisites

Before working on this lab, you must have:

- ■ Introductory Visual Basic or Visual C# language skills. For example, the ability to declare variables and write procedures, loops, and branching statements.
- ■ Introductory Windows Forms skills. For example, the ability to create a simple form with multiple controls.

For more information

See the topics Visual Basic Language Features and Windows Forms Walkthroughs in the Visual Studio .NET documentation.

Scenario

Northwind Traders has an e-commerce Web site that allows customers to order products from an online catalog. Because it is a publicly available Web site, when a user first visits the site, he or she can browse catalogs and fill a shopping cart before any customer data exists in the Northwind customer database.

The site automatically tracks basic information about customers and the products that they have added to their shopping carts. If a customer wants to place an order, additional customer information must be gathered. Only during the final checkout stage is the customer and order data saved into the Northwind database. While the customer continues to shop, the data is stored temporarily in the middle tier on the Web server. The DataSet class in ADO.NET provides this capability.

Estimated time to complete this lab: 30 minutes

Exercise 1
Building the Custom DataSet

In this exercise, you will create the structure of the DataSet. The DataSet will contain a DataTable called Customer that will hold customer contact details, and a DataTable called CartItems that will hold all of the items that a customer chooses from the online catalog.

Scenario

You will create a custom DataSet that can track the contents of a shopping cart for a visitor to the Northwind Traders e-commerce Web site.

▶ **Open the starter application**

- Open the solution **BuildingDataSets** in the folder
  <install folder>\Labs\Lab04_1\Starter\xx\ where xx is either VB or CS.

▶ **Create a custom DataSet**

1. Drag a **DataSet** control from the **Toolbox** on to **Form1** and choose the **Untyped dataset** option.
2. Change the **(Name)** property to **dsShoppingCart**.
3. Use the Properties window and the **Tables** collection to add two tables to the DataSet with the following properties.

(Name)	TableName
dtCustomer	Customer
dtCartItems	CartItems

▶ **Create the columns for the Customer table**

- Add the following columns to the **Customer** table.

Column	Property	Value
CustomerID	(Name)	dcCustomerID
	ColumnName	CustomerID
	AllowDBNull	False
	MaxLength	5
CompanyName	(Name)	dcCompanyName
	ColumnName	CompanyName
	AllowDBNull	False
	MaxLength	40
	Unique	True
Address	(Name)	dcAddress
	ColumnName	Address
	MaxLength	60
City	(Name)	dcCity
	ColumnName	City
	MaxLength	15

▶ **Create the columns for the cart items table**

1. Add the following columns to the CartItems table.

Column	Property	Value
CustomerID	(Name)	dcCustomerID2
	ColumnName	CustomerID
	AllowDBNull	False
	MaxLength	5
ProductID	(Name)	dcProductID
	ColumnName	ProductID
	DataType	System.Int32
	AllowDBNull	False
UnitPrice	(Name)	dcUnitPrice
	ColumnName	UnitPrice
	DataType	System.Decimal
	AllowDBNull	False
Quantity	(Name)	dcQuantity
	ColumnName	Quantity
	DataType	System.Int32
	AllowDBNull	False
Cost	(Name)	dcCost
	ColumnName	Cost
	DataType	System.Decimal
	ReadOnly	True
	Expression	UnitPrice * Quantity

2. Save all of the changes to the solution.

Exercise 2
Opening and Saving the DataSet

In this exercise, you will write code to save the DataSet to your local hard disk and open an existing DataSet file.

Scenario

On the Northwind Traders e-commerce Web site, the DataSet will be stored temporarily in a Microsoft ASP.NET session. In the Windows Application, you will persist the DataSet to disk to simulate the situation.

▶ **Continue building the application**

1. If you do not already have the solution open, open the solution **BuildingDataSets** in the folder <install folder>\Labs\Lab04_1\Solution\ Ex1\xx\ where xx is either VB or CS.

2. Open the **Form1** class module by using the Code editor.

▶ **Add code to open an existing DataSet file**

In this step, you will write a procedure that will open an existing DataSet.

1. Declare a variable with the following properties.

Scope	Name	Data type
Public	Filename	System.String

Note This variable will be a property of the form used to store the filename of the XML file that is used to persist the DataSet when the application is not running.

2. Create a new public method called **OpenFromFile**.

```
' Visual Basic
Public Sub OpenFromFile()
End Sub

// Visual C#
public void OpenFromFile()
{
}
```

3. Inside the **OpenFromFile** method, add code to empty the tables in the DataSet named **dsShoppingCart**.

Note   You must clear the CartItems table first, because in a later lab you will add a ForeignKeyConstraint that will enforce referential integrity, which means that a cart item cannot exist without a related customer record.

```
' Visual Basic
Me.dsShoppingCart.Tables("CartItems").Clear()
Me.dsShoppingCart.Tables("Customer").Clear()

// Visual C#
this.dsShoppingCart.Tables["CartItems"].Clear();
this.dsShoppingCart.Tables["Customer"].Clear();
```

4. Read the XML data from the file specified in the Filename variable.

```
' Visual Basic
Me.dsShoppingCart.ReadXml(Me.Filename)

// Visual C#
this.dsShoppingCart.ReadXml(this.Filename);
```

5. Add exception handling for common errors such as an invalid file name.

```
' Visual Basic
Try

Catch Xcp As System.Exception
   MessageBox.Show(Xcp.ToString(), _
       "Failed to open: " & Me.Filename, _
       MessageBoxButtons.OK, MessageBoxIcon.Exclamation)
End Try

// Visual C#
try
{

}
catch (System.Exception Xcp)
{
   MessageBox.Show(Xcp.ToString(),
       "Failed to open: " + this.Filename,
       MessageBoxButtons.OK, MessageBoxIcon.Exclamation);
}
```

▶ **Add code to save the DataSet to a file**

1. Create a new public method called **SaveToFile**.

2. Inside the **SaveToFile** method, add code to write the XML data to the file name specified in the Filename variable.

```
' Visual Basic
Me.dsShoppingCart.WriteXml(Me.Filename)
```

```
// Visual C#
this.dsShoppingCart.WriteXml(this.Filename);
```

3. Add exception handling for common errors such as an invalid file name.

▶ **Before continuing to the next exercise**

• Save all the changes to the solution.

Exercise 3
Coding the Menus in the Windows Application

In this exercise, you will write code to add functionality to the menus in the Windows Application. The **File** menu allows management of the DataSet file. The **View** menu enables the user to toggle the view of the two tables of the DataSet in the DataGrid.

Scenario

The DataSet contains two tables that need to be edited by users, but the Windows Application only has a single DataGrid, so the **View** menu will be used to toggle the display of each table.

▶ **Continue building the application**

1. If you do not already have the solution open, open the solution **BuildingDataSets** in the folder `<install folder>\Labs\Lab04_1\Solution\Ex2\xx\` where xx is either VB or CS.

2. Open the **Form1** class module by using the Code editor.

3. Create a private procedure called **SetFormCaption** that contains code to display the **Filename** property of the **dsShoppingCart** object in the title bar of the form, combined with the fixed string " – Shopping Cart : Test WinApp".

```
' Visual Basic
Private Sub SetFormCaption()
   Me.Text = Me.Filename & _
       " - Shopping Cart : Test WinApp"
End Sub
```

```
// Visual C#
private void SetFormCaption()
{
   this.Text = this.Filename +
       " - Shopping Cart : Test WinApp";
}
```

► **Code the View menu items**

1. Program the **Click** event of the **Customer** menu item to perform the following actions:

   a. Set the DataGrid to bind to a new DataView based on the **Customer** table.

   b. Place a check mark next to the **Customer** menu item.

   c. Clear the check mark next to the **Cart Items** menu item.

   ```
   ' Visual Basic
   Me.grd.DataSource = New DataView( _
       Me.dsShoppingCart.Tables("Customer"))

   Me.mnuCustomer.Checked = True
   Me.mnuCartItems.Checked = False

   // Visual C#
   this.grd.DataSource = new DataView(
       this.dsShoppingCart.Tables["Customer"]);

   this.mnuCustomer.Checked = true;
   this.mnuCartItems.Checked = false;
   ```

2. Program the **Click** event of the **Cart Items** menu item to perform the following actions:

   a. Set the DataGrid to bind to a new DataView based on the **CartItems** table.

   b. Clear the check mark next to the **Customer** menu item.

   c. Place a check mark next to the **Cart Items** menu item.

▶ **Create a new DataSet object**

1. Program the **Click** event of the **New** menu item to perform the following actions:

   a. Empty the tables in the DataSet.

   b. Set the **Filename** property to **ShoppingCart1.ds**.

   c. Call the **SetFormCaption** procedure.

   d. Call the **Click** event for the **Customer** menu item to simulate a customer selecting that menu item.

```vb
' Visual Basic
Me.dsShoppingCart.Tables("CartItems").Clear()
Me.dsShoppingCart.Tables("Customer").Clear()
Me.Filename = "ShoppingCart1.ds"
Me.SetFormCaption()
Me.mnuCustomer_Click(sender, e)
```

```csharp
// Visual C#
this.dsShoppingCart.Tables["CartItems"].Clear();
this.dsShoppingCart.Tables["Customer"].Clear();
this.Filename = "ShoppingCart1.ds";
this.SetFormCaption();
this.mnuCustomer_Click(sender, e);
```

2. Program the **Load** event of the **Form1** object to call the **mnuNew_Click** procedure.

► **Open an existing DataSet file**

In this procedure, you will code the **Open** menu item. You will use the **OpenFileDialog** control to allow the user to choose which file to open.

Note   The **ShowDialog** method of the **OpenFileDialog** control returns a System.Windows.Forms.DialogResult.OK value when the **OK**, **Open**, or **Save** buttons are clicked.

---

1. Show the **dlgOpen** dialog box by adding code to the **Click** event of the **Open** menu item.

2. If the user clicks the **Open** button, perform the following actions:

   a. Set the **Filename** property to the file name selected in the **Open** dialog box.

   b. Call the **OpenFromFile** procedure.

   c. Call the **SetFormCaption** procedure.

   d. Call the **Click** event of the **Customer** menu item to simulate a customer selecting that menu item.

```
' Visual Basic
If Me.dlgOpen.ShowDialog() = DialogResult.OK Then
    Me.Filename = Me.dlgOpen.FileName
    Me.OpenFromFile()
    Me.SetFormCaption()
    Me.mnuCustomer_Click(sender, e)
End If

// Visual C#
if (this.dlgOpen.ShowDialog() == DialogResult.OK)
{
    this.Filename = this.dlgOpen.FileName;
    this.OpenFromFile();
    this.SetFormCaption();
    this.mnuCustomer_Click(sender, e);
}
```

▶ **Save a DataSet file**

1. Show the **Save** dialog box by adding code to the **Click** event of the **Save As** menu item.

2. If the user clicks the **Save** button on the **Save** dialog box, perform the following actions:

   a. Set the **Filename** property to the file name selected in the **Save As** dialog box.

   b. Call the **SaveToFile** procedure.

   c. Call the **SetFormCaption** procedure.

3. Program the **Click** event of the **Save** menu item to call the **SaveToFile** procedure.

▶ **Test creating a DataSet file**

1. Build the application and correct any build errors.

2. Set a break point at the beginning of the **InitializeComponent** and **mnuSaveAs_Click** procedures.

3. Run the application.

4. Step through the code line by line until the form appears.

5. Toggle between the two **DataTables** by pressing the F7 and SHIFT+F7 keys, or by using the **Customer** and **Cart Items** menu items on the **View** menu. Notice that the DataGrid automatically recognizes the DataTable structure.

6. Enter some data into the grid for a customer and several cart items. Notice that the rules for data types and NULL values are enforced automatically. The unique constraint on the Customer table prevents a user from adding two customers with the same company name.

7. Use the **Save As** menu item to save the DataSet as a file called **MyFirstDataSet.ds**. (The .ds file extension should be appended automatically if you do not enter it.) Step through the code line by line until the form reappears.

8. Close the application.

▶ **Test editing and opening a DataSet file**

1. Run Windows Explorer and open the file **MyFirstDataSet.ds** with Notepad.

2. Use Notepad to edit the **CompanyName** value of the customer you entered. Save the changes to the file and close Notepad.

3. In Visual Studio .NET, clear all existing break points and set a new break point at the beginning of the **mnuOpen_Click** procedure.

4. Run your application again and open the file **MyFirstDataSet.ds**.

   Notice that your application recognizes the change that you made in Notepad.

5. Choose the **New** menu item. The DataGrid should be emptied.

6. Close the application.

Lesson: Defining Data Relationships

- **Using Foreign Key Constraints to Restrict Actions**
- **How to Create a Foreign Key Constraint**
- **What Is a DataRelation Object?**
- **How to Create a DataRelation Object**
- **How to Navigate Related DataTables**

Introduction

Before you modify data in a DataTable, it is necessary to first define the relationships between data to ensure data integrity.

Lesson objectives

After completing this lesson, you will be able to:

- Create a **ForeignKeyConstraint** object.
- Create a **DataRelation** object.
- Navigate related DataTables.

Using Foreign Key Constraints to Restrict Actions

- **A ForeignKeyConstraint enforces referential integrity**
    - If the EnforceConstraints property of a DataSet is True
- **Restricting actions performed in related tables**
    - DeleteRule and UpdateRule properties

Action	Description
Cascade	Deletes or updates related rows. This is the default.
SetNull	Sets values in related rows to DBNull.
SetDefault	Sets values in related rows to the DefaultValue.
None	No action is taken, but an exception is raised.

Introduction

A *foreign key constraint* restricts the action performed in related tables when data in a table is either updated or deleted. For example, if a value in a row of one table is updated or deleted, and that same value is also used in one or more related tables, you can use the **DeleteRule** or **UpdateRule** property of a **ForeignKeyConstraint** to determine what happens in the related tables.

A **ForeignKeyConstraint** can restrict, as well as propagate, changes to related columns. Depending on the properties set for the **ForeignKeyConstraint** of a column, and if the **EnforceConstraints** property of the DataSet is true, performing certain operations on the parent row will result in an exception. For example, if the **DeleteRule** property of the **ForeignKeyConstraint** is **None**, a parent row cannot be deleted if it has any child rows.

Restricting actions performed in related tables

In a parent-child relationship between two columns, you establish the action to be taken by setting the **DeleteRule** property of the foreign key constraint to one of the values in the following table.

Action	Description
Cascade	Deletes or updates related rows. This is the default.
SetNull	Sets values in related rows to **DBNull**.
SetDefault	Sets values in related rows to the **DefaultValue**.
None	No action is taken, but an exception is raised

How to Create a Foreign Key Constraint

- **Use Properties window**
  - DataSet must have at least two tables
  - Parent table must have a primary key
  - Add a ForeignKeyConstraint to the child table
  - Choose the matching columns
  - Choose Update and Delete rules
- **Write code**

<u>Visual Basic Example</u>   <u>Visual C# Example</u>

Introduction

When creating a **ForeignKeyConstraint**, you can pass the DeleteRule and UpdateRule values to the constructor as arguments, or you can set them as properties, as in the following example.

Example

The following code shows how to create a **ForeignKeyConstraint** on the CustomerID column of the Orders table. The DeleteRule value is then set to prevent the deletion of any customer who has existing orders.

```
' Visual Basic
dtCustomers = dsNorthwind.Tables("Customers")
dtOrders = dsNorthwind.Tables("Orders")

Dim fkcCustomersOrders As New ForeignKeyConstraint( _
   "FK_CustomersOrders", dtCustomers.Columns("CustomerID"), _
   dtOrders.Columns("CustomerID"))

fkcCustomersOrders.DeleteRule = Rule.None
dtOrders.Constraints.Add(fkcCustomersOrders)
```

To delete constraints programmatically

▶ **To delete constraints by using the Remove or Clear methods of the Constraints collection**

```
' Visual Basic

' Clear a named constraint in a DataTable
dtCustomers.Constraints.Remove("FK_CustomersOrders")

' Clear all constraints in a DataTable
dtCustomers.Constraints.Clear()
```

What Is a DataRelation Object?

- **Definition**
  - A DataRelation object defines a navigational relationship, NOT a constraint relationship
- **Used by presentation objects (for example, a DataGrid) to allow easier navigation (for example, "drill down" capability from parent rows to child rows)**
- **Used by expression columns to calculate aggregates**
- **A DataSet has a Relations collection**

Definition

A **DataRelation** object defines the navigational relationship between two tables. Typically, two tables are linked through a single field that contains the same data. For example, a table that contains address data might have a single field that contains codes that represent countries/regions. A second table that contains country and region data would have a single field that contains the code that identifies the country or region; it is this code that is inserted into the corresponding field in the first table.

The **DataRelation** object can make available the records related to a record with which you are working. It provides child records if you are in a parent record, and a parent record if you are working with a child record.

DataSets and DataRelation objects

Although a DataSet contains tables and columns in a relational structure similar to that of a database, the DataSet does not inherently include the ability to relate tables. However, you can create DataRelation objects that establish a relationship between a parent (master) and a child (detail) table based on a common key.

For example, a DataSet that contains customer data might have a Customers table and an Orders table. Even if the tables contain a key in common (in this example, CustomerID), the DataSet itself does not keep track of the records in one table that relate to those in another. However, you can create a DataRelation object that references the parent and child tables (and their keys), and then use this object to work with the related tables.

How to Create a DataRelation Object

- **Use the Properties window**
- **Or, write code**

```
dsNorthwind.Relations.Add( _
   "FK_CustomersOrders", _
   dtCustomers.Columns("CustomerID"), _
   dtOrders.Columns("CustomerID"), _
   True) ' create a ForeignKeyConstraint too
```

Introduction

To create a **DataRelation** object, you use the **DataRelation** constructor or the **Add** method of the Relations collection of a DataSet.

Example

The following example creates a **DataRelation** object:

```
' Visual Basic
dsNorthwind.Relations.Add("FK_CustomersOrders", _
   dtCustomers.Columns("CustomerID"), _
   dtOrders.Columns("CustomerID"), True)
```

```
// Visual C#
dsNorthwind.Relations.Add("FK_CustomersOrders",
   dtCustomers.Columns["CustomerID"],
   dtOrders.Columns["CustomerID"], true);
```

Practice

In this exercise, you will add a relationship between the Categories and Products tables in a simple application that uses the Northwind database.

1. Open the following starter solution. Run the solution and notice that there is no way to access the products table.

   <install folder>\Practices\Mod04_2\Lesson1\Starter\
   CreateADataRelation.sln

2. Open the form in Code view.

3. Add code to the **Form1_Load** event handler that will create a **DataRelation** and **ForeignKeyConstraint** between **Categories** and **Products** tables on their **CategoryID** columns.

4. Run and test the application. You should see a list of eight categories in the grid. Note that you can click the [+] icon next to a category and drill down to see only the products for that category.

The solution for this practice is at the following location:

<install folder>\Practices\Mod04_2\Lesson1\CreateADataRelation\

How to Navigate Related DataTables

- ■ **The GetChildRows method of the DataRow**
  - • Pass a DataRelation name as the parameter
- ■ **Example:**

```
Dim drCustomer As DataRow
Dim drOrder As DataRow
For Each drCustomer In _
          dsNorthwind.Tables("Customer").Rows
  For Each drOrder In drCustomer.GetChildRows( _
          "FK_CustomersOrders")
    ' process row
  Next
Next
```

Introduction

In many application scenarios, you want to work with data from more than one table, and often with data from related tables. This is called a *master-detail* relationship between a parent and child table. An example is retrieving a customer record and also viewing related order information.

The disconnected DataSet model enables you to work with multiple tables in your application and to define a relationship between the tables. You can then use the relationship to navigate between related records.

Definition

The **GetChildRows** method of the DataRow enables you to retrieve related rows from a child table.

Example

The following example loops through each customer and processes each order in the Orders table that is related to that customer:

```
Dim drCustomer As DataRow
Dim drOrder As DataRow

For Each drCustomer In dsNorthwind.Tables("Customer").Rows
  For Each drOrder In drCustomer.GetChildRows( _
        "FK_CustomersOrders")

    ' process row

  Next
Next
```

To delete DataRelation objects, use the **Remove** or **Clear** methods of the **Relations** collection for a DataSet.

Lesson: Modifying Data in a DataTable

- How to Insert a New Row
- How to Position on a Row
- Modifying Data in a Table
- How to Delete a Row
- What Are the RowState and RowVersion Properties?
- How to Handle the DataTable Events

Introduction

After creating a DataTable in a DataSet, you can perform the same activities that you would perform when using a table in a database: add, view, edit, and delete data; monitor errors and events; and query the data. When modifying data in a DataTable, you can also verify whether the changes are accurate, and determine whether to programmatically accept or reject the changes.

Lesson objectives

After completing this lesson, you will be able to:

- Insert a new record into a DataTable.
- Find records in a DataTable.
- Update data in DataTables.
- Delete a record in a DataTable.
- Handle the **RowDeleted** event.
- Accept or reject changes to DataTables.

How to Insert a New Row

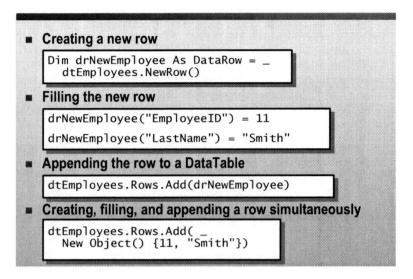

- **Creating a new row**
```
Dim drNewEmployee As DataRow = _
    dtEmployees.NewRow()
```
- **Filling the new row**
```
drNewEmployee("EmployeeID") = 11
drNewEmployee("LastName") = "Smith"
```
- **Appending the row to a DataTable**
```
dtEmployees.Rows.Add(drNewEmployee)
```
- **Creating, filling, and appending a row simultaneously**
```
dtEmployees.Rows.Add( _
    New Object() {11, "Smith"})
```

Introduction

After you create a DataTable and define its structure by using columns and constraints, you can add new rows of data to the table.

Creating a new row

To add a new row to a DataTable, you declare a new variable of the type DataRow. A new DataRow object is returned when you call the **NewRow** method. The DataTable then creates the DataRow object based on the structure of the table, as defined by the **DataColumnCollection**.

```
Dim drNewEmployee As DataRow = dtEmployees.NewRow()
```

Filling the new row

After adding a new row to a DataTable, you can manipulate the new row by using an index or the column name.

```
drNewEmployee(0) = 11
drNewEmployee(1) = "Smith"

drNewEmployee("EmployeeID") = 11
drNewEmployee("LastName") = "Smith"
```

Appending the row to a DataTable

After data is inserted into the new row, the **Add** method is used to add the row to the **DataRowCollection**.

```
dtEmployees.Rows.Add(drNewEmployee)
```

Creating, filling, and appending a row by using one line of code

You can also call the **Add** method to add a new row by passing in an array of values, typed as Object:

```
dtEmployees.Rows.Add(New Object() {11, "Smith"})
```

This technique creates a new row inside the table, and sets its column values to the values in the object array. Note that values in the array are matched sequentially to the columns, based on the order in which they appear in the table.

How to Position on a Row

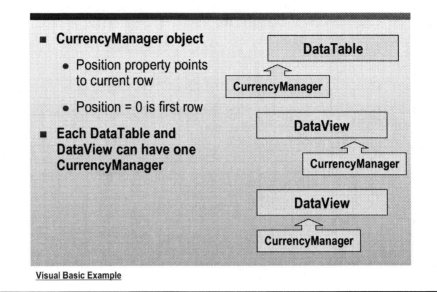

- **CurrencyManager object**
  - Position property points to current row
  - Position = 0 is first row
- **Each DataTable and DataView can have one CurrencyManager**

DataTable

CurrencyManager

DataView

CurrencyManager

DataView

CurrencyManager

<u>Visual Basic Example</u>

Introduction

To modify data, you must first find the rows that you want to modify.

In a Windows Form application, the data binding layer manages navigation through rows in a data source. The **CurrencyManager** object associated with a table or view in a DataSet includes a **Position** property that can be used to navigate through rows.

Because the DataSet can contain multiple data sources, or because the controls on a form can be bound to two or more data lists, the form can have multiple currency managers.

Finding rows in a Windows Form application

To find a row in a Windows Form application, set the **Position** property of the **CurrencyManager** object for the bound data to the row position where you want to go.

Example

The following is an example of setting the **Position** property of the **CurrencyManager** object. The code assumes a form with four buttons that enable the user to move to the first, previous, next, and last rows in the Customers table.

```vbnet
' Visual Basic

Private cmCustomers As CurrencyManager

Private Sub Form1_Load() Handles Form1.Load
  txtCompanyName.DataBindings.Add( _
      "Text", dtCustomers, "CompanyName")
  cmCustomers = CType(Me.BindingContext( _
      dtCustomers), CurrencyManager)
  cmCustomers.Position = 0
End Sub

Private Sub btnMoveNext()
  If cmCustomers.Position <> cmCustomers.Count - 1 Then
      cmCustomers.Position += 1
  End If
End Sub

Private Sub btnMoveFirst()
    cmCustomers.Position = 0
End Sub

Private Sub btnMovePrevious()
    If cmCustomers.Position <> 0 Then
      cmCustomers.Position -= 1
    End if
End Sub

Private Sub btnMoveLast()
    cmCustomers.Position = cmCustomers.Count - 1
End Sub
```

Modifying Data in a Table

> - **The BeginEdit method of DataRow class**
>   - Disables the raising of events and exceptions
> - **EndEdit and CancelEdit methods of DataRow class**
>   - Enable the raising of events and exceptions
> - **How to modify data in a table**
>
> ```
> Dim drEmployee As DataRow = dtEmployees.Rows(3)
> drEmployee.BeginEdit()
> drEmployee("FirstName") = "John"
> drEmployee("LastName") = "Smith"
> drEmployee.EndEdit()
> ```

Introduction

You can modify data in a DataSet by using code as well as through bound controls.

The DataRow class

The DataRow class is used to manipulate individual records.

The BeginEdit, EndEdit, and CancelEdit methods

The DataRow class provides three methods for suspending and reactivating the state of the row while editing: **BeginEdit**, **EndEdit**, and **CancelEdit**.

You call **BeginEdit** to suspend any events or exceptions while editing data. You use the Items collection to specify the column names of the data you want to modify and the new values. You use **EndEdit** to reactivate any events or exceptions, and **CancelEdit** to rollback any changes and reactivate any events or exceptions.

How to modify data in a table

The following example shows how to use the **BeginEdit** method, the Items collection, and the **EndEdit** method:

```
' get the third employee
Dim drEmployee As DataRow = dtEmployees.Rows(3)

drEmployee.BeginEdit()
drEmployee("FirstName") = "John"
drEmployee("LastName") = "Smith"
drEmployee.EndEdit()
```

How to Delete a Row

- **The Remove method of the DataRowCollection class**
    - Completely removes the row from the collection
- **Example:**

```
dtEmployees.Rows.Remove(drEmployee)
```

- **The Delete method of the DataRow class**
    - Marks the row as deleted
    - Hidden, but still accessible if necessary
- **Example:**

```
drEmployee.Delete
```

Introduction

You can use two methods to delete a DataRow object from a DataTable object: the **Remove** method of the **DataRowCollection** object, and the **Delete** method of the DataRow object. Although the **Remove** method deletes a DataRow from the **DataRowCollection**, the **Delete** method only marks the row for deletion.

The **Delete** method is typically used with data in a disconnected environment.

The Remove method

The **Remove** method of the **DataRowCollection** takes a DataRow as an argument and removes it from the collection as shown in the following example:

```
' Visual Basic
' get the third employee
Dim drEmployee As DataRow = dtEmployees.Rows(3)
dtEmployees.Rows.Remove(drEmployee)

// Visual C#
DataRow drEmployee = dtEmployees.Rows(3);
dtEmployees.Rows.Remove(drEmployee);
```

The Delete method

In contrast, the following example demonstrates how to call the **Delete** method on a DataRow to change its **RowState** to **Deleted**:

```
' Visual Basic
drEmployee.Delete

// Visual C#
drEmployee.Delete;
```

What Are the RowState and RowVersion Properties?

- **RowState property of a DataRow**
  - Added, Deleted, Detached, Modified, Unchanged
- **DataViewRowState enumeration**
  - Used with a DataView to filter rows of a certain state
  - CurrentRows, OriginalRows, and so on
- **DataRowVersion enumeration is used when retrieving values using the Item property**
  - Current, Default, Original, Proposed
- **HasVersion method of a DataRow**
- **AcceptChanges and RejectChanges methods**

Introduction

The DataRow class includes the **RowState** property. The **RowState** property's values indicate whether and how the row has changed, and in what way, since the DataTable was first created or loaded from the database.

The DataRowState enumeration

Edits made to column values in a DataRow are immediately placed in the Current state of the row. At this point, the **RowState** is set to Modified.

Deleted rows remain in the DataTable but are hidden, because they are marked as being deleted. It is still possible to retrieve the original row before it was deleted.

New rows are initially marked as Detached. When they are appended to the DataTable, they are marked as Added.

The DataViewRowState enumeration

The DataViewRowState values are used either to retrieve a particular version of data from a DataRow, or to determine what versions exist.

Set the **RowStateFilter** property of the DataView to specify which version or versions of data you want to view. You can use the Boolean operator **Or** with the values to get more than one version.

The DataTable uses DataViewRowState in the **Select** method.

The DataRowVersion enumeration

The **DataRowVersion** values are used when retrieving the value found in a DataRow by using the **Item** property (the DataRow indexer) or the **GetChildRows** method of the DataRow object. There are four possible values.

- **Current**. The row contains current values.
- **Default**. The row contains its default values.
- **Original**. The row contains its original values.
- **Proposed**. The row contains a proposed value.

The **DataRowVersion** informs you what version of a DataRow exists. Versions change under the following circumstances:

- After calling the DataRow object's **BeginEdit** method, if you change the value, the Current and Proposed values become available.

- After calling the DataRow object's **CancelEdit** method, the Proposed value is deleted.

- After calling the DataRow object's **EndEdit** method, the Proposed value becomes the Current value.

- After calling the DataRow object's **AcceptChanges** method, the Proposed value becomes the Current value. The Original value persists.

- After calling the DataTable object's **AcceptChanges** method, the Original value becomes identical to the Current value.

- After calling the DataRow object's **RejectChanges** method, the Proposed value is discarded, and the version becomes Current.

Testing the row version

You can test whether a DataRow has a particular row version by calling the **HasVersion** method and passing a **DataRowVersion** as an argument. For example, **DataRow.HasVersion(DataRowVersion.Original)** will return **false** for newly added rows.

The AcceptChanges and RejectChanges methods

After verifying the accuracy of changes made to data in a DataTable, you can commit the changes by using the **AcceptChanges** method of the DataRow, DataTable, or DataSet. This sets the Current row values to be the Original values, and sets the **RowState** to Unchanged.

Accepting or rejecting changes deletes any RowError information and sets HasErrors to **false**. Accepting or rejecting changes can also affect updating data in the data source.

If **ForeignKeyConstraints** exist on the DataTable, changes committed or rejected by using **AcceptChanges** and **RejectChanges** are propagated to child rows of the DataRow according to the **AcceptRejectRule** of the **ForeignKeyConstraint**.

How to Handle the DataTable Events

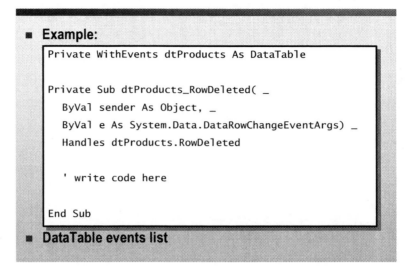

- **Example:**

```
Private WithEvents dtProducts As DataTable

Private Sub dtProducts_RowDeleted( _
   ByVal sender As Object, _
   ByVal e As System.Data.DataRowChangeEventArgs) _
   Handles dtProducts.RowDeleted

   ' write code here

End Sub
```

- **DataTable events list**

Introduction

You might need to build functionality into your application that handles events that occur on a DataTable when data is being changed or deleted.

To handle DataTable events

To handle DataTable events, use the **WithEvents** statement when declaring an object. Then, create a procedure that uses the **Handles** statement to associate the procedure with the event.

Example

The following example shows how to handle the **RowDeleted** event:

```
Private WithEvents dtProducts As DataTable

...

Private Sub dtProducts_RowDeleted( _
  ByVal sender As Object, _
  ByVal e As System.Data.DataRowChangeEventArgs) _
  Handles dtProducts.RowDeleted

  ' write code here

End Sub
```

List of DataTable events

The DataTable object provides a series of events that can be processed by an application. The following table describes DataTable events.

Event	Description
ColumnChanged	Occurs when a value has been inserted successfully into a column.
ColumnChanging	Occurs when a value has been submitted for a column.
RowChanged	Occurs after a row in the table has been edited successfully.
RowChanging	Occurs when a DataRow is changing.
RowDeleted	Occurs after a row in the table has been deleted.
RowDeleting	Occurs when a row in the table is marked for deletion.

Practice

The Northwind Traders Operations Manager wants more complex validation rules to apply when products are changed than can be provided by simple constraints. In this practice, you will handle the **ColumnChanging** DataTable event.

You want to see categories in the grid, and have the ability to drill down and see the related products, so the grid must stay bound to the Categories table. However, you also want to see an event fired when a product is changed. Therefore, an event-handling pointer to the Products table must be created that responds to the **Column_Changing** event.

1. Open the solution you built for the previous practice, or open the solution at the following location:

   <install folder>\Practices\Mod04_2\Lesson1\CreateADataRelation\

2. Open the form in Code view.

3. Declare a private DataTable variable called **dtProducts** with the capability of responding to events.

   ```
   Private WithEvents dtProducts As DataTable
   ```

4. Add code to the **Form1_Load** event handler to point the **dtProducts** variable to the **Products** table in the **dsCatProd** DataSet.

   ```
   dtProducts = dsCatProd.Tables("Products")
   ```

5. Add code to handle the **dtProducts ColumnChanging** event by displaying a message box that shows the original value and the proposed new value of a modified product row.

   ```
   MessageBox.Show("From: " & e.Row.Item(e.Column) & _
     ", To: " & e.ProposedValue.ToString(), e.Column.ColumnName)
   ```

6. Run and test the application by editing one of the product names.

Note You will need to drill down to find a product to edit. If you edit a category name, the event will not occur. For example, changing the name of the Beverages category will not trigger the event. Changing the name of the product, Chai, will trigger the event.

The solution for this practice is at the following location:

<install folder>\Practices\Mod04_2\Lesson2\HandlingDataTableEvents\

Lesson: Sorting and Filtering

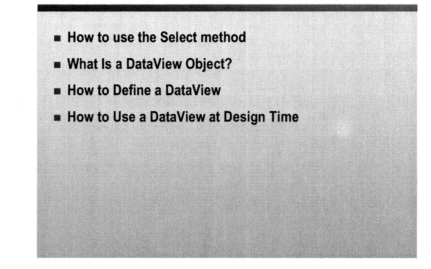

- How to use the Select method
- What Is a DataView Object?
- How to Define a DataView
- How to Use a DataView at Design Time

Introduction

You can achieve sorting and filtering by using a method and an object. A DataView object acts similarly to the way a view acts in SQL Server. It is an object that presents a subset of data from a DataTable. A DataView object acts similarly to a layer on top of the DataTable, providing a filtered and sorted view of the table contents.

Lesson objectives

After completing this lesson, you will be able to:

- Sort and filter data by using the **Select** method.
- Describe what a DataView object is.
- Create a DataView object.
- Sort and filter a DataTable by using a DataView object.

How to Use the Select Method

- **DataTables have a Select method**
  - Gets an array of DataRow objects that match the filter in the order of the sort, and that match the specified state
- **Three optional parameters**
  - Filter expression, for example, "City='London'"
  - Sort, for example, "CompanyName ASC"
  - DataViewRowState, for example, Deleted

Introduction

The **Select** method of a DataSet object gets an array of DataRow objects. This method creates a set of pointers to rows within the original DataSet. It does not actually copy anything, but only points to the changes, so it is very efficient.

Example of selecting modified rows in a DataSet

The following example selects rows from the Customers table. The **Select** method gets all of the deleted customers whose **City** is London. The example loops through these customers, and displays the original **CompanyName** of each customer.

```
' Visual Basic
Dim selRows As DataRow() = _
  dtCustomers.Select("City='London'", _
  "CompanyName ASC", DataViewRowState.Deleted)

Dim row As DataRow
For Each row In selRows
  MessageBox.Show("Company name: " & _
      row("CompanyName", DataRowVersion.Original))
Next
```

```
// Visual C#
DataRow[] selRows = dsCustomers.Customers.Select(
  "City='London'", "CompanyName ASC",
  DataViewRowState.Deleted);

foreach (DataRow row in selRows) {
  MessageBox.Show("Company name: " +
      row["CompanyName", DataRowVersion.Original]); }
```

What Is a DataView Object?

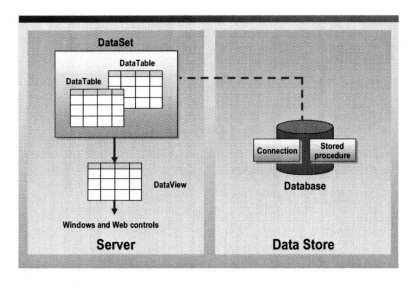

Introduction

A DataView object is similar to a view in SQL Server. It is an object that presents a subset of data from a DataTable. A DataView object acts similarly to a layer on top of the DataTable, providing a filtered and sorted view of the table contents. This capability enables you to have two controls bound to the same DataTable, but showing different versions of the data.

Another benefit of the DataView object is to allow data binding on both Windows Forms and Web Forms.

Example

A sales associate at Northwind Traders travels throughout her assigned region. While in a particular city, she might only want to see the contact information (name, company, phone number, address) for the clients in that city. You can use a DataView object to filter clients based on the city where the sales associate will be working on a particular day.

How to Define a DataView

- **Creating a DataView by using form controls**
- **Creating a DataView programmatically**

```
Dim dvProducts As New _
    DataView(dsNorthwind.Tables("Products"))
dvProducts.Sort = "UnitPrice"
dvProducts.RowFilter = "CategoryID > 4"
grdProducts.DataSource = dvProducts
```

- **Applying a DataView to a DataTable**

```
dvProducts.Table = _
    dsNorthwind.Tables("Products")
```

Introduction

You can create a DataView object in two ways:

- By using the Visual Studio .NET development environment graphical tools
- Programmatically

Creating a DataView by using form controls

▶ **To add a DataView to a form or component graphically**

The easiest way to create a DataView is to use the graphical tools provided by the Visual Studio .NET development environment.

1. In the Visual Studio .NET development environment, in the **Toolbox**, drag a **DataView** item from the **Data** tab onto the form or component.

2. If you want to configure the DataView at design time (rather than in code at run time), select the DataView and use the Properties window to configure the DataView.

Creating a DataView programmatically

The following is an example of creating a DataView programmatically:

```
Dim dvProducts As New DataView(dsNorthwind.Tables("Products"))
dvProducts.Sort = "UnitPrice"
dvProducts.RowFilter = "CategoryID > 4"
grdProducts.DataSource = dvProducts
```

Applying a DataView to a DataTable

A DataView can be created independently of a DataTable and applied later to different DataTables dynamically.

To apply a DataView to a DataTable, set the **Table** property of the DataView, as shown in the following example:

```
Dim dvProducts As New DataView()
dvProducts.Table = dsNorthwind.Tables("Products")
```

How to Use a DataView at Design Time

- **DataViews allow sorting and filtering at design time**

- **A DataView cannot span multiple DataTables, unlike the View object in SQL Server**

  - Use presentation-level objects instead (for example, the DataGrid control, report designers, and so on)

- **Every DataTable has a DefaultView property**

Introduction

Sorting with a DataView object enables you to set sort criteria at design time, and provides an object that you can use for data binding.

You can filter and sort a DataTable by using a DataView object that you have explicitly added to a form or component. Doing this enables you to set filter and sort options at design time.

Alternatively, you can use the default DataView, called DefaultView, which is available for every table in a DataSet. When you use the default view, you can specify filter and sort options programmatically.

Filtering and sorting by using a DataView object

▶ **To filter and sort by using a DataView object**

1. If you want to set DataView options at design time, add a DataView object to the form or component.

2. Set the DataView **Sort** property by using a sort expression. The sort expression can include the names of DataColumns or a calculation. If you set the sort expression at design time, the DataView reflects the change immediately.

3. Set the DataView **RowFilter** property by using a filter expression. The filter expression should evaluate to **true** or **false**, as in the following expression:

   ```
   dvProducts.RowFilter = "CategoryID = 3"
   ```

4. To filter based on a version or state of a record, set the **RowStateFilter** property to a value from the **DataViewRowState** enumeration, such as the following:

   ```
   dvProducts.RowStateFilter = DataViewRowState.CurrentRows
   ```

Filtering and sorting by using the default DataView

The following example shows how to set the DataView filter and sort order at run time by using the default DataView:

```
dtCustomers.DefaultView.Sort = "City"
```

Practice

The Northwind Traders Sales Director wants the ability to filter products in the company's catalog based on customer requirements.

1. Open the solution you built for the previous practice, or open the solution at the following location:

   <install folder>\Practices\Mod04_2\Lesson2\HandlingDataTableEvents\

2. Open the form in Code view.

3. Add code to the **Form1_Load** event handler to create a new DataView called **dvExpensiveProducts** based on the dtProducts variable.

   ```
   Dim dvExpensiveProducts As New DataView(dtProducts)
   ```

4. Add code to sort the DataView on the **UnitsInStock** column.

   ```
   dvExpensiveProducts.Sort = "UnitsInStock"
   ```

5. Add code to filter the DataView so that only products that cost more than $50 are displayed.

   ```
   dvExpensiveProducts.RowFilter = "UnitPrice>50"
   ```

6. Modify the statement that binds the DataGrid. Bind the DataGrid to the data view, as follows:

   ```
   DataGrid1.DataSource = dvExpensiveProducts
   ```

7. Run and test the application.

   How many products have a unit price greater than $50?

The solution for this practice is at the following location:

<install folder>\Practices\Mod04_2\Lesson3\SortAndFilterUsingADataView\

Review

- Working in a Disconnected Environment
- Building DataSets and DataTables
- Binding and Saving a DataSet
- Defining Data Relationships
- Modifying Data in a DataTable
- Sorting and Filtering

1. What is the difference between a DataTable and a DataView?

2. What types of constraints can you create in a DataSet?

3. What are some uses for a custom expression?

4. How do you display the contents of a DataTable in a grid control?

5. What are the four possible restricting actions for a **ForeignKeyConstraint**?

6. Are **ForeignKeyConstraint** objects always enforced?

7. What does a DataRelation object do?

8. What does a **CurrencyManager** object do?

9. What is the difference between the **Delete** and **Remove** methods?

10. What is the difference between the **RowState** and **RowVersion** properties?

Lab 4.2: Manipulating DataSets

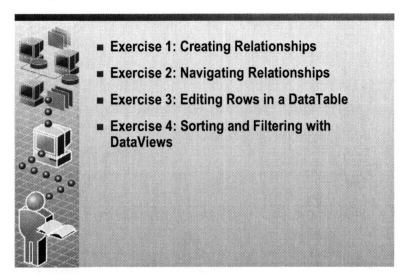

- Exercise 1: Creating Relationships
- Exercise 2: Navigating Relationships
- Exercise 3: Editing Rows in a DataTable
- Exercise 4: Sorting and Filtering with DataViews

Objectives

After completing this lab, you will be able to:

- Define a relationship.
- Navigate a relationship by using code.
- Modify data in a DataTable.
- Sort and filter a DataTable by using a DataView object.

Estimated time to complete this lab: 60 minutes

Exercise 1
Creating Relationships

In this exercise, you will add a relationship between the DataTables you created in Lab 4.1, "Building, Binding, Opening, and Saving DataSets."

Scenario

The Northwind Traders database is normalized to reduce data redundancy and duplication. To extract useful information, you must join the data together in the disparate tables by using relationships before displaying it to users.

▶ **Continue building the application**

- Open the solution you created in Lab 4.1, or open the solution **BuildingDataSets** in the folder
  <install folder>\Labs\Lab04_2\Starter\xx\ where xx is either VB or CS.

▶ **Give the Customer table a primary key**

A primary key must be defined for the column of the parent table that forms part of a relationship.

1. Open the **Form1** class module.

2. In the **Form1_Load** procedure, programmatically create a primary key by using the following information.

Attribute	Value
Name	PK_Customer
Table	dtCustomer
Column	CustomerID

```
' Visual Basic
Me.dtCustomer.Constraints.Add("PK_Customer", _
    Me.dtCustomer.Columns("CustomerID"), True)
```

```
// Visual C#
this.dtCustomer.Constraints.Add("PK_Customer",
    this.dtCustomer.Columns["CustomerID"], true);
```

▶ **Relate the Customer and CartItems tables**

1. In the **Form1_Load** procedure, create a relationship (including a ForeignKeyConstraint with default rules) between the **Customer** and **CartItems** tables by using the information in the following table.

Attribute	Value
Name	FK_Customer_CartItems
Parent Table	dtCustomer
Parent Column	CustomerID
Child Table	dtCartItems
Child Column	CustomerID

```
' Visual Basic
Me.dsShoppingCart.Relations.Add("FK_Customer_CartItems", _
    Me.dtCustomer.Columns("CustomerID"), _
    Me.dtCartItems.Columns("CustomerID"), True)
```

```
// Visual C#
this.dsShoppingCart.Relations.Add("FK_Customer_CartItems",
    this.dtCustomer.Columns["CustomerID"],
    this.dtCartItems.Columns["CustomerID"], true);
```

▶ **Test the relationship**

1. Run the application.

2. Add a new customer record, or open a DataSet file that you created previously.

3. Notice that the DataGrid recognizes the relationship and automatically provides the ability to expand to a customer's shopping cart items.

4. Add a new cart item for a customer. Notice that the **CustomerID** field is automatically completed if the drill down feature is used.

5. Test the primary key by attempting to add another customer with a duplicate CustomerID value.

Exercise 2
Navigating Relationships

In this exercise, you will use the relationship defined between the two tables in Exercise 1 to provide a summation of the total order value of a customer's shopping cart items. You will use two techniques: programmatically navigating the object model, and adding an expression column that can automatically summarize child rows.

Scenario

To make its e-commerce Web site more convenient for users, Northwind Traders wants to give its customers the ability to view a running total of the order value of their shopping cart items.

▶ **Start with the solution to the previous exercise**

- If you did not complete the previous exercise, open the solution **BuildingDataSets** in the folder <install folder>\Labs\Lab04_2\Solution\Ex1\xx\ where xx is either VB or CS.

▶ **Display a shopping cart order total**

1. Open the **Form1** class module in Designer view.

2. Add a new menu item to the **View** menu by using the following information.

Menu	Property	Value
mnuSubtotal	(Name)	mnuSubtotal
	Text	Cart &Subtotal
	Shortcut	F9

▶ **Calculate the subtotal**

1. Add code to handle the **Click** event for the **Cart Subtotal** menu item.

2. Declare the following local variables. Initialize the variable named dSubtotal to zero.

Name	Data type
sCustomerID	System.String
drCustomer	System.Data.DataRow
drCartItem	System.Data.DataRow
dSubtotal	System.Decimal

```
' Visual Basic
Dim sCustomerID As System.String
Dim drCustomer As System.Data.DataRow
Dim drCartItem As System.Data.DataRow
Dim dSubtotal As System.Decimal = 0
```

```
// Visual C#
System.String sCustomerID;
System.Data.DataRow drCustomer;
// drCartItem will be declared later
System.Decimal dSubtotal = 0;
```

3. Set the string variable to be the CustomerID value of the currently selected customer in the DataGrid.

Tip   The **CurrentRowIndex** property returns the current row in a DataGrid.

```
' Visual Basic
sCustomerID = Me.grd(Me.grd.CurrentRowIndex, 0)
```

```
// Visual C#
sCustomerID = (System.String)
  this.grd[this.grd.CurrentRowIndex, 0];
```

4. Set the customer DataRow variable to point to the correct row in the **Customer** DataTable by using the CustomerID retrieved in the previous line as a criteria value for a DataRow selection filter.

Tip Use the **Select** method provided by the DataTable class. The **Select** method returns an array of DataRows. Even if only one DataRow matches the select filter, you must use array syntax to retrieve an individual DataRow.

```
' Visual Basic
drCustomer = Me.dsShoppingCart.Tables("Customer").Select( _
    "CustomerID='" & sCustomerID & "'")(0)
```

```
// Visual C#
drCustomer = this.dsShoppingCart.Tables["Customer"].Select(
    "CustomerID='" + sCustomerID + "'")[0];
```

5. Write a **For Each** statement to loop through all of the child rows returned by a call to the **GetChildRows** method of the Customer DataRow. Inside the loop, increment the subtotal variable by the value in the Cost column of the DataRow.

```
' Visual Basic
For Each drCartItem In _
        drCustomer.GetChildRows("FK_Customer_CartItems")
    dSubtotal += drCartItem.Item("Cost")
Next
```

```
// Visual C#
foreach (System.Data.DataRow drCartItem in
    drCustomer.GetChildRows("FK_Customer_CartItems"))
    dSubtotal += (System.Decimal) drCartItem["Cost"];
```

6. Use a message box to show the company name of the customer and the amount the customer owes based on the items currently in his or her shopping cart.

```
' Visual Basic
MessageBox.Show(drCustomer("CompanyName") & " owes " _
    & dSubtotal.ToString("$0.00"), "Cart Subtotal")
```

```
// Visual C#
MessageBox.Show(drCustomer["CompanyName"] + " owes "
    + dSubtotal.ToString("$0.00"), "Cart Subtotal");
```

7. Add code for a generic exception handler for this procedure.

▶ **Add a cart total to the Customer table**

1. In the **Form1_Load** procedure, programmatically add a new column to the
   Customer table with the following attributes.

DataColumn	Property	Value
CartSubtotal	ColumnName	CartSubtotal
	DataType	System.Decimal
	Expression	Sum(Child.Cost)

```vb
' Visual Basic
Me.dtCustomer.Columns.Add(New DataColumn( _
    "CartSubtotal", GetType(System.Decimal), _
    "Sum(Child.Cost)"))
```

```csharp
// Visual C#
this.dtCustomer.Columns.Add(new DataColumn(
    "CartSubtotal", typeof(System.Decimal),
    "Sum(Child.Cost)"));
```

▶ **Test the cart totals**

1. Run the application.

2. Open an existing DataSet, or add a new customer record and add some cart
   items and then return to the customer view.

Note The DataGrid automatically calculates the cart subtotal and displays
the results in the grid as an additional column.

---

3. On the **View** menu, click **Cart Subtotal**. The same subtotal value should be
   returned.

Exercise 3
Editing Rows in a DataTable

In this exercise, you will provide a simple method to add new cart items to the shopping cart. To supply the basic values required for a cart item, you will open an existing DataSet file that contains sample categories and products.

Scenario

When browsing the Northwind Traders e-commerce Web site, a customer will want the ability to add an item to his or her shopping cart with a single click.

▶ **Start with the solution to the previous exercise**

- If you did not complete the previous exercise, open the solution **BuildingDataSets** in the folder <install folder>\Labs\Lab04_2\Solution\Ex2\xx\ where xx is either VB or CS.

▶ **Open the existing DataSet file**

1. Open the **Form1** class module.

2. Declare a class-level variable named **dsCatProd** by using the standard DataSet class as the data type.

   ```
   ' Visual Basic
   Private dsCatProd As DataSet
   ```

   ```
   // Visual C#
   private DataSet dsCatProd;
   ```

3. Add code to the **Form1_Load** event to set the **dsCatProd** variable to point to a new instance of the DataSet class.

   ```
   ' Visual Basic
   Me.dsCatProd = New DataSet()
   ```

   ```
   // Visual C#
   this.dsCatProd = new DataSet();
   ```

4. Call the **ReadXml** method of the **dsCatProd** object to open the existing DataSet file (including the schema) from the following location on your training computer:

   <install folder>\Labs\Lab04_2\CatProd.ds

   ```
   ' Visual Basic
   Me.dsCatProd.ReadXml("\Program Files\MSDNTrain\2389\" & _
       "Labs\Lab04_2\catprod.ds", XmlReadMode.ReadSchema)
   ```

   ```
   // Visual C#
   this.dsCatProd.ReadXml(@"\Program Files\MSDNTrain\2389\" +
       @"Labs\Lab04_2\catprod.ds", XmlReadMode.ReadSchema);
   ```

▶ **Code the View menu items**

1. Add code to the **mnuCustomer_Click** event to clear the check mark next to the **mnuProducts** menu item.

2. Add code to the **mnuCartItems_Click** event to clear the check mark next to the **mnuProducts** menu item.

3. Add code to the **mnuProducts_Click** event to place a check mark next to the **mnuProducts** menu item, and then clear the check marks next to the **mnuCustomer** and **mnuCartItems** menu items.

4. Add code to the **mnuProducts_Click** event to set the DataGrid to bind to the **Products** table in the **dsCatProd** DataSet through an intermediate DataView object.

```
' Visual Basic
Me.grd.DataSource = New _
    DataView(Me.dsCatProd.Tables("Products"))

// Visual C#
this.grd.DataSource = new
    DataView(this.dsCatProd.Tables["Products"]);
```

▶ **Create the menu to add a product to the cart**

1. Use the Menu Editor to insert an **Edit** menu by using the following information.

Menu	Property	Value
mnuEdit	(Name)	mnuEdit
	Text	&Edit
mnuAddToCart	(Name)	mnuAddToCart
	Text	&Add To Cart
	Shortcut	Ins

Note   The **Add To Cart** menu should only be available when the products are displayed in the DataGrid, so you will now write code to disable the menu when it should not be available.

2. Add code to handle the **Edit** menu's **Select** event that sets the **Enabled** property of the **Add To Cart** menu item to have the same value as the **Checked** property of the **Products** menu item.

```
' Visual Basic
Private Sub mnuEdit_Select(ByVal sender As Object, _
   ByVal e As System.EventArgs) Handles mnuEdit.Select

   mnuAddToCart.Enabled = mnuProducts.Checked
End Sub
```

```
// Visual C#
private void mnuEdit_Select(
   object sender, System.EventArgs e)
{
   mnuAddToCart.Enabled = mnuProducts.Checked;
}

// add the following code to InitializeComponent
this.mnuEdit.Select += new
   System.EventHandler(this.mnuEdit_Select);
```

▶ **Test the changes**

1. Run the application.
2. Use the **View** menu to toggle the DataGrid to show the products available on the Northwind Traders e-commerce Web site.
3. Ensure that the **Add To Cart** menu is only available when products are shown in the DataGrid.

▶ **Add a product to the shopping cart**

1. Add code to handle the **Click** event for the **Add To Cart** menu item.
2. Declare local variables to store the CustomerID, ProductID, UnitPrice, and Quantity that the user selects. Use the generic **System.Object** data type for all four.

```
' Visual Basic
Dim CustomerID As System.Object
Dim ProductID As System.Object
Dim UnitPrice As System.Object
Dim Quantity As System.Object
```

```
// Visual C#
System.Object CustomerID;
System.Object ProductID;
System.Object UnitPrice;
System.Object Quantity;
```

3. Set the CustomerID to the value in the first column of the first row of the **Customer** DataTable.

> **Note** To simplify this example, assume that there is only one customer row. If you have time at the end of this lab, you can add code to allow the user to select a customer in addition to a product and quantity.

```
' Visual Basic
CustomerID = Me.dtCustomer.Rows(0).Item(0)

// Visual C#
CustomerID = this.dtCustomer.Rows[0][0];
```

4. Set the ProductID variable to the **ProductID** column (the first column) of the product currently selected in the DataGrid.

```
' Visual Basic
ProductID = Me.grd(Me.grd.CurrentRowIndex, 0)

// Visual C#
ProductID = this.grd[this.grd.CurrentRowIndex, 0];
```

5. Set the UnitPrice variable to the **UnitPrice** column (the sixth column) of the product currently selected in the DataGrid.

```
' Visual Basic
UnitPrice = Me.grd(Me.grd.CurrentRowIndex, 5)

// Visual C#
UnitPrice = this.grd[this.grd.CurrentRowIndex, 5];
```

6. Use the **InputBox** method to prompt the user for a quantity and store the value in the Quantity variable.

> **Tip** Visual C# does not include native support for the **InputBox** method. You must add a reference to the **Microsoft Visual Basic .NET Runtime** assembly, and then use a fully qualified method call. See the following code for an example.

```
// Syntax for the InputBox method when used in Visual C#
// Note: all five parameters are mandatory
Microsoft.VisualBasic.Interaction.InputBox("Prompt",
    "Title", "DefaultResponse", XPos, YPos);

' Visual Basic
Quantity = InputBox("How many " & _
    Me.grd(Me.grd.CurrentRowIndex, 1) & " do you want?", _
    "Add To Cart")

// Visual C#
Quantity = Microsoft.VisualBasic.Interaction.InputBox(
    "How many " + this.grd[this.grd.CurrentRowIndex, 1] +
    " do you want?", "Add To Cart", "", 0, 0);
```

7. Try to add the values as an array of objects by using the **Add** method of the **Rows** collection of the **CartItems** DataTable. Catch any exceptions.

```
' Visual Basic
dsShoppingCart.Tables("CartItems").Rows.Add( _
    New Object() _
    { CustomerID, ProductID, UnitPrice, Quantity } )
```

```
// Visual C#
dsShoppingCart.Tables["CartItems"].Rows.Add(
    new Object[]
    { CustomerID, ProductID, UnitPrice, Quantity } );
```

▶ **Test the application**

1. Run the application.

2. Enter a new customer or open an existing file.

3. View the products.

4. Select a product in the DataGrid.

5. On the **Edit** menu, click **Add To Cart**.

6. When prompted, enter a quantity.

7. Repeat the procedure for several products.

8. Switch the view to see the cart items.

Exercise 4
Sorting and Filtering with DataViews

In this exercise, you will add the ability to filter the products list. The DataGrid automatically provides basic sorting capability, but you will provide the user with the ability to view all products, to filter out discontinued or out-of-stock products, or both.

Scenario

When browsing the Northwind Traders e-commerce Web site, a customer will want the ability to view the products in different ways; for example, products that match some criteria sorted with the cheapest products first. Customers might only want to see products that are in stock, or that have not been discontinued.

▶ **Start with the solution to the previous exercise**

- If you did not complete the previous exercise, open the solution **BuildingDataSets** in the folder
<install folder>\Labs\Lab04_2\Solution\Ex3\xx\ where xx is either VB or CS.

▶ **Open the existing DataSet file**

1. Open the **Form1** class module in Designer view.

2. Add two menu items to the **View** menu by using the following information.

Menu	Property	Value
mnuDiscontinued	(Name)	mnuDiscontinued
	Text	&Discontinued
	Checked	True
mnuOutOfStock	(Name)	mnuOutOfStock
	Text	&Out Of Stock
	Checked	True

Add menu separators where appropriate (optional).

Note These menu items should only be available when the products are displayed in the DataGrid. You will now write code to disable these menu items when the products are not displayed.

---

3. Add code to handle the **Select** event of the **View** menu.

4. Add code to set the **Enabled** property of the two menu items to have the same value as the **Checked** property of the **Products** menu item on the **View** menu.

▶ **Toggle the display of discontinued and out-of-stock products**

1. Add a new private procedure named **FilterMenus**. This procedure must be able to handle the **System.EventHandler** delegate. Set the procedure to handle the **mnuDiscontinued.Click, mnuOutOfStock.Click**, and **mnuProducts.Click** events.

```vb
' Visual Basic
Private Sub FilterMenus( _
    ByVal sender As System.Object, _
    ByVal e As System.EventArgs) _
    Handles mnuDiscontinued.Click, _
    mnuOutOfStock.Click, mnuProducts.Click

End Sub
```

```csharp
// Visual C#
private void FilterMenus(object sender, System.EventArgs e)
{

}

// add the following to the InitializeComponent function

this.mnuProducts.Click += new
    System.EventHandler(this.FilterMenus);

this.mnuDiscontinued.Click += new
    System.EventHandler(this.FilterMenus);

this.mnuOutOfStock.Click += new
    System.EventHandler(this.FilterMenus);
```

Tip Multiple procedures can handle an event. For example, we now have two procedures that handle the **mnuProducts.Click** event: **FilterMenus** and **mnuProducts_Click**.

---

2. Toggle the **Checked** property of the sender object, if the sender is not **mnuProducts**.

```vb
' Visual Basic
If Not sender Is mnuProducts Then
    sender.Checked = Not sender.Checked
End If
```

```csharp
// Visual C#
MenuItem mi = (MenuItem)sender;
if (mi != mnuProducts) mi.Checked = !(mi.Checked);
```

Tip If you are using Visual C#, you must declare a System.Windows.Forms.MenuItem variable, cast the **sender** object to it, and then use that variable instead, because, unlike Visual Basic, Visual C# does not support late binding.

---

3. Declare a local DataView variable named **dvProducts** and instantiate it by using the **Products** DataTable.

```
' Visual Basic
Dim dvProducts As New _
   DataView(Me.dsCatProd.Tables("Products"))
```

```
// Visual C#
DataView dvProducts = new
   DataView(this.dsCatProd.Tables["Products"]);
```

4. If the **Discontinued** menu item is not selected, set the **RowFilter** property of the DataView variable to only show rows where the **Discontinued** column is **False**.

5. If the **Out Of Stock** menu item is not selected, set the **RowFilter** property of the DataView variable to only show rows where the **UnitsInStock** column is greater than zero.

6. If both the **Discontinued** and the **Out Of Stock** menu items are not selected, set the **RowFilter** property of the DataView variable to only show rows where the **Discontinued** column is **False** and the **UnitsInStock** column is greater than zero.

```
' Visual Basic
If Not mnuOutOfStock.Checked And _
      Not mnuDiscontinued.Checked Then
   dvProducts.RowFilter = _
      "Discontinued=False And UnitsInStock>0"
ElseIf Not mnuOutOfStock.Checked Then
   dvProducts.RowFilter = "UnitsInStock>0"
ElseIf Not mnuDiscontinued.Checked Then
   dvProducts.RowFilter = "Discontinued=False"
End If
```

```
// Visual C#
if (!mnuOutOfStock.Checked && !mnuDiscontinued.Checked)
   dvProducts.RowFilter =
      "Discontinued=False And UnitsInStock>0";
else if(!mnuOutOfStock.Checked)
   dvProducts.RowFilter = "UnitsInStock>0";
else if(!mnuDiscontinued.Checked)
   dvProducts.RowFilter = "Discontinued=False";
```

7. Set the **DataSource** property of the data grid to **dvProducts**.

```
' Visual Basic
Me.grd.DataSource = dvProducts

// Visual C#
this.grd.DataSource = dvProducts;
```

8. In the **mnuProducts_Click** procedure, delete the line of code that sets the **DataSource** of the DataGrid, because the **FilterMenus** procedure now does this.

▶ **Test the application**

1. Run the application.

2. Use the **View** menu to display the **Products** table.

3. Use the **View** menu to toggle the display of discontinued and/or out-of-stock products.

msdn training

Module 5: Reading and Writing XML with ADO.NET

Contents

Microsoft

Overview

- **■ Creating XSD Schemas**
- **■ Loading Schemas and Data into DataSets**
- **■ Writing XML from a DataSet**

Introduction

Microsoft® ADO.NET uses XML as the format for managing and moving data from a data source to a DataSet object and back. In addition, you can work directly with data in XML format in an ADO.NET application. This module explains how to use XML Schema Definition Language (XSD) to create files that provide structure for working with data in XML documents and DataSets.

Objectives

After completing this module, you will be able to:

- Generate an XSD schema from a DataSet by using graphical tools.
- Save a DataSet structure to an XSD schema file.
- Create and populate a DataSet from an XSD schema and XML data.
- Save DataSet data as XML.
- Write and load changes by using a **DiffGram**.

Lesson: Creating XSD Schemas

- **What Is an XSD Schema?**
- **What Are Typed DataSets?**
- **How XSD Schema Information Maps to Relational Structure**
- **Generating an XSD Schema with Visual Studio**

Introduction

XSD schemas provide the mapping between relational data in DataSets and data in XML documents. XSD schemas define the structure of the data in a DataSet, so that the data can be expressed and used in XML format.

Lesson objectives

After completing this lesson, you will be able to:

- Provide a definition of an XSD schema.
- Give examples of when to use an XSD schema.
- Create and save an XSD schema by using Microsoft Visual Studio® .NET.
- Create and save an XSD schema by using code.

What Is an XSD Schema?

- **An XSD schema can contain:**
  - A representation of relationships between data items
  - A representation of constraints
  - A specification of data types
- **Use an XSD schema to:**
  - Import data and know the structure of the data
  - Describe the structure of data you export
- **Practice**

XSD Example   XML Document Example

Introduction

When you create a new DataSet, no tables or other structures are defined. The structure can be loaded from an XSD schema, or you can create the structure by using code.

Definition

An *XSD schema* is a document that describes the structure of an XML document, as well as the constraints on data in that document.

What can an XSD schema contain?

An XSD schema can contain the following information:

- A representation of relationships between data items, similar to the foreign key relationships between tables in a relational database.

- A representation of constraints similar to the primary key and unique constraints in a relational model.

- A specification of the data types of each individual element and attribute in an XML document that complies with the XSD schema.

Why use an XSD schema?

There are two basic reasons to use XSD schemas:

- To import data and know the structure of the data that you import.

  When you receive data in XML format and want to load that data into a DataSet, you can use a schema to define the structure of the data that you are reading.

- To describe the structure of data that you are exporting to another consumer.

  When you want to send data from a DataSet and put it into an XML data document, you can provide a schema to describe the data.

  In both of these cases, you could infer schema information from the structure of the data in the XML file, rather than using an existing schema. However, you should use a schema when one exists to avoid the added cost of inferring the schema. In addition, the inferred schema might not contain the same level of detail as a complete XSD schema.

Example of an XSD   The following example shows a two-level XSD schema:
schema

```xml
<?xml version="1.0" standalone="yes"?>
<xsd:schema id="PersonPet" xmlns:xsd="http://www.w3.org/2001/XMLSchema"
xmlns:msdata="urn:schemas-microsoft-com:xml-msdata">
  <xsd:element name="PersonPet" msdata:IsDataSet="true">
    <xsd:complexType>
      <xsd:choice maxOccurs="unbounded">
        <xsd:element name="Person">
          <xsd:complexType>
            <xsd:sequence>
              <xsd:element name="ID" msdata:AutoIncrement="true" type="xsd:int" />
              <xsd:element name="Name" type="xsd:string" minOccurs="0" />
              <xsd:element name="Age" type="xsd:int" minOccurs="0" />
            </xsd:sequence>
          </xsd:complexType>
        </xsd:element>
        <xsd:element name="Pet">
          <xsd:complexType>
            <xsd:sequence>
              <xsd:element name="ID" msdata:AutoIncrement="true" type="xsd:int" />
              <xsd:element name="OwnerID" type="xsd:int" minOccurs="0" />
              <xsd:element name="Name" type="xsd:string" minOccurs="0" />
              <xsd:element name="Type" type="xsd:string" minOccurs="0" />
            </xsd:sequence>
          </xsd:complexType>
        </xsd:element>
      </xsd:choice>
    </xsd:complexType>
    <xsd:unique name="Constraint1" msdata:PrimaryKey="true">
      <xsd:selector xpath=".//Person" />
      <xsd:field xpath="ID" />
    </xsd:unique>
    <xsd:unique name="Pet_Constraint1" msdata:ConstraintName="Constraint1"
msdata:PrimaryKey="true">
      <xsd:selector xpath=".//Pet" />
      <xsd:field xpath="ID" />
    </xsd:unique>
  </xsd:element>
  <xsd:annotation>
    <xsd:appinfo>
      <msdata:Relationship name="PersonPet" msdata:parent="Person"
msdata:child="Pet" msdata:parentkey="ID" msdata:childkey="OwnerID" />
    </xsd:appinfo>
  </xsd:annotation>
</xsd:schema>
```

Example of an XML document based on a schema

The following example shows an XML data document that is based on the schema in the preceding example:

```
<PersonPet>
  <Person>
    <ID>0</ID>
    <Name>Mark</Name>
    <Age>18</Age>
  </Person>
  <Person>
    <ID>1</ID>
    <Name>William</Name>
    <Age>12</Age>
  </Person>
  <Person>
    <ID>2</ID>
    <Name>James</Name>
    <Age>7</Age>
  </Person>
  <Person>
    <ID>3</ID>
    <Name>Levi</Name>
    <Age>4</Age>
  </Person>
  <Pet>
    <ID>0</ID>
    <OwnerID>0</OwnerID>
    <Name>Frank</Name>
    <Type>cat</Type>
  </Pet>
  <Pet>
    <ID>1</ID>
    <OwnerID>1</OwnerID>
    <Name>Rex</Name>
    <Type>dog</Type>
  </Pet>
  <Pet>
    <ID>2</ID>
    <OwnerID>2</OwnerID>
    <Name>Cottontail</Name>
    <Type>rabbit</Type>
  </Pet>
  <Pet>
    <ID>3</ID>
    <OwnerID>3</OwnerID>
    <Name>Sid</Name>
    <Type>snake</Type>
  </Pet>
  <Pet>
```

Code continued on the following page

```
            <ID>4</ID>
            <OwnerID>3</OwnerID>
            <Name>Tickles</Name>
            <Type>spider</Type>
        </Pet>
        <Pet>
            <ID>5</ID>
            <OwnerID>1</OwnerID>
            <Name>Tweetie</Name>
            <Type>canary</Type>
        </Pet>
    </PersonPet>
```

Practice

Create an XML file based on a schema by using the Visual Studio XML Editor.

▶ **Create an XML file based on a target schema**

1. Start Visual Studio .NET and create a new Microsoft Visual Basic® or Microsoft Visual C#™ Empty Project.

2. On the **File** menu, click **Add Existing Item**. Add *install folder*\Practices\Mod05**PhoneList.xsd** to the project. Double-click the file in the Solution Explorer to open an editor window. The editor opens by default in DataSet view, showing a graphical representation of the schema for the DataSet.

3. Switch to the XML view and examine the schema. Note that a <customers> element has three child elements and one attribute.

4. On the **File** menu, click **Add New Item**. Add a new XML file named **PhoneList.xml** to the project.

5. Right-click the new XML document, and then click **Properties**.

6. Change the Target Schema to **http://tempuri.org/PhoneList.xsd**, and then click **OK**. Notice that Visual Studio automatically adds a schema reference and a parent tag to the XML document.

▶ **Add data to the XML document**

1. Type a < symbol between the <CustomerData> tags. Visual Studio suggests an appropriate XML element based on the target schema. Press the TAB key to insert the <customers> element into the XML document.

2. Type a space. Visual Studio suggests an XML attribute based on the target schema. Press the TAB key to insert the **ContactName** attribute into the XML document.

3. Type a = symbol. Visual Studio inserts a set of quotation marks. Type your own name as a value for the **Contact Name** attribute between these quotation marks.

4. Type a > symbol after your name in quotation marks. Visual Studio adds a closing tag for the <customers> element.

5. Between the <**customers**> and </**customers**> tags, type a < symbol. Visual Studio suggests appropriate child elements based on the target schema. Double-click the suggested tag to insert a <CompanyName> child element into the XML document.

6. Type a > symbol to add a closing tag for the <**CompanyName**> element. Add data for the company name.

7. Use the Visual Studio XML Editor to complete the information for this customer.

8. Save the changes.

9. Switch the XML Editor to Data view and type the name of another customer.

10. Switch the XML Editor to XML view. Notice that the tags and data are entered for you.

What Are Typed DataSets?

- **Why build a typed DataSet?**
  - Save data and its definition for others to consume
  - Validate data in a document
  - Text format, operating-system agnostic
- **Ways to create a typed DataSet**

Introduction

In the .NET world, applications communicate by sending XML documents. When you send an XML document to someone, you must send something that describes the structure of the data, data types, relationships, and constraints that are contained in the document.

You provide this description by including an XSD schema or an inline schema with your data.

Definition

A *typed DataSet* is an instance of an existing DataSet class for which schema information has been defined.

Why build a typed DataSet?

When you import data from an XML file, you must know how it maps to a relational structure. That information is usually contained in an XSD schema, or in an inline schema with the XML document. You use this schema information to build your DataSet on the client application. When you retrieve data from an XML Web service, database, or XML data document, the typed DataSet on the client is already structured to accept and store the information.

**Generating a typed
DataSet class**

To create a typed DataSet, you must first define a new DataSet class that contains schema information. After defining the class, you create a new instance of the DataSet and populate it with data.

▶ **To create a typed DataSet**

1. Create or obtain an XSD schema that describes the data that you expect to retrieve. You use an XSD schema to define tables, columns, data types, constraints, and relationships in a DataSet. This schema could also be inferred from the structure of data in an XML file.

2. Generate a new DataSet based on that schema information. When you use Visual Studio .NET, the development environment generates a class to describe the DataSet. The name that you give to the DataSet is the name of the class.

3. Create a new instance of the DataSet class. When you create a new DataSet based on this class, you create a typed DataSet that inherits the tables, columns, and other structure from the parent class.

4. Populate the DataSet instance with data.

How XSD Schema Information Maps to Relational Structure

How XSD information maps to relational structure

- ComplexTypes map to tables
- Nested ComplexTypes map to nested tables
- Key/Unique constraints map to UniqueConstraints
- KeyRef elements map to ForeignKeyConstraint

XSD Schema

Introduction	When you use a schema to define your DataSet, certain types of schema tags generate certain relational objects.
<complexType> elements map to tables	Within an XSD schema, there is an element called <complexType>. A complexType name usually maps to a table name. A complexType definition can contain elements and attributes, which usually map to column names.
Nested <complexType> elements map to nested tables	A complexType can also contain other complexTypes. In this case, the nested complexType maps to a child table in a parent-child relationship in the relational model.
<key> and <unique> constraints map to UniqueConstraint	Schemas can contain <key> and <unique> elements, often at the end of the schema. These elements map to primary keys and unique constraints in the relational model.
<keyref> maps to ForeignKeyConstraint	<keyref> elements define the relationships between data items in the schema. <keyref> elements map to foreign key constraints in the relational model.

Example   The following example shows how to use an XSD schema that defines the parts
                               of a relational table named Orders:

```
<!-- The element name followed by a complexType defines the "Orders" table -->

<xsd:element name="Orders" minOccurs="0" maxOccurs="unbounded">
   <xsd:complexType>

      <xsd:sequence>

         <xsd:element name="OrderID" type="xsd:int"/>

         <!--This next block defines the OrderDetails table -->
         <xsd:element name="OrderDetails" minOccurs="0" maxOccurs="unbounded">
            <xsd:complexType>
               <xsd:sequence>
                  <xsd:element name="ProductID" type="xsd:int"/>
                  <xsd:element name="UnitPrice" type="xsd:number"/>
                  <xsd:element name="Quantity"  type="xsd:short"/>
               </xsd:sequence>
            </xsd:complexType>
         </xsd:element>

         <xsd:element name="OrderDate" type="xsd:dateTime" minOccurs="0"/>

      </xsd:sequence>

      <xsd:attribute name="CustomerID" type="xsd:string" use="prohibited" />

   </xsd:complexType>

<xsd:unique name="Orders_Constraint">        <!-- Each OrderID is unique -->
   <xsd:selector xpath=".//Orders" />
   <xsd:field xpath="OrderID" />
</xsd:unique>

<xsd:key name="OrderDetails_Constraint">     <!-- Primary key -->
   <xsd:selector xpath=".//OrderDetails" />
   <xsd:field xpath="OrderID" />
   <xsd:field xpath="ProductID" />
</xsd:key>

</xsd:element>
```

Generating an XSD Schema with Visual Studio .NET

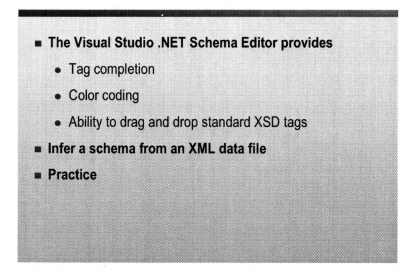

- **The Visual Studio .NET Schema Editor provides**
  - Tag completion
  - Color coding
  - Ability to drag and drop standard XSD tags
- **Infer a schema from an XML data file**
- **Practice**

Introduction

You can use tools in the Visual Studio .NET development environment to create and edit XML schema (XSD) documents. You can also use a simple text editor, such as Microsoft Notepad, to create a schema document.

Using the Visual Studio Schema Designer

The XML Designer, which contains the Schema Editor, provides the following advantages:

- Tag completion
- Color coding
- Ability to drag and drop standard XSD tags (such as elements, attributes, complex types, simple types, keys, and relations) into an XSD document.

Inferring an XSD from an XML data file

If you have an XML data file and do not have a schema for the data, you can infer an XML schema (XSD) from the data file by following these steps:

1. Add a copy of the XML document into the Solution Explorer, and then view the document.

2. Viewing the document in XML view, right-click the file, and then select **Create Schema** to add an XSD file to the project.

Practice

Create an XML schema (XSD) by using the Visual Studio XML Editor.

► Create a new XML schema

1. Start Visual Studio .NET, and then create a new Empty Project.

2. On the **File** menu, click **Add New Item**. Add a new XML Schema named **PurchaseOrder.xsd** to the project.

3. Drag a new element from the Toolbox onto the designer surface. Change the element name to **PurchaseOrder**.

4. Drag a complexType to the designer surface. Change the complexType name to **Address**.

5. In the **Address** complexType, click the first cell on the first row, and then click **element** in the drop-down list. This is a child element.

6. In the second cell on the first row, where you enter the name of the child element, type **Name**.

7. In the third cell on the first row, where you choose the data type of the child element, choose **string**.

8. Add the following three additional child elements to the **Address** complex type.

Name	Data type
City	String
Street	String
Zip	Integer

9. Add the following child elements to the <**PurchaseOrder**> element.

Name	Data type
BillTo	Address
ShipTo	Address

10. Add a **Country** attribute of type String to the **Address** complex type. Notice that the <BillTo> and <ShipTo> elements are updated to reflect changes in the data type.

11. Switch to the XML view to view the XSD schema.

12. Save **PurchaseOrder.xsd**, and then quit Visual Studio.

Lesson: Loading Schemas and Data into DataSets

- **Loading a Schema into a DataSet**
- **Loading XSD Information from a File**
- **Examining Metadata**
- **Demonstration: Examining DataSet Structure**
- **Loading XML Data into a DataSet**

Introduction

A typed DataSet is one that is based on an XSD schema. In this lesson, you will learn how to create and use typed DataSets.

Lesson objectives

After completing this lesson, you will be able to:

- Load an XSD schema into a DataSet.
- Examine metadata.
- Load data in XML format into a DataSet.

Loading a Schema into a DataSet

- **Why load an XSD schema into a DataSet?**
  - To create a relational data structure in the DataSet
- **Ways to load schema information into a DataSet**
  - Use an XSD schema
  - Infer a schema from XML data
  - Manually create the structure of the DataSet by adding code to build tables and create relationships

---

Why load an XSD schema into a DataSet?

You might need to load data from an XML data file into a DataSet object. Before you load the data, you must create a relational data structure in the DataSet.

Ways to load a schema into a DataSet

You can load a schema into a DataSet by:

- Using an XSD schema.

  When you load an XSD file into a DataSet, the DataSet generates tables, relationships, and constraints based on the data structure described in the XSD schema. This relational representation does not capture all of the detail that is represented by an XSD file, but uses only the information that is required to construct tables, columns, data types, unique constraints, and foreign keys in the relational model. The XSD schema can exist in a separate XSD file, or as an inline schema that precedes the data in an XML data file.

- Inferring a schema from XML data.

  If you have some XML data but no schema, you can generate a schema based on the structure of the XML data. In some cases, the data might be ambiguous or inconsistent. Therefore, if an appropriate schema exists, you should use this schema rather than inferring one from the XML data.

- Manually creating the structure of the DataSet by using code to build tables and create relationships.

Loading XSD Information from a File

- **Use ReadXMLSchema to load an existing XSD schema into a DataSet**

- **Syntax of ReadXMLSchema**

```
DataSet.ReadXMLSchema

(ByVal filename as string | stream as stream |
    reader as textreader | reader as xmlreader)
```

Visual Basic Example   Visual Basic Example

Introduction

You use the **ReadXmlSchema** method of the DataSet object to load an XSD schema into a DataSet. This method is overloaded so that you can you use any of the following to supply the XSD information: a file name, a stream, a **TextReader** subclass object, or an **XmlReader** subclass object.

How to load an existing XSD schema into a DataSet

The following example shows the syntax for using the **ReadXmlSchema** method of the DataSet object:

```
DataSet.ReadXMLSchema (ByVal filename as string | stream as
stream | reader as textreader | reader as xmlreader)
```

Example of loading an XSD schema from a file

The following example shows how to load an XSD schema from a file:

```
This code loads an XSD schema from a file into a dataset. The
XSD schema describes the structure of a purchase order.
Private Const PurchaseSchema As String = _
                                "C:\sampledata\Purchase.xsd"
Private myDS as DataSet

Private Sub Load_XSD()
  Try
      myDS = New DataSet()
      Console.WriteLine ("Reading the Schema file")
      myDS.ReadXmlSchema(PurchaseSchema)
  Catch e as Exception
      Console.WriteLine("Exception: " & e.ToString())
  End Try
End Sub
```

Example of loading an XSD schema by using a Stream object

The following code loads an XSD schema into a DataSet by using a **Stream** object. In some applications, you might receive schema information in the form of a stream, from a Web service, or another Internet application.

```
Private Const PurchaseSchema As String = _
                            "C:\sampledata\Purchase.xsd"
Private myDS as DataSet

Private Sub Load_XSD()
  Dim myStreamReader As StreamReader = Nothing
  Try
      myStreamReader = New StreamReader(PurchaseSchema)
      myDS = New DataSet()
      Console.WriteLine ("Reading the Schema file")
      myDS.ReadXmlSchema(myStreamReader)
  Catch e as Exception
      Console.WriteLine("Exception: " & e.ToString())
  Finally
      If Not myStreamReader Is Nothing Then
          myStreamReader.Close()
      End If
  End Try
End Sub
```

Examining Metadata

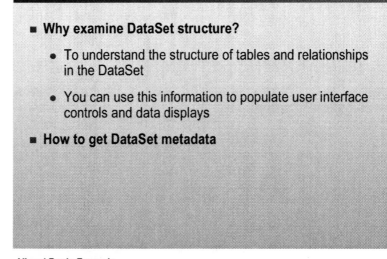

- **Why examine DataSet structure?**
  - To understand the structure of tables and relationships in the DataSet
  - You can use this information to populate user interface controls and data displays
- **How to get DataSet metadata**

Visual Basic Example

Why examine DataSet structure?

After you have loaded a schema into a DataSet object, or created an instance of a typed DataSet subclass, you can examine the structure of the tables and relationships in the DataSet.

The DataSet object contains information such as table names, column names, and data types. You can use this information to populate user interface controls and data displays.

How to retrieve DataSet metadata

You can use the following properties of the DataSet object to return information about the DataSet structure.

DataSet property	What this gives you
Tables	Allows you to reference the DataTable collection of a DataSet.
Relations	Allows you to reference the **DataRelation** collection of a DataSet.
Tables.Count	Returns the number of tables in a DataSet.
Tables(*index*).TableName	Returns the name of a table in the DataTable collection.
Tables(*tablename* | *index*).Columns(*index*)	Allows you to reference the DataColumn collection.
Tables(*index*).Columns(index).ColumnName	Returns the name of a column.
Tables(*index*).Columns(index).DataType	Returns the data type of a column.
Tables(*index*).Columns.Count	Returns the number of columns in a table.

Example The following example prints out the structure of a DataSet named **myDS**:

```
Private Sub DisplayTableStructure()

    Console.WriteLine("Table structure")

    'Print the number of tables
    Console.WriteLine("Tables count=" & myDS.Tables.Count.ToString())

    'Print the table and column names
    Dim i, j As Integer

    For i = 0 To (myDS.Tables.Count - 1)
        'Print the table names
        Console.WriteLine("TableName='" & myDS.Tables(i).TableName & "'.")
        Console.WriteLine("Columns count=" & myDS.Tables(i).Columns.Count.ToString())

        For j = 0 To (myDS.Tables(i).Columns.Count - 1)
            'Print the column names and data types
            Console.WriteLine( vbTab & _
                " ColumnName='" & myDS.Tables(i).Columns(j).ColumnName & _
                " DataType='"   & myDS.Tables(i).Columns(j).DataType.ToString() )
        Next
        Console.WriteLine()
    Next
End Sub
```

Demonstration: Examining DataSet Structure

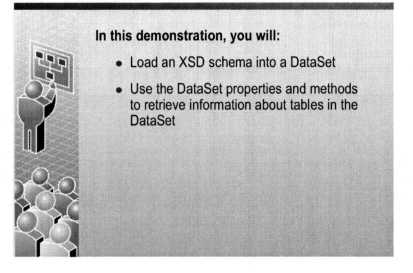

In this demonstration, you will:

- Load an XSD schema into a DataSet
- Use the DataSet properties and methods to retrieve information about tables in the DataSet

Introduction

In this demonstration, you will load an XSD schema into a DataSet. You will then use DataSet properties and methods to retrieve information about the tables in the DataSet.

1. Open *<install folder>*\DemoCode\Module5**PersonPet.xsd** with Notepad and explain how the XSD tags are mapped to relational objects in the DataSet.

2. Open *<install folder>*\ DemoCode\Module5\ExistingSchema**ExistingSchema.sln** with Visual Studio .NET.

3. Double-click the **Get Schema** button and show the code.

4. Point out that the **ParseSchema** procedure loads the DataSet **myDS** with schema information from **PersonPet.xsd**.

5. Explain the code in the **Button1_click** procedure. Point out that **Tables**, **Columns**, **ColumnName**, and **Count** properties are used to return information about the number of tables and the columns in each table.

6. Point out that a set of nested loops is used to reference each column in each table.

7. Run the application and observe the results.

8. Quit Visual Studio .NET.

Loading XML Data into a DataSet

- **Use ReadXML to load data from a file or stream**

- **Simplified syntax**

```
Dataset.ReadXML(Stream | FileName | TextReader
    | XMLReader, { ByVal mode as XMLReadMode })
```

- **XMLReadMode specifies what to load**
  - ReadSchema
  - IgnoreSchema
  - InferSchema
  - DiffGram
  - Fragment

Visual Basic Example   Visual Basic Example   Visual Basic Example

Loading data and schemas by using the Dataset.ReadXML method

You can use the **ReadXml** method of the DataSet object to load data from an XML file into a DataSet. When you use this method, you can load data from XML files that contain only XML data, or from files that contain XML data as well as an inline schema.

An *inline schema* is an XSD schema that appears at the beginning of the XML data file. This schema describes the XML information that appears after the schema in the XML file.

Simplified syntax

The **ReadXml** method is overloaded and can be used to read from a stream object, an XML file, a **TextReader** subclass object, or an **XmlReader** subclass object, as shown in the following example:

```
Dataset.ReadXml(Stream | FileName | TextReader | XmlReader, {
ByVal mode as XmlReadMode })
```

Use the *XmlReadMode* parameter to specify what the XML file contains and what information should be loaded from the file. This parameter is optional. If no **XmlReadMode** value is supplied, the default value **Auto** is used.

XmlReadMode parameter values

The following table shows the values for the *XmlReadMode* parameter of the **ReadXml** method of the DataSet object.

XmlReadMode value	Description
ReadSchema	Reads any inline schema and then loads the schema and data. 1. If the DataSet already contains a schema, any new tables that are defined by an inline schema are added to the DataSet. 2. If the inline schema defines a table that is already in the DataSet, an exception is thrown. 3. If the DataSet does not contain a schema, and there is no inline schema, no data is read.
IgnoreSchema	Ignores any inline schema and loads data into the existing DataSet. Any data that does not match the existing schema is discarded.
InferSchema	Ignores any inline schema and infers a new schema based on the structure of the XML data. If the DataSet already defines a schema, tables are added to this schema. The data is then loaded into the DataSet.
DiffGram	Reads a DiffGram and adds the data to the current schema in the DataSet.
Fragment	Reads XML fragments and appends data to appropriate DataSet tables. This setting is typically used to read XML data generated directly from Microsoft SQL Server™.
Auto	Examines the XML file and chooses the most appropriate option. 1. If the DataSet contains a schema or the XML contains an inline schema, ReadSchema is used. 2. If the DataSet does not contain a schema and the XML does not contain an inline schema, InferSchema is used. For best performance, specify an **XmlReadMode** rather than using **Auto**.

Example of loading a schema and data into a DataSet

The following example first loads a schema into a new DataSet by using the **ReadXmlSchema** method, and then loads the data from an XML file by using the **ReadXml** method with the **IgnoreSchema** option of the *XmlReadMode* parameter.

```
Private Const PurchaseSchema As String = _
                            "C:\sampledata\Purchase.xsd"

Private Sub ReadXmlDataOnly()
  Try
      myDS = New DataSet()
      Console.WriteLine("Reading the Schema file")
      myDS.ReadXmlSchema(PurchaseSchema)

      Console.WriteLine("Loading the XML data file")
      myDS.ReadXml("C:\sampledata\PurchaseData.xml", _
              XmlReadMode.IgnoreSchema)

      DataGrid1.DataSource = myDS.Tables(0)

  Catch e as Exception
      Console.WriteLine("Exception: " & e.ToString())
  End Try
End Sub
```

Example of reading inline schema and XML data

The following example reads both an inline schema and XML data from an XML file into a DataSet. In this case, **PurchaseOrder.xml** contains an inline schema in addition to XML data.

```
Private Sub ReadXmlDataAndSchema()
  Try
      myDS = New DataSet()

      myDS.ReadXml("C:\sampledata\PurchaseOrder.xml", _
              XmlReadMode.ReadSchema)

  Catch e as Exception
      Console.WriteLine("Exception: " & e.ToString())
  End Try
End Sub
```

Example of inferring a schema

The following example shows how to infer a schema from XML data. In this example, PurchaseOrder.xml contains XML data but no inline schema. When the data is read into a DataSet, the DataSet infers a schema from the structure of the XML data.

```
Private Sub ReadXmlDataInferSchema()
  Try
      myDS = NEW DataSet()

      myDS.ReadXml("C:\sampledata\PurchaseOrder.xml", _
                   XmlReadMode.InferSchema)

  Catch e as Exception
      Console.WriteLine("Exception: " & e.ToString())
  End Try
End Sub
```

Lesson: Writing XML from a DataSet

- **Writing a Schema to a File, Reader, or Stream**
- **Writing DataSet Information to a File or Stream**
- **Demonstration: Writing an Inline Schema and Data to a File**
- **Writing DataSet Changes**

Introduction

In this lesson, you will learn how to write data in XML format from a DataSet.

Lesson objectives

After completing this lesson, you will be able to:

- Write a schema to a file, reader, or stream.
- Write information in a DataSet object to a file or stream.
- Write DataSet changes.

Writing a Schema to a File, Reader, or Stream

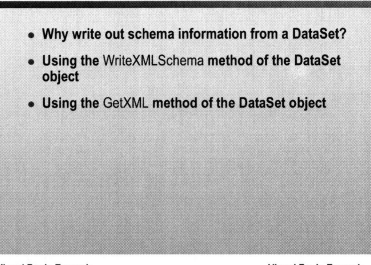

- Why write out schema information from a DataSet?
- Using the WriteXMLSchema method of the DataSet object
- Using the GetXML method of the DataSet object

Visual Basic Example   Visual Basic Example

Why write out schema information from a DataSet?

An application might create and populate a DataSet from several different sources. Therefore, the structure of a DataSet can be fairly complex.

If a DataSet is required to run an application in the future, or to allow other applications and services to integrate with XML data, you might want to save the structure and data that is contained in the DataSet to one or more files. By using this strategy, you can easily re-create the structure of the DataSet or construct a new typed DataSet from the XSD file and then load the data when you need it. You can use two different methods of the DataSet object to generate an XSD file:

- **WriteXmlSchema**
- **GetXmlSchema**

Using the WriteXmlSchema method of the DataSet object

Syntax

You can use the **WriteXmlSchema** method of the DataSet object to save a DataSet schema to an XSD file, stream, or reader object. This method takes a single parameter that specifies the destination of the schema information.

The following example shows the syntax for the **WriteXmlSchema** method of the DataSet object:

```
WriteXmlSchema (ByVal filename As String | stream As Stream |
writer As TextWriter | writer As XmlWriter)
```

Example

This code sample loads a DataSet by using an inline schema and data from an XML file. The schema is then saved to an XSD file by using the **WriteXmlSchema** method of the DataSet object.

```
Private Sub SaveXSDSchema()
  Try
      myDS = New DataSet()

      'Load an inline schema and data from an XML file
      myDS.ReadXml("C:\sampledata\PurchaseOrder.xml", _
          XmlReadMode.ReadSchema)

      'Save the schema to an XSD file
      myDS.WriteXmlSchema("C:\sampledata\POSchema.xsd")

  Catch e as Exception
      Console.WriteLine("Exception: " & e.ToString())
  End Try
End Sub
```

Using the GetXmlSchema method of the DataSet object
Syntax

To extract schema information from a DataSet and store it as a string, use the **GetXmlSchema** method of the DataSet object.

```
Public Function GetXmlSchema() as String
```

This method has no parameters.

Example

The following code fragment uses the **GetXmlSchema** method of the DataSet object to generate a string that contains schema information:

```
Private Sub XSDSchemaToString()
  Try
      Dim StrPurchaseSchema as String
      myDS = New DataSet()

      'Load an inline schema and data from an XML file
      myDS.ReadXml("C:\sampledata\PurchaseOrder.xml", _
          XmlReadMode.ReadSchema)

      'Get the schema from the DataSet and load it
      'into a string
      StrPurchaseSchema = myDS.GetXmlSchema()

  Catch e as Exception
      Console.WriteLine("Exception: " & e.ToString())
  End Try
End Sub
```

Writing DataSet Information to a File or Stream

- **Write data and schema information from a DataSet to a file or stream by using the WriteXML method**

- **Partial syntax of writing DataSet Information to a file or stream**

```
Overloads Public Sub WriteXml (ByVal filename as
    String | stream as Stream | writer as XmlWriter |
    writer as TextWriter, {ByVal mode as
    XmlWriteMode})
```

- ***XmlWriteMode* specifies what to persist**

  - IgnoreSchema

  - WriteSchema

  - DiffGram

Visual Basic Example

Introduction

You can write data and schema information from a DataSet to a file or stream by using the **WriteXml** method of the DataSet object.

Partial syntax

The following example shows partial syntax for the **WriteXml** method of the DataSet object:

```
Overloads Public Sub WriteXml (ByVal filename As String |
stream As Stream | writer as TextWriter | writer as XmlWriter,
{ByVal mode As XmlWriteMode})
```

XmlWriteMode values

When you use the **WriteXml** method, you can specify an optional value for the *XmlWriteMode* parameter. This parameter specifies whether to generate a file that contains only XML data, XML data with an inline XSD schema, or a DiffGram.

The following table describes the different values for the *XmlWriteMode* parameter of the **WriteXml** method of the DataSet object.

XmlWriteMode value	What is generated
IgnoreSchema	An XML file containing the data from a DataSet. No schema information is included. If the DataSet is empty, no file is created.
WriteSchema	An XML file containing an inline schema and the data from a populated DataSet. If the DataSet contains only schema information, an inline schema is written to the output file. If the DataSet does not include schema information, no file is created.
DiffGram	An XML file in the form of a DiffGram, containing both the original and current values for the data.

Example of writing XML data to a file

The following example saves the data stored in a DataSet as an XML file, but does not write any schema information:

```
Private Sub SaveXMLDataOnly()
  Try
      Dim StrPurchaseSchema as String
      myDS = New DataSet()

      'Load an inline schema and data from an XML file
      myDS.ReadXml("C:\sampledata\PurchaseOrder.xml", _
          XmlReadMode.ReadSchema)

      'Save the data portion of the DataSet to a file
      myDS.WriteXml("C:\sampledata\CurrentOrders.xml", _
          XmlWriteMode.IgnoreSchema)

  Catch e as Exception
      Console.WriteLine("Exception: " & e.ToString())
  End Try
End Sub
```

Demonstration: Writing an Inline Schema and Data to a File

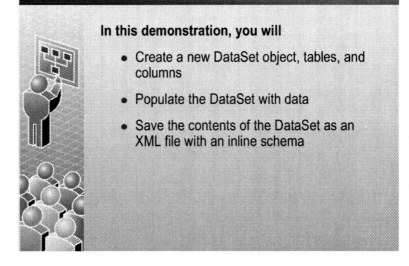

In this demonstration, you will

- Create a new DataSet object, tables, and columns
- Populate the DataSet with data
- Save the contents of the DataSet as an XML file with an inline schema

Introduction

This demonstration shows how to save schema and data information from a DataSet.

1. Start Visual Studio .NET, and open *<install folder>*\DemoCode\Module5\CreateAndSaveSchema\CreateAndSaveSchema.sln.

2. View the code for **Form1**.

3. Examine the code in the **LoadDataSet** procedure. Point out that this builds a schema by using code rather than by importing an XSD file. Also examine the code that loads data into the tables.

4. Examine the code behind the **Create Schema** button. Point out the code that generates a schema file. Also point out the code that generates an XML data file.

5. Run the application and examine the output files located in *<install folder>*\DemoCode\Module5.

6. Close Visual Studio .NET.

Writing DataSet Changes

- **What is a DiffGram?**

  - A file or a stream in XML format that represents changes made to a DataSet

- **Creating a DiffGram**

  - Set the **WriteXml** method of the DataSet object with the *XmlWriteMode* parameter set to **DiffGram.**

Example of DiffGram   Visual Basic Example

Why save DataSet changes?

A DataSet is a local information cache. During the lifetime of an application, the data rows in the DataSet are often modified or deleted, and new rows may be added.

Although you can send changes in a DataSet back to the database by using an **OleDbConnection** or **SqlConnection** object and an **OleDbDataAdapter** or **SqlDataAdapter** object, not every application uses a database to store and retrieve information. You might want to store the changes in an XML file.

Scenario

A salesperson has an application that loads a product stock list from an XML file that he receives in an e-mail message each morning. The application generates a DataSet from this file. During the day, the sales application is not connected to the Internet. At the end of the day, the salesman uses the application to generate an XML document that reflects the changes that he made to the original DataSet, and then sends this file in an e-mail message to the regional sales manager.

Definition of a DiffGram

A *DiffGram* is an XML format, such as a file or stream, that represents changes made to a DataSet. It contains the original and current data for an element or attribute, and a unique identifier that associates the original and current versions of an element or attribute to each other.

A DiffGram is useful when you want to send data across a network and preserve the various versions of the data (Original or Current), in addition to the Row State values (Added, Modified, Deleted, Unchanged) of the DataRows in a DataSet.

Example of a DiffGram

In the **CustomerDataSet**, the row with a CustomerID of ALFKI was modified. In the resulting DiffGram, the new version of the row appears at the top of the document and the original version appears inside the <**diffgr:before**> tag near the end of the document:

```
<diffgr:diffgram
  xmlns:msdata="urn:schemas-microsoft-com:xml-msdata"
  xmlns:diffgr="urn:schemas-microsoft-com:xml-diffgram-v1">

  <CustomerDataSet>
    <Customers diffgr:id="Customers1"msdata:rowOrder="0"
               diffgr:hasChanges="modified">
      <CustomerID>ALFKI</CustomerID>
      <CompanyName>New Company</CompanyName>
    </Customers>
    <Customers diffgr:id="Customers2" msdata:rowOrder="1">
      <CustomerID>ANATR</CustomerID>
      <CompanyName>Ana Trujillo Emparedados y
helados</CompanyName>
    </Customers>
  </CustomerDataSet>

  <diffgr:before>
    <Customers diffgr:id="Customers1" msdata:rowOrder="0">
      <CustomerID>ALFKI</CustomerID>
      <CompanyName>Alfreds Futterkiste</CompanyName>
    </Customers>
  </diffgr:before>
</diffgr:diffgram>
```

Creating a DiffGram

To generate a DiffGram from a DataSet, set the **WriteXml** method of the DataSet object with the *XmlWriteMode* parameter set to **DiffGram**.

Example

```
Private Sub SaveDataSetChanges()
  Try
      Dim StrPurchaseSchema as String
      myDS = New DataSet()

      'Load an inline schema and data from an XML file
      myDS.ReadXml("C:\sampledata\Customers.xml", _
          XmlReadMode.ReadSchema)

      'Make a change to information in the DataSet
      'Delete a row
      myDS.Tables(1).Rows(1).Delete

      'Save the data portion of the DataSet as a Diffgram
      myDS.WriteXml("C:\sampledata\CustomerChanges.xml", _
          XmlWriteMode.DiffGram)

  Catch e as Exception
      Console.WriteLine("Exception: " & e.ToString())
  End Try
End Sub
```

Review

- **Creating XSD Schemas**
- **Loading Schemas and Data into DataSets**
- **Writing XML from a DataSet**

1. You want to create an XSD schema from data in an XML document. The document does not contain an inline schema, and no external XSD document exists. What are the ways that you can generate a schema by using Visual Studio .NET?

2. An XPath query returns results from a Microsoft SQL Server™ database. How can you load the results into a DataSet?

3. Should you create XML files with an inline schema, or generate a separate XSD file?

4. You have data stored in a relational database. You want to retrieve this data and filter it by using an Extensible Stylesheet Language for Transformations (XSLT) style sheet before sending it to a client. How can you do this?

Lab 5.1: Working with XML Data in ADO.NET

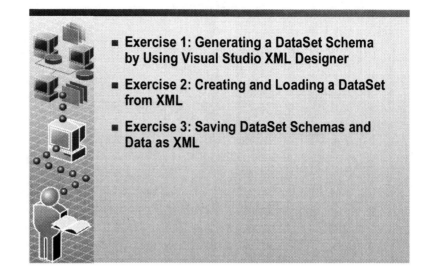

- **Exercise 1: Generating a DataSet Schema by Using Visual Studio XML Designer**
- **Exercise 2: Creating and Loading a DataSet from XML**
- **Exercise 3: Saving DataSet Schemas and Data as XML**

Objectives

After completing this lab, you will be able to:

- Create XSD schemas and XML data files by using Visual Studio .NET.
- Load schemas and data into a DataSet.
- Write XSD schemas and XML data to a file.
- Process relational data by using XML techniques.

Prerequisites

Before working on this lab, you must have:

- Basic knowledge of the structure of an XML document.
- Basic knowledge of the purpose of an XSD schema.

Estimated time to complete this lab: 60 minutes

Exercise 1
Generating a DataSet Schema by Using Visual Studio XML Designer

In this exercise, you will infer a DataSet schema from an XML data file. You will use the tools in the Visual Studio XML Designer to import the data and infer a schema for the data. After you generate a schema, you will use it to display data from the file in a data grid control.

▶ **Infer a schema from an XML file by using the XML Designer**

1. Start Visual Studio .NET, and then create a new Microsoft Windows® Application named **CreateSchema** in <install folder>\Labs\Lab05\Starter.

2. Drag <install folder>\Labs\Lab05\customers.xml into the new project. Alternatively, you can click **File**, and then click **Add Existing Item...** to add customers.xml to the project.

3. Examine the structure of the file. It contains customer, order, and order detail data, but no explicit definition of a schema. Notice that hierarchical data can be mapped to three tables with parent-child relationships in a relational model.

4. Switch to the Data View of the XML Designer.

5. Notice that the XML Designer has identified the three tables. Use the DataGrid to traverse the parent-child relationship of the three tables.

6. Right-click the document and then click **Create Schema** to generate an XSD file based on the current data.

7. In the Solution Explorer, double-click **customers.xsd**.

8. Switch to the XML view and examine the schema generated by Visual Studio .NET.

▶ **Create a new DataSet by using the XML Designer**

1. Switch to the DataSet view of the **Customers.xsd** schema.

2. Right-click the design surface, and then click **Generate Dataset**.

3. In the Solution Explorer, click the **Show All Files** button. Confirm that a class was generated for the DataSet.

▶ **Display DataSet data in a DataGrid control**

1. In Solution Explorer, double-click **Form1**.

2. Drag and drop a new DataGrid onto the form. Set the **Dock** property of the DataGrid to **Fill** to dock the DataGrid to the entire form.

3. Drag and drop a new DataSet from the Toolbox to the form. Base this DataSet on the **CreateSchema.CustomerData** DataSet.

4. Right-click the DataGrid on the form. Click **Properties**, and then set the **DataSource** property to **CustomerData1.customers**. Note that the Customers table is the parent of the Orders and OrderDetails tables.

5. Examine the DataGrid on the form. Note that Visual Studio .NET uses the schema information to populate the column headers automatically.

6. View the code for the form. Expand the code generated by the Windows form designer. Find the following code:

   "InitializeComponent()"

7. Add the following code after the call to **InitializeComponent()**:

```
'VB code
Me.CustomerData1.ReadXml("..\customers.xml")
```

```
// C# code
this.customerData1.ReadXml("..\\..\\customers.xml");
```

8. Save, build, and then run the application. You should see data from customers.xml in the data grid.

Exercise 2
Creating and Loading a DataSet from XML

In this exercise, you will load schema information into a DataSet and then load the data from an XML file.

Scenario

A salesman uses a Windows Application to collect orders for products that are sold by Northwind Traders. The salesman does not have a reliable Internet connection. Instead, the application loads customer and order information from an XML file. This XML file contains only sales data; a separate file contains schema information. You will build a part of a Windows application that allows you to load and view the existing customer and order information.

▶ **Display the Customer Information form**

1. Create a new Visual Basic or Visual C# Windows Application named **LoadingDataSets** in the folder <install folder>\Labs\Lab05\Starter.

2. Set the following properties of the **Form1**.

Property	Value
Text	Sales Information

3. Add a DataGrid control with the following characteristics.

Property	Value
Anchor	Top, Left
Dock	Left

4. Add a button to the form with the following characteristics.

Property	Value
Name	btnLoadData
Text	Display Customer Information

5. Add a button to the form with the following characteristics.

Property	Value
Name	btnClose
Text	Close

6. Add code to the **btnClose_Click** event to close the application.

▶ **Declare namespaces, variables, and constants**

1. At the beginning of the source file for **Form1**, add two **Imports** statements (Visual Basic) or **using** statements (Visual C#) as follows:

```
'VB code
Imports System.Xml
Imports System.IO

// C# code
using System.Xml;
using System.IO;
```

2. Add the following declarations to the form.

Variable or constant name	Type	Value
myDocument	String Constant	\Program Files\MSDNTrain\2389 \Labs\Lab05\customers.xml
myLoadSchema	String Constant	\Program Files\MSDNTrain\2389\Labs\Lab05\cust omerSchema.xsd
myDS	DataSet Variable	none

▶ **Create and load a DataSet**

1. Create a **Try/Catch** block for the **btnLoadData** click event procedure.

2. Create a new instance of a DataSet named **myDS**.

3. Write code to load a schema file into the DataSet by using the information in the following table. You might want to code this step as a separate subroutine. Make sure to include code to handle errors. (Hint: use the **ReadXmlSchema** method.)

Parameter	Value
File variable	myLoadSchema

4. Write code to load the XML data into the DataSet by using the information in the following table. (Hint: Use the **ReadXml** method.)

Parameter	Value
File variable	myDocument
XmlReadMode	IgnoreSchema

5. Bind the data grid to the **Customers** table in the DataSet.

6. Save, build, and then run the application.

7. Click the **Display Customer Information** button. The data grid displays three customers, as defined in Customers.xml.

▶ **Infer a schema for the Customer DataSet**

1. Modify your code to infer a schema for the XML data rather than loading a separate schema file.

2. Save, build, and then run the application.

3. Click the **Display Customer Information** button. The data grid displays three customers, as it did before.

Exercise 3
Saving DataSet Schemas and Data as XML

In this exercise, you will add code to the Windows Application created in the previous exercise to save the schema and data contained in the DataSet. You will save the schema to a separate XSD file, and save an inline schema with an XML data file.

Scenario

At the end of each business day, the salesman for Northwind traders saves sales information to an XML file and then sends the data in an e-mail message to the company's central office for fulfillment. To accommodate this activity, you will extend the Windows Application to generate XML data files and XSD schema files.

▶ **Open the starter code**

- For this exercise, you can use the code that you wrote for the previous exercise, or you can use the project <install folder>**Labs\Lab05\Solution\Ex2***xx*\ where *xx* is VB or CS. Open the project file in Visual Studio .NET.

▶ **Save schema information**

1. Add a button to the form with the following characteristics.

Property	Value
Name	btnSaveSchema
Text	Save Schema

2. Add code to the **Click** event of this button that saves the DataSet schema. Use the information in the following table.

Property	Value
File name	\Program Files\MSDNTrain\2389\Labs\Lab05\ ResultSchema.xsd

3. Save, build, and then run the application.

4. Examine the resulting XSD file to confirm that it reflects the structure of the Customers DataSet.

▶ **Save data as XML**

1. Add a button to the form with the following characteristics.

Property	Value
Name	btnSaveData
Text	Save Data

2. Add code to the **Click** event of this button that saves only the DataSet data. Use the information in the following table.

Property	Value
File name	\Program Files\MSDNTrain\2389\Labs\Lab05\ResultData.xml

3. Save, build, and then run the application.

4. Examine the resulting XML file to confirm that it reflects the data in the Customers DataSet.

▶ **Save data and a schema as XML**

1. Modify your code to save both the DataSet data and an inline schema. Use the information in the following table.

Property	Value
File name	\Program Files\MSDNTrain\2389\Labs\Lab05\ ResultInlineSchema.xml

2. Save, build, and then run the application.

3. Examine the resulting XML file to confirm that it reflects the data and schema information.

Course Evaluation

Your evaluation of this course will help Microsoft understand the quality of your learning experience.

At a convenient time between now and the end of the course, please complete a course evaluation, which is available at http://www.metricsthatmatter.com/survey.

Microsoft will keep your evaluation strictly confidential and will use your responses to improve your future learning experience.

msdn training

Module 6: Building DataSets from Existing Data Sources

Contents

Microsoft

Overview

- **Configuring a DataAdapter to Retrieve Information**
- **Populating a DataSet Using a DataAdapter**
- **Configuring a DataAdapter to Update the Underlying Data Source**
- **Persisting Changes to a Data Source**
- **How to Handle Conflicts**

Introduction

In the Microsoft® .NET environment, data can move from a central data source to a local DataSet. To move the data, there must be a bridge from the data source to the DataSet. That bridge is the DataAdapter.

Objectives

After completing this module, you will be able to:

- Configure a DataAdapter to retrieve information.
- Populate a DataSet by using a DataAdapter.
- Configure a DataAdapter to modify information.
- Persist data changes to a data source.
- Manage data conflicts.

Lesson: Configuring a DataAdapter to Retrieve Information

- **Multimedia: Overview of Creating and Populating a DataSet**
- **What is a DataAdapter?**
- **The XxxDataAdapter Object Model**
- **DataAdapter Properties and Methods**
- **How to Create a DataAdapter That Uses a New SELECT Statement**
- **How to Create a DataAdapter That Uses an Existing Stored Procedure**

Introduction

When you create an instance of a DataAdapter object, you can set it up to pull information from an existing data source.

Lesson objectives

After completing this lesson, you will be able to:

- Define a DataAdapter.
- Define useful properties of a DataAdapter object.
- Define useful methods of a DataAdapter object.
- Create a DataAdapter by using a new connection string and a **SELECT** statement.
- Create a DataAdapter by using an existing connection and an existing stored procedure.

Multimedia: Overview of Creating and Populating a DataSet

This animation provides an overview of how the **Fill** method of a DataAdapter object creates a DataTable in a DataSet and then populates that DataTable; how changes are tracked in a DataSet; and how those changes are made in the central data source by using the **InsertCommand**, **UpdateCommand**, and **DeleteCommand** of the DataAdapter.

What Is a DataAdapter?

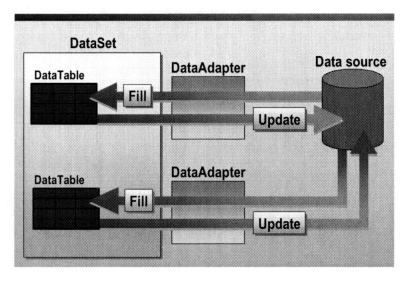

Introduction

The DataSet object represents a local copy of data from a data source and is one of the key innovations of the Microsoft .NET Framework. By itself, the DataSet object is useful for reference. However, to serve as a true data-management tool, a DataSet must be able to interact with a data source. To accomplish this, .NET provides the DataAdapter class.

Definition

A DataAdapter object serves as a bridge between a DataSet and a data source for retrieving and saving data. The DataAdapter class represents a set of database commands and a database connection that you use to fill a DataSet and update the data source. DataAdapter objects are part of the Microsoft ADO.NET data providers, which also include connection objects, data-reader objects, and command objects.

Each DataAdapter exchanges data between a single DataTable object in a DataSet and a single result set from a SQL statement or stored procedure.

Scenario

You use DataAdapters to exchange data between a DataSet and a data source. A common example of this occurs when an application reads data from a database into a DataSet, and then writes changes from the DataSet back to the database. However, a DataAdapter can retrieve and update data from any data source, such as from a Microsoft BizTalk™ Server application to a DataSet.

Primary DataAdapters for databases

Microsoft Visual Studio® .NET makes two primary DataAdapters available for use with databases. In addition, other DataAdapters can be integrated with Visual Studio. The primary DataDdapters are:

- **OleDbDataAdapter**, which is suitable for use with any data source that is exposed by an OLE DB provider.

- **SqlDataAdapter**, which is specific to a Microsoft SQL Server™ version 7.0 or later database. The SqlDataAdapter is faster than the OleDbDataAdapter because it works directly with SQL Server and does not go through an OLE DB layer.

Example

Suppose that you have a SQL table to which you want to make multiple modifications. To do so, you take a copy of a subset of the table and store that copy in a middle tier or a user tier as a DataSet.

Non-example

A search function on your corporate Web site needs to return a list of matches on a Web page. It would be inappropriate to use a DataAdapter and DataSet in this situation because the results will be thrown away as soon as the page is created. There is no reason to cache this data in a DataSet.

The XxxDataAdapter Object Model

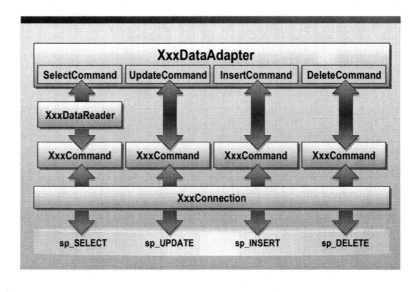

Introduction

The XxxDataAdapter class provides easy to manage disconnected functionality. It is used to populate datasets, and then update the underlying data source with any changes made to the dataset.

Example of using a data adapter

You can use a data adapter to populate a DataSet and to send data updates back to the data source. For example, to use a DataSet with a SQL Server .NET Data Provider:

1. Create a **SqlConnection** object to connect to a SQL Server database.

2. Create a **SqlDataAdapter** object. The object contains properties that can point to four **SqlCommand** objects. These objects specify SQL statements to **SELECT**, **INSERT**, **DELETE**, and **UPDATE** data in the database.

3. Create a DataSet object that contains one or more tables.

4. Use the **SqlDataAdapter** object to fill a DataSet table by calling the **Fill** method. The **SqlDataAdapter** implicitly executes the **SqlCommand** object that contains a **SELECT** statement.

5. Modify the data in the DataSet. You can do this programmatically, or by binding the DataSet to a user interface control such as a **DataGrid** and then changing the data in the grid.

6. When you are ready to send the data updates to the database, use the **SqlDataAdapter** to call the **Update** method. The **SqlDataAdapter** object implicitly uses its **SqlCommand** objects to execute **INSERT**, **DELETE**, and **UPDATE** statements on the database.

DataAdapter Properties and Methods

- **DataAdapter properties**
  - SelectCommand
  - InsertCommand
  - UpdateCommand
  - DeleteCommand
- **Methods used by DataAdapters**
  - Fill
  - Update

Introduction

Although the DataAdapter class contains many properties and methods, you will most likely use a certain subset of each.

DataAdapter properties

You use DataAdapters to act on records from a data source. You can specify which actions you want to perform by using one of four DataAdapter properties, which execute a SQL statement or call a stored procedure. The properties are actually objects that are instances of the **SqlCommand** or **OleDbCommand** class:

- **SelectCommand**. Refers to a command object that retrieves rows from the data source.

- **InsertCommand**. Refers to a command object that writes inserted rows from the DataSet into the data source.

- **UpdateCommand**. Refers to a command object that writes modified rows from the DataSet into the data source.

- **DeleteCommand**. Refers to a command object that deletes rows in the data source.

Methods used by a DataAdapter

You use DataAdapter methods to fill a DataSet or to transmit changes in a DataSet table to a corresponding data store. These methods include:

- **Fill**. Use this method of a **SqlDataAdapter** or **OleDbDataAdapter** to add or refresh rows from a data source and place them in a DataSet table. The **Fill** method uses the **SELECT** statement specified in the **SelectCommand** property.

- **Update**. Use this method of a **DataAdapter** object to transmit changes to a DataSet table to the corresponding data source. This method calls the corresponding **INSERT**, **UPDATE**, or **DELETE** command for each specified row in a DataSet DataTable.

Practice

When you create a DataAdapter, you do not necessarily need to create **Command** objects for all of the data modification commands (**SelectCommand**, **InsertCommand**, **UpdateCommand**, and **DeleteCommand**).

Describe a scenario where you would only need to create a **Command** object for the **SelectCommand** property.

Describe another scenario where you would only need to create two **Command** objects: one for the **SelectCommand** property, and one for the **UpdateCommand** property.

Describe another scenario where you would need to create all four **Command** objects: one each for **SelectCommand**, **InsertCommand**, **UpdateCommand**, and **DeleteCommand**.

How to Create a DataAdapter That Uses a New SELECT Statement

- **You can create a DataAdapter to execute a new SELECT statement**
  - Read-only data access for disconnected applications
- **Two ways to create the DataAdapter**
  - Use the Data Adapter Configuration Wizard
  - Write the code yourself
- **You must specify**
  - A new or existing connection
  - The SELECT statement for the query

Visual Basic Example   Visual C# Example

Introduction

You can create a DataAdapter object to execute a new **SELECT** statement. This provides disconnected applications with read-only access to the data in the database.

You can create the DataAdapter by using the Data Adapter Configuration Wizard, or programmatically in your code. You must specify a connection to the required database. You can also specify a new **SELECT** statement to retrieve data from the database.

Scenario

A mobile worker needs to read addresses and telephone numbers for her company's offices around the world. She needs to view this information on the road, where there is no database connectivity available. She never needs to update the addresses or telephone numbers.

How to create a DataAdapter by using the Data Adapter Configuration Wizard

To create a DataAdapter by using the Data Adapter Configuration Wizard, follow these steps:

1. Drag a **SqlDataAdapter** control or **OleDbDataAdapter** control from the Toolbox onto your form.
2. On the Welcome screen for the Data Adapter Configuration Wizard, click **Next**.
3. On the Choose Your Data Connection screen, click **New Connection**.
4. In the **Data Link Properties** dialog box, enter the connection details for the required database, and then click **OK**.
5. Return to the Choose Your Data Connection screen and click **Next**.
6. On the Choose a Query Type screen, choose **Use SQL statements**, and then click **Next**.
7. On the Generate the SQL statements screen, type an appropriate SQL query statement, and then click **Advanced Options**.

8. In the **Advanced SQL Generation Options** dialog box, clear the **Generate Insert, Update, and Delete statements** check box, and then click **OK**.

9. Return to the Generate the SQL statements screen and click **Next**.

10. On the View Wizard Results screen, click **Finish**.

How to create a DataAdapter programmatically

To create a DataAdapter programmatically, follow these steps:

1. Create a new **SqlDataAdapter** object or **OleDbDataAdapter** object.

2. Create a new **SqlConnection** object or **OleDbConnection** object. Specify the connection string to connect to the required database.

3. Create a new **SqlCommand** object or **OleDbCommand** object. Specify a **SELECT** statement to retrieve the required data from the database.

4. Call the **AddParameter** method on the command object to specify any parameters that are required by the **SELECT** statement.

5. Assign the new command object to the **SelectCommand** property of the DataAdapter object.

Example of creating a DataAdapter programmatically

The following example uses a **SqlDataAdapter** object to define a query on the Products table in the Northwind database. The database connection is specified by a **SqlConnection** object, and the query is specified by a **SqlCommand** object.

```
' Visual Basic
Imports System.Data.SqlClient
...
Dim daProducts As New SqlDataAdapter()

Dim cnNorthwind As New SqlConnection( _
    "data source=(local);initial catalog=Northwind;" & _
    "integrated security=SSPI")

Dim cmSelect As New SqlCommand( _
    "SELECT * FROM Products", cnNorthwind)

daProducts.SelectCommand = cmSelect
```

```
// Visual C#
using System.Data.SqlClient;
...
SqlDataAdapter daProducts = new SqlDataAdapter();

SqlConnection cnNorthwind = new SqlConnection(
    "data source=(local);initial catalog=Northwind;" +
    "integrated security=SSPI");

SqlCommand cmSelect = new SqlCommand(
    "SELECT * FROM Products", cnNorthwind);

daProducts.SelectCommand = cmSelect;
```

How to Create a Data Adapter That Uses an Existing Stored Procedure

- **You can create a DataAdapter programmatically to execute an existing stored procedure by:**
  - Specifying a stored procedure for SelectCommand
  - Specifying stored procedures for InsertCommand, UpdateCommand, and DeleteCommand if required
- **Create the DataAdapter by using the wizard, or in code**
- **You must specify:**
  - A new or existing connection
  - The stored procedure(s)
- **Practice**

Visual Basic Example   Visual C# Example

Introduction

You can create a DataAdapter to execute an existing stored procedure. This enables disconnected applications to retrieve complex table joins, by using existing functionality in the database.

You can create the DataAdapter by using the Data Adapter Configuration Wizard, or programmatically in your code. You must specify a connection to the required database, and the name of the stored procedure that you want to call to retrieve the data from the database.

Scenario

An organization has a suite of stored procedures that retrieve consolidated data from several tables in the database. Mobile workers need read-only access to this consolidated data, in a disconnected application.

How to create a DataAdapter by using the Data Adapter Configuration Wizard

To create a DataAdapter by using the Data Adapter Configuration Wizard, follow these steps:

1. Drag a **SqlDataAdapter** control or **OleDbDataAdapter** control from the Toolbox onto your form.

2. On the Welcome screen for the Data Adapter Configuration Wizard, click **Next**.

3. On the Choose Your Data Connection screen, select an existing connection (or click **New Connection** and specify a new connection, if necessary).

4. On the Choose a Query Type screen, choose **Use existing stored procedures**, and then click **Next**.

5. On the Bind Commands to Existing Stored Procedures screen, choose an existing stored procedure for the **Select** operation. (If the stored procedure does not yet exist, create it now in the Server Explorer.) Click **Next**.

6. On the View Wizard Results screen, click **Finish**.

How to create a DataAdapter programmatically

To create a DataAdapter programmatically, follow these steps:

1. Create a new **SqlDataAdapter** object or **OleDbDataAdapter** object.

2. Create a new **SqlConnection** object or **OleDbConnection** object (or use an existing **XxxConnection** object if one is available).

3. Create a new **SqlCommand** object or **OleDbCommand** object. Specify the following properties for the command object.

Property	Description
Connection	The **XxxConnection** object
CommandText	The name of the stored procedure you wish to call
CommandType	**System.Data.CommandType.StoredProcedure**

4. Call the **AddParameter** method on the command object to specify any parameters that are required by the stored procedure.

5. Assign the new command object to the **SelectCommand** property of the DataAdapter object.

Example of creating a DataAdapter programmatically

The following example creates a **SqlDataAdapter** object, and uses an existing stored procedure named **GetProductsAndCategories** to query the database. An existing **SqlConnection** object named **cnNorthwind** is used to connect to the database.

```
' Visual Basic
Imports System.Data
Imports System.Data.SqlClient
...
Dim daProdCat As New SqlDataAdapter()

Dim cmSelect As New SqlCommand()
cmSelect.Connection = cnNorthwind
cmSelect.CommandText = "GetProductsAndCategories"
cmSelect.CommandType = CommandType.StoredProcedure

daProdCat.SelectCommand = cmSelect

// Visual C#
using System.Data;
using System.Data.SqlClient;
...
SqlDataAdapter daProdCat = new SqlDataAdapter();

SqlCommand cmSelect = new SqlCommand();
cmSelect.Connection = cnNorthwind;
cmSelect.CommandText = "GetProductsAndCategories";
cmSelect.CommandType = CommandType.StoredProcedure;

daProdCat.SelectCommand = cmSelect;
```

Practice

Northwind Traders needs to build a disconnected data application that allows users to view information in the product catalog.

In this practice, you will create a Windows Application that contains two DataAdapters. The first DataAdapter will retrieve category information from the Northwind database. The second DataAdapter will retrieve product information from the same database.

▶ **Create a Windows Application that contains two DataAdapters**

1. Create a new Windows Application solution named **CatalogViewer** at the following location:

   <install folder>\Practices\Mod06_1\

2. Drag a **DataGrid** onto the form.

3. Drag a **Button** onto the form, and change its **Text** property to **Fill**.

4. Drag a **SqlDataAdapter** control from the Toolbox onto the form, and use the Data Adapter Configuration Wizard to set the following properties.

Property	Value
Server Name	(local)
Log On	Use Windows NT® Integrated security
Database	Northwind
Query Type	Use SQL statements
Load Statement	SELECT * FROM Categories
Advanced Options	All options enabled

5. Select the new DataAdapter, and in the Property window, change its **Name** to **daCategories**.

6. In the Server Explorer, create a new stored procedure in the Northwind database as follows:

```
CREATE PROCEDURE dbo.usp_GetProducts
AS
   SELECT * FROM Products
```

7. In the Form Designer, drag another **SqlDataAdapter** control onto the form. Use the Data Adapter Configuration Wizard to set the following properties.

Property	Value
Connection	Use the connection you created earlier.
Query Type	Use existing stored procedures.
Select stored procedure	usp_GetProducts

8. Select the new DataAdapter, and in the Property window, change its **Name** to **daProducts**.

9. Save all of the files in your solution.

10. View the code that has been generated by Visual Studio .NET.

The solution for this practice is located at
<install folder>\Practices\Mod06_1\Lesson1\CatalogViewer\

Lesson: Populating a DataSet Using a DataAdapter

- Multimedia: How the Fill Method of a DataAdapter Creates and Populates a DataTable in a DataSet
- How to Fill a DataSet Table by Using a DataAdapter
- How to Infer Additional Constraints for a DataSet
- How to Fill a Dataset Efficiently
- How to Fill a DataSet from Multiple DataAdapters

Introduction

After you choose the type of DataAdapter you want to use (either **SqlDataAdapter** or **OleDbDataAdapter**) and configure it to perform the tasks you need, you are ready to populate the DataSet for which you created the DataAdapter.

Lesson objectives

When you complete this lesson, you will be able to:

- Diagram how the **Fill** method works.
- Infer additional constraints for a DataSet.
- Call the **Fill** method of the DataAdapter to populate a DataSet efficiently.
- Populate a DataSet from multiple DataAdapters.

MultiMedia: How the Fill Method of a DataAdapter Creates and Populates a DataTable in a DataSet

Introduction

A DataAdapter object is the bridge between a DataSet and a data source. A DataSet contains one or more DataTables, each of which contains DataRows. This animation shows how the **Fill** method of a DataAdapter object creates and populates a DataTable.

How to Fill a DataSet Table Using a DataAdapter

- **You can fill a DataSet table by using a DataAdapter**
  - Call the Fill method on the DataAdapter
- **The Fill method executes the SelectCommand**
  - Fills the DataSet table with the structure and content of the query result
- **To optimize performance**
  - aDataSet.EnforceConstraints=False
  - Call the BeginLoadData method on the DataTable

Visual Basic Example   Visual C# Example

Introduction

You can fill a DataSet table by using a DataAdapter. Call the **Fill** method on the DataAdapter, specifying the DataSet table that you wish to fill.

Definition of the Fill method

The **Fill** method implicitly executes the SQL query in the **SelectCommand** of the DataAdapter. The results of the query are used to define the structure of the DataSet table, and to populate the table with data.

Syntax for the Fill method

The **Fill** method is overloaded. The following are some of the overloaded versions of **Fill**:

```
rowsAffected = aDataAdapter.Fill(aDataSet)
rowsAffected = aDataAdapter.Fill(aDataSet, strDataTableName)
rowsAffected = aDataAdapter.Fill(aDataTable)
```

Performance considerations

When you fill a DataSet, the DataAdapter enforces constraints such as primary key uniqueness. To improve performance, set the DataSet property **EnforceConstraints** to **false** before you fill the DataSet. This disables constraint checking while the data is loaded.

```
aDataSet.EnforceConstraints = False
```

Another way to improve performance is to call the **BeginLoadData** method on the DataTable. This turns off events and exceptions while data is loaded into the table, and also disables constraints checking. Call **EndLoadData** after the data has been loaded.

```
aDataTable.BeginLoadData()
...
aDataTable.EndLoadData()
```

Example of filling a DataSet by using a DataAdapter

The following example creates a DataSet containing a single table named Customers. The table is filled by using a DataAdapter named **daCustomers**. The **BeginLoadData** method is called to optimize performance.

After the table has been filled, a **DataGrid** control is bound to the table. The **DataGrid** will display the customer information on the screen.

```vb
' Visual Basic
Dim dsCustomers As New DataSet()
dsCustomers.Tables.Add(New DataTable("Customers"))

dsCustomers.Tables(0).BeginLoadData()
daCustomers.Fill(dsCustomers, "Customers")
dsCustomers.Tables(0).EndLoadData()

DataGrid1.DataSource = dsCustomers.Tables(0).DefaultView
```

```csharp
// Visual C#
DataSet dsCustomers = new DataSet();
dsCustomers.Tables.Add(new DataTable("Customers"));

dsCustomers.Tables[0].BeginLoadData();
daCustomers.Fill(dsCustomers, "Customers");
dsCustomers.Tables[0].EndLoadData();

dataGrid1.DataSource = dsCustomers.Tables[0].DefaultView;
```

How to Infer Additional Constraints for a DataSet

- **You can fill a DataSet even if the schema is not known at design time**
  - The DataSet schema is created at run time
- **Set the MissingSchemaAction property to control how the schema is created**
  - Add, AddWithKey, Error, or Ignore
- **Call FillSchema to build a new DataSet schema**
  - FillSchema executes SelectCommand on the DataAdapter, to determine the structure of the data

Visual Basic Example   Visual C# Example

Introduction

You can fill a DataSet even if the schema is not known at design time. The DataSet schema can be created at run time, based on the structure of the retrieved data.

You can control how a DataSet schema is created and modified at run time. Before you fill the DataSet, do one of the following:

- Set the **MissingSchemaAction** property on the DataAdapter.
- Call the **FillSchema** method on the DataAdapter.

Scenario

A Windows Application periodically needs to download data from a remote service or application. The structure of the data might change slightly over time. The Windows Application can download the XML Schema to determine the latest structure of the data.

Note   Generating a DataSet schema at run time is less efficient than building a typed DataSet class at design time. You will learn about typed DataSets later in this lesson.

Definition of the MissingSchemaAction property

You set the **MissingSchemaAction** property to control how the schema is created. The **MissingSchemaAction** property specifies the action to take when you retrieve DataTables or DataColumns that are not present in the DataSet schema.

You use one of the following values for the **MissingSchemaAction** property.

MissingSchemaAction value	Description
Add	Adds extra tables and columns to the DataSet schema, but does not preserve primary key information.
	If you add the same rows to the DataSet several times, the rows are appended each time rather than being modified. This is because the DataSet does not check for primary keys, and therefore does not detect that the same rows are being loaded.
AddWithKey	Extra tables and columns are added to the schema. Primary key information is added to the DataTable to overcome the limitations of the **Add** property value described earlier.
	The **AllowDBNull**, **AutoIncrement**, **MaxLength**, **ReadOnly**, and **Unique** properties are set for the new columns, as defined in the data source. The **PrimaryKey** property is also set for primary key columns.
	If there are no primary keys, but the result set contains unique columns that are all non-nullable, the unique columns are assigned the **PrimaryKey** property. If any unique columns are nullable, a **UniqueConstraint** is added to the **ConstraintCollection** for the DataSet, but the **PrimaryKey** property is not set.
Error	Generates a **SystemException**. This is useful if the retrieved data must comply with a predefined DataSet schema.
Ignore	Ignores extra tables and columns in the result set.

Syntax for the MissingSchemaAction property

The following example shows the syntax for the **MissingSchemaAction** property of a DataAdapter object:

```
aDataAdapter.MissingSchemaAction =
                MissingSchemaAction.Add |
                MissingSchemaAction.AddWithKey |
                MissingSchemaAction.Error |
                MissingSchemaAction.Ignore
```

**Example of using
MissingSchemaAction**

The following example creates an untyped DataSet, and uses a DataAdapter named **daCustomers** to fill the DataSet. The **MissingSchemaAction** property is set to **AddWithKey**, so that the DataSet schema is amended when the DataSet is filled. This creates the necessary tables and columns in the DataSet to accommodate the data as it is loaded.

```
' Visual Basic
Dim dsCustomers As New DataSet()
daCustomers.MissingSchemaAction = _
                            MissingSchemaAction.AddWithKey
daCustomers.Fill(dsCustomers)
DataGrid1.DataSource = dsCustomers.Tables(0).DefaultView
```

```
// Visual C#
DataSet dsCustomers = new DataSet();
daCustomers.MissingSchemaAction =
                            MissingSchemaAction.AddWithKey;
daCustomers.Fill(dsCustomers);
dataGrid1.DataSource = dsCustomers.Tables[0].DefaultView;
```

**Definition of the
FillSchema method**

You call the **FillSchema** method to build a new DataSet schema. The **FillSchema** method executes the **SelectCommand** object on the DataAdapter to determine the schema of the data retrieved by that command. The **FillSchema** method takes a SchemaType parameter, which can be one of the following values.

SchemaType parameter	Description
Mapped	Applies any existing table mappings to the retrieved schema, and configures the DataSet with the transformed schema.
Source	Ignores any existing table mappings in the DataAdapter, and configures the DataSet with the retrieved schema.

**Syntax for the
FillSchema method**

The following is the syntax for the **FillSchema** method:

```
aDataTableArray = aDataAdapter.FillSchema(
                    aDataSet,
                    SchemaType.Mapped | SchemaType.Source)
```

Example of using the FillSchema method

The following example creates an untyped DataSet. The schema for the DataSet is defined by calling the **FillSchema** method on a DataAdapter. Calling the **Fill** method on the DataAdapter retrieves the data for the DataSet.

```
' Visual Basic
Dim dsCustomers As New DataSet()
daCustomers.FillSchema(dsCustomers, SchemaType.Mapped)
daCustomers.Fill(dsCustomers)
DataGrid1.DataSource = dsCustomers.Tables(0).DefaultView
```

```
// Visual C#
DataSet dsCustomers = new DataSet();
daCustomers.FillSchema(dsCustomers, SchemaType.Mapped);
daCustomers.Fill(dsCustomers);
dataGrid1.DataSource = dsCustomers.Tables[0].DefaultView;
```

Performance considerations

The **MissingSchemaAction** property and the **FillSchema** method are slow, because they build the DataSet schema at run time. For this reason, you should avoid using these techniques if possible. A more efficient solution is to use strongly typed DataSets, where the schema for the DataSet is defined at design time. This enables the DataSet to retrieve data quickly into a known schema, rather than having to deduce the schema first.

How to Fill a Dataset Efficiently

- **Define an explicit schema before you fill the DataSet**
  - DataTables, DataColumns, and DataRelations are known before the data is loaded
  - Enables the data to be loaded more efficiently
- **To define an explicit DataSet schema**
  - Create a typed DataSet class:

```
dsCustomers.Customers.BeginLoadData()
daCustomers.Fill(dsCustomers.Customers)
dsCustomers.Customers.EndLoadData()
DataGrid1.DataSource =
dsCustomers.Customers.DefaultView
```

  - Or, create the DataTables, DataColumns, and DataRelations programmatically

Visual Basic Example   <u>**Visual C# Example**</u>

Introduction

The most efficient way to fill a DataSet is to define an explicit schema before filling the DataSet. This means that the DataTables, DataColumns, and DataRelations are already known before the DataSet is filled.

There are two ways to define an explicit schema for a DataSet:

- Create a typed DataSet in the Form Designer.
- Create the DataTables, DataColumns, and DataRelations programmatically.

Scenario

A disconnected application retrieves customer information from a central database. The structure of the data is known in advance. You can therefore create a typed DataSet, with a schema that conforms to the structure of the retrieved data. This enables data to be loaded efficiently at run time.

How to create a typed DataSet in the Form Designer

To create a typed DataSet in the Form Designer, follow these steps:

1. Drag a **SqlDataAdapter** control or **OleDbDataAdapter** control from the Toolbox onto your form.
2. Configure the DataAdapter as required, by using the Data Adapter Configuration Wizard.
3. Right-click the new DataAdapter object, and then click **Generate Dataset**.
4. In the **Generate Dataset** dialog box, specify a name for the new DataSet class.
5. Choose the tables that you wish to add to the DataSet.
6. Ensure that the **Add this dataset to the designer** check box is selected.
7. Click **OK**. This will create a typed DataSet class, inherited from DataSet. An instance of this class will also be created and added to your application.

8. Right-click the new DataSet object, and then click **View Schema**.

9. In the XML Designer, examine the XSD schema for the DataSet. Modify and extend the XSD schema, if necessary, by dragging XSD schema elements from the Toolbox onto the XML Designer.

10. In your application, write code to fill the DataSet by using a Data Adapter.

Example of filling a typed DataSet

The following example fills a typed DataSet object named dsCustomers. The DataSet has a single table named Customers. The **BeginLoadData** method is called before the data is loaded, to optimize performance.

```
' Visual Basic
dsCustomers.Customers.BeginLoadData()
daCustomers.Fill(dsCustomers.Customers)
dsCustomers.Customers.EndLoadData()
DataGrid1.DataSource = dsCustomers.Customers.DefaultView
```

```
// Visual C#
dsCustomers.Customers.BeginLoadData();
daCustomers.Fill(dsCustomers.Customers);
dsCustomers.Customers.EndLoadData();
dataGrid1.DataSource = dsCustomers.Customers.DefaultView;
```

How to define a DataSet schema programmatically

To define a DataSet schema programmatically, write the following code:

1. Create a DataTable object.

2. Create a DataColumn object for each column you require in the table.

3. Add these columns to the table. To do this, call the **Add** method on the **Columns** collection in the DataTable object.

4. Define constraints on the table. To do this, call the **Add** method on the **Constraints** collection in the DataTable object.

5. Repeat steps 1 to 4 as necessary to create additional DataTable objects.

6. Create a DataSet object.

7. Add the DataTable objects to the DataSet. To do this, call the **Add** method on the **Tables** collection in the DataSet object.

8. Define relations between columns in the DataSet. To do this, call the **Add** method on the **Relations** collection in the DataSet object.

Example of defining a DataSet schema programmatically

The following example shows how to create a DataSet schema programmatically. The DataSet contains a single table named Customers. The table has three columns named CustomerID, CompanyName, and ContactName (all strings). The CustomerID column is a primary key.

After the DataSet schema has been defined, the DataSet is filled by using a DataAdapter named daCustomers. A DataGrid control is then bound to the DataSet.

```vb
' Visual Basic
' Create the DataTable and DataColumns
Dim table As New DataTable("Customers")
Dim c1 As New DataColumn("CustomerID",  GetType(String))
Dim c2 As New DataColumn("CompanyName", GetType(String))
Dim c3 As New DataColumn("ContactName", GetType(String))

' Add DataColumns and Constraints to the DataTable
table.Columns.Add(c1)
table.Columns.Add(c2)
table.Columns.Add(c3)
table.Constraints.Add("PK_CustomerID", c1, True)

' Create the DataSet, and add the DataTable to it
Dim dsCustomers As New DataSet()
dsCustomers.Tables.Add(table)

' Fill DataSet by using a DataAdapter, and bind to a DataGrid
dsCustomers.Tables(0).BeginLoadData()
daCustomers.Fill(dsCustomers, "Customers")
dsCustomers.Tables(0).EndLoadData()
DataGrid1.DataSource = dsCustomers.Tables(0).DefaultView
```

```csharp
// Visual C#
// Create the DataTable and DataColumns
DataTable table = new DataTable("Customers");
DataColumn c1 = new DataColumn("CustomerID",  typeof(String));
DataColumn c2 = new DataColumn("CompanyName", typeof(String));
DataColumn c3 = new DataColumn("ContactName", typeof(String));

// Add DataColumns and Constraints to the DataTable
table.Columns.Add(c1);
table.Columns.Add(c2);
table.Columns.Add(c3);
table.Constraints.Add("PK_CustomerID", c1, true);

// Create the DataSet, and add the DataTable to it
DataSet dsCustomers = new DataSet();
dsCustomers.Tables.Add(table);

// Fill DataSet by using a DataAdapter, and bind to a DataGrid
dsCustomers.Tables[0].BeginLoadData();
daCustomers.Fill(dsCustomers, "Customers");
dsCustomers.Tables[0].EndLoadData();
dataGrid1.DataSource = dsCustomers.Tables[0].DefaultView;
```

How to Fill a DataSet from Multiple DataAdapters

- **You can use multiple DataAdapters to fill a DataSet**
  - Each DataAdapter fills a separate table in the DataSet
- **Call the Fill method on each DataAdapter**
  - Specify the table to fill in the DataSet
- **Visual Basic example**

```
daCustomers.Fill(dsCustomerOrders.Customers)
daOrders.Fill(dsCustomerOrders.Orders)
DataGrid1.DataSource = dsCustomerOrders.Customers
```

- **Practice**

Introduction

You can use multiple DataAdapters to fill a DataSet. Each DataAdapter fills a separate table in the DataSet. Because each DataAdapter maps to a single DataSet table, you can control the order in which updates are written back to the database. This helps you to preserve referential integrity between related tables in the database.

Scenario

A salesperson needs to retrieve customer information, and information about orders placed by each customer, from the central database. To meet this requirement, you create a disconnected application that contains two DataAdapters: one to retrieve customer records, and the other to retrieve order records.

You then create a typed DataSet that contains two tables (Customers and Orders), and define a relation to associate orders with customers. After you create the typed DataSet, you use the two DataAdapters to fill the tables in the DataSet.

Example

The following example populates a typed DataSet by using two DataAdapters named daCustomers and daOrders. The Dataset has a Customers table and an Orders table. The Customers table is populated with the daCustomers DataAdapter. The Orders table is populated with the daOrders DataAdapter.

After the DataSet has been populated, a DataGrid control is bound to the Customers table in the DataSet. The DataGrid will display the customers and the orders placed by each customer.

```
' Visual Basic
daCustomers.Fill(dsCustomerOrders.Customers)
daOrders.Fill(dsCustomerOrders.Orders)
DataGrid1.DataSource = dsCustomerOrders.Customers.DefaultView
```

```
// Visual C#
daCustomers.Fill(dsCustomerOrders.Customers);
daOrders.Fill(dsCustomerOrders.Orders);
dataGrid1.DataSource = dsCustomerOrders.Customers.DefaultView;
```

Practice

In this practice, you will continue to build a Windows Application that allows users to view the Northwind Traders online product catalog. The solution for this practice is located at

<install folder>\Practices\Mod06_1\Lesson2\CatalogViewer\

▶ **Using the DataAdapter without a strongly typed DataSet**

In the first part of this practice, you will see how the **MissingSchemaAction** property influences how a DataAdapter fills a DataSet.

1. Open the Windows Application solution you created in the previous practice. Alternatively, you can use the sample solution **CatalogViewer.sln** from the previous practice, which is located in the following location:

   <install folder>\Practices\Mod06_1\Lesson1\CatalogViewer

2. Open **Form1** in the Form Designer, right-click **daCategories**, and then click **Preview Data**.

3. Click **Fill DataSet**. This button calls the **Fill** method of the DataAdapter, so it is a useful way of testing a DataAdapter.

   How many bytes of memory does the DataSet require?

   How many rows are returned?

4. Click **Fill DataSet** again. This simulates refreshing the DataSet with the latest data in the underlying database.

   How many bytes of memory does the DataSet require now?

   How many rows are returned? Why are rows being duplicated?

5. Close the Data Adapter Preview window.

6. Set the **MissingSchemaAction** property of the **daCategories** DataAdapter to **AddWithKey**.

7. Right-click **daCategories** and then click **Preview Data**.

8. Click **Fill DataSet** twice.

   Are rows still being duplicated?

9. Close the Data Adapter Preview window.

10. Set the **MissingSchemaAction** property of the two DataAdapters to **Error**, because the Add and AddWithKey values for this property have a negative impact on performance. You will use a DataSet schema instead.

In the next part of this practice, you will generate a strongly typed DataSet based on the structure of the data retrieved by the DataAdapter.

▶ **Generate a strongly typed DataSet**

1. Right-click **daCategories** and then click **Generate Dataset**.

2. Set the name of the new DataSet to **CatalogDataSet**, and select both **daCategories** and **daProducts** DataAdapters.

3. Select the new DataSet in the Form Designer. In the Property window, change its **Name** to **dsCatalog**.

4. Right-click **dsCatalog** and then click **View Schema**. This will open the XSD file that was generated for you by the wizard.

5. In the **usp_GetProducts** box, change **usp_GetProducts** to **Products**.

6. Right-click the **Products** box, click **Add-New Relation**, and then click **OK** in the **Edit Relation** dialog box.

7. Click the background of the Schema Designer to select the DataSet. In the Property window, expand the **key** collection. Rename the two constraints as **PK_Categories** and **PK_Products**.

8. Save the XSD schema file.

In the final part of this practice, you will use the DataAdapter to fill the DataSet with data from the data store.

▶ **Fill a DataSet with data from a data store**

1. Return to the Form Designer and add a Click event handler for the **Fill** button.

2. In the event handler, call the **Fill** method of the two DataAdapters. Also bind the DataGrid control to the **Categories** table in the DataSet.

    ```
    daCategories.Fill(dsCatalog.Categories)
    daProducts.Fill(dsCatalog.Products)
    DataGrid1.DataSource = dsCatalog.Categories
    ```

3. Run and test your application. Verify that the DataGrid recognizes the relationship between categories and products.

4. Use Server Explorer to change some data in the Products table in the SQL Server Northwind database. Verify that you can use the **Fill** button on your form to refresh the DataSet, and see changes that were made to the underlying data.

The solution for this practice is located at

<install folder>\Practices\Mod06_1\Lesson2\CatalogViewer\

Lab 6.1: Retrieving Data into a Disconnected Application

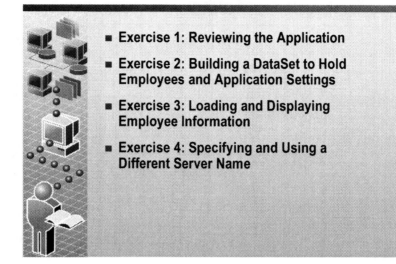

- **Exercise 1: Reviewing the Application**
- **Exercise 2: Building a DataSet to Hold Employees and Application Settings**
- **Exercise 3: Loading and Displaying Employee Information**
- **Exercise 4: Specifying and Using a Different Server Name**

Objectives

After completing this lab, you will be able to:

- Create and configure a DataAdapter.
- Generate a typed DataSet from the DataAdapter.
- Use the XML Designer to adjust the schema in the DataSet.
- Use the DataAdapter to fill the DataSet.
- Save the DataSet data as an XML **DiffGram**.

Prerequisites

Before working on this lab, you must have:

- Microsoft Visual Basic® or Microsoft Visual C#™ programming skills.
- Familiarity with the Visual Studio .NET development environment.
- Basic knowledge about XSD schemas.

For more information

See the DataSet and SqlDataAdapter topics in the Visual Studio .NET documentation.

Scenario

Northwind Traders has many salespeople who travel to visit customers. The salespeople need to be able to update customer data, including orders, while they are away from the office. Each salesperson typically has responsibility for a limited subset of the total central sales database. Therefore, it is unnecessary to give every salesperson a complete copy of the central database.

The application must allow salespeople to update the data while traveling, and then synchronize the data with the central sales database when they return to the home office.

In this lab, you will retrieve data into DataSets in a disconnected application. In Lab 6.2, Retrieving and Updating Customers and Orders Data, you will update the database by using the data in the DataSets.

Estimated time to complete this lab: 60 minutes

Exercise 1
Reviewing the Application

In this exercise, you will review a complete solution to this lab so that you clearly understand how it works. This solution will show how the application loads data into the disconnected application.

You will then review a starter solution that will be the starting point for the application you will complete in the other exercises of Labs 6.1 and 6.2.

Scenario

Northwind Traders salespeople use the "On The Road" Windows Application to track customer order information when they are traveling and do not have access to the central database servers.

The application runs on the salespeople's laptop computers. While in the office, a salesperson can connect to the corporate network and get the latest order data for his or her customers. This will be a subset of the order data that is stored on the central database server. The salesperson creates the subset of data by choosing his or her name from a list of employees, and this information is used to return customer and order data for that employee only.

When the application closes, it automatically saves a copy of the current DataSet to the local disk drive of the salesperson's laptop computer. The next time the salesperson executes the application, it automatically opens the saved DataSet so that he or she can immediately continue working on the data.

While on the road, salespeople can add new orders and edit and delete existing orders. When salespeople return to the home office, they can choose a menu item to update the central database with the changes that they have made to the DataSet. You will implement this functionality in Lab 6.2, Retrieving and Updating Customers and Orders Data.

The application allows salespeople to specify the server name that hosts the central database. It also has an **About** dialog box to display version information.

Application Startup Decision Tree

This is the decision tree for when the "On The Road" application starts up.

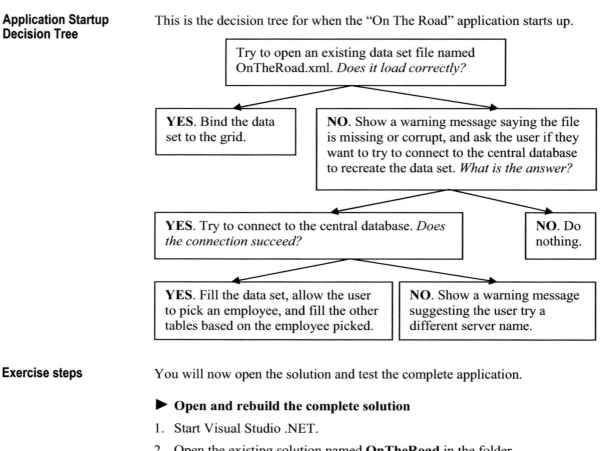

Try to open an existing data set file named OnTheRoad.xml. *Does it load correctly?*

YES. Bind the data set to the grid.

NO. Show a warning message saying the file is missing or corrupt, and ask the user if they want to try to connect to the central database to recreate the data set. *What is the answer?*

YES. Try to connect to the central database. *Does the connection succeed?*

NO. Do nothing.

YES. Fill the data set, allow the user to pick an employee, and fill the other tables based on the employee picked.

NO. Show a warning message suggesting the user try a different server name.

Exercise steps

You will now open the solution and test the complete application.

▶ **Open and rebuild the complete solution**

1. Start Visual Studio .NET.

2. Open the existing solution named **OnTheRoad** in the folder <install folder>\Labs\Lab06_2\Solution\Ex3\xx\OnTheRoad, where *xx* is either VB or CS. This project contains the complete solution for all of the work that you will do in Labs 6.1 and 6.2.

3. Rebuild the solution.

4. Exit Visual Studio .NET.

5. Start the Microsoft SQL Server Query Analyzer.

6. Connect to the **(local)** server by using **Windows Authentication**.

7. Open the script named **lab6setup.sql** located at:

   <install folder>\Labs\Lab06_1\

8. Run the script.

9. Exit the Microsoft SQL Server Query Analyzer.

▶ **Test the application settings**

1. In Windows Explorer, navigate to one of the following folders:

   <install folder>\Labs\Lab06_2\Solution\Ex3\VB\OnTheRoad\bin\

   or

   <install folder>\Labs\Lab06_2\Solution\Ex3\CS\OnTheRoad\bin\debug\

2. There are files named **OnTheRoad.exe** (the application executable) and **OnTheRoad.pdb** (program debug database). If there is a file named **OnTheRoad.xml**, delete it. (This is where the DataSet is saved while the salesperson is on the road.)

3. Double-click the executable **OnTheRoad.exe** to run it.

4. You will see a warning message telling you that a DataSet was not found, and offering to connect to the central database to create one. Click **No**.

5. On the **Tools** menu, click **Options**. Notice that you can change the server name for the central database, and that it is currently set to **(local)**. Click **Cancel** because you do not want to change this option yet.

6. Close the application.

7. In Windows Explorer, notice that a file was created named **OnTheRoad.xml**. Double-click the file to open it in Microsoft Internet Explorer.

8. In Internet Explorer, review the contents of the file **OnTheRoad.xml**. Notice that it currently contains the ID of the currently selected employee (defaults to zero) and the server name for the central database.

9. Close Internet Explorer.

10. Double-click the executable **OnTheRoad.exe** to run it again.

11. When the warning message appears, click **No** because you are still not ready to connect to the central database.

12. On the **Tools** menu, click **Options**, and change the server name to the name of your computer.

13. Close the application.

14. Double-click the file **OnTheRoad.xml** to open it in Internet Explorer again, and note that the server name has changed.

▶ **Test the local DataSet caching**

1. Rerun the executable, and when the warning message appears, click **Yes** to connect to the central database and download a list of employees.

2. In the **Get from central database** dialog box, choose **Dodsworth, Anne** for the employee name, and then click **OK**. You will see all of the customers (and their orders and order details) managed by Anne.

3. Close the application. This will automatically save the DataSet into the same XML file that stored the application settings.

4. Reopen the file **OnTheRoad.xml** with Internet Explorer.

5. On the **Edit** menu, click **Find (on This Page)...** to search for the XML elements that begin with <Products, <Employees, <Customers, <Orders, <OrderDetails, and <AppSettings. Review the contents.

6. Run the executable again. Notice that the warning message no longer appears because the XML file contains a complete and valid DataSet.

7. In the Data Table, expand the customer with the company name of **Around The Horn**. Notice that this customer currently has two orders. Change the order date of the first order to today's date.

8. Expand the first order and add a third order detail row, for a product ID **1**, with a unit price of **25** and a quantity of **4**. Click the first or second row to make sure that the change is made to the DataSet.

9. On the **File** menu, click **Update to central database**. In the central database, one row will be added to the OrderDetails table, and one row in the Orders table will be modified.

10. When prompted to refresh your local copy of the data, click **Yes**. This will make sure any changes made by other users will be reflected in your application.

11. In the Server Explorer, verify that the changes were successfully made.

Note   Lab 6.1 only deals with retrieving data from the central database. Lab 6.2, Retrieving and Updating Customers and Orders Data, deals with updating the central database.

▶ **Remove the stored procedures used by the solution**

1. Start the Microsoft SQL Server Query Analyzer.

2. Connect to the **(local)** server by using **Windows Authentication**.

3. Open the script named **lab6reset.sql** located at:

   <install folder>\Labs\Lab06_1\

4. Run the script.

5. Exit the Microsoft SQL Server Query Analyzer.

► **Review the starter solution**

1. Start the Visual Studio .NET development environment.

2. Open the existing project named **OnTheRoad** in the folder <install folder>\Labs\Lab06_1\Starter\xx\OnTheRoad, where *xx* is either VB or CS.

3. Open each of the following files in Designer view and notice that they each provide a very simple dialog box user interface for performing certain tasks.

Form	Description
About	Shows version information.
Logon	Allows the user to pick a named employee from a list, and retrieves the customer data associated with that employee from the central database.
Options	Allows the user to change the SQL Server name of the central database.

4. Open the file named **MainForm** in Designer view, and review the menu and its items. The menu items will perform the following tasks.

Menu	Task
File – Get from central database…	Shows the Logon form.
File – Update to central database	Updates the central database with the latest changes made in the grid.
File – Exit	Ends the application.
Tools – Options…	Shows the Options form.
Help – About…	Shows the About form.

► **Test the starter solution**

1. Run the starter solution.

2. Click the **Help** menu item, and choose **About**. The About dialog box is displayed

3. Click the **File** menu item, and choose **Exit** (none of the other menu items have any functionality yet).

Exercise 2
Building a DataSet to Hold Employees and Application Settings

In this exercise, you will build a custom DataSet that initially contains two tables: one table for storing a list of all employees' IDs and complete names, and one table to store application settings. You will create and configure a DataAdapter so that it populates the Employees table. You will populate the application settings table programmatically in your code.

You will also write code to save the DataSet to an XML document when the application closes.

Scenario

You will create a custom DataSet class and schema that can track the application specific options (for example, the employee using the application and the server name for the central database).

▶ **Start with an existing Windows Application solution**

• Open the solution **OnTheRoad** in the folder
<install folder>\Labs\Lab06_1\Starter\xx\OnTheRoad where xx is either VB or CS.

▶ **Change the project settings**

You will start by changing some project settings so that your code strictly enforces data type conversions and allows the debugging of SQL Server stored procedures called by the code.

1. In the Solution Explorer, right-click the project name and then click **Properties**.

2. *For Visual Basic projects only.* Select **Build** properties and switch **Option Strict** on. This will enforce the explicit conversion of data types.

3. For *Visual Basic projects only.* Select **Configuration Properties**, **Debugging** and switch **SQL Server debugging** on.

4. For *Visual C# projects only.* Select Configuration Properties, Debugging and set Enable SQL Debugging to True.

5. Click **OK**.

▶ **Build the DataAdapter for filling the employees table**

1. Open the **MainForm** class in Designer view and drag a **SqlDataAdapter** from the Toolbox onto the form. This will run the Data Adapter Configuration Wizard.

2. Choose a data connection to the Northwind database on your local SQL Server.

3. Choose **Use SQL statements**, click **Next**, and type the following statement:

```
SELECT
    EmployeeID, LastName + ', ' + FirstName AS FullName
FROM
    Employees ORDER BY LastName, FirstName
```

4. Click the **Advanced Options** button, clear the **Generate Insert, Update and Delete statements** check box, and then click **OK**. This application will not allow changes to be made to the Employees table.

5. Click **Finish**. The wizard creates a DataAdapter and a connection, and displays these in the tray beneath your form. The wizard also generates a command to execute your SQL query, but this command is not displayed in the tray.

6. Right-click the connection and then click **Properties**. In the Properties window, change the **(Name)** property to **cnNorthwind**.

7. Modify the DataAdapter properties. Change the **(Name)** property to **daEmployees**. Also, expand the **SelectCommand** property and set its **(Name)** to **cmSelectEmployees**.

8. Review the code written by the wizard.

▶ **Generate the custom DataSet schema and class**

1. Right-click the DataAdapter and choose **Generate Dataset**. Change the name to **NWDataSet**, select the **Add this dataset to the designer** check box, and then click **OK**.

Note This will add a new XSD (DataSet schema) file to the project named **NWDataSet.xsd**. An associated class file will also be created, but is hidden by default. Use the **Show All Files** button in the toolbar of the Solution Explorer to toggle the display of hidden files.

---

2. Select the new DataSet object in the Form Designer tray, and view its properties. Change its **(Name)** property to **dsNorthwind**.

▶ **Store the two application settings**

While the application is running, the two application settings can be held in memory by using simple fields that can be added to the form class. When the application is not running, these settings will be stored with the DataSet in an XML file.

1. Open the **MainForm** class in Code view and declare two variables named **EmployeeID** and **ServerName** with appropriate data types.

```
' Visual Basic
Friend EmployeeID As System.Int32 = 0
Friend ServerName As System.String = "(local)"

// Visual C#
internal System.Int32 EmployeeID = 0;
internal System.String ServerName = "(local)";
```

2. Right-click the DataSet named **dsNorthwind** and then click **View Schema**. This will launch the XML Designer and allow you to change the schema.

3. Drag a new **element** from the **XML Schema** section of the Toolbox onto the Designer, and name it **AppSettings**.

4. Add two child elements to **AppSettings** named **EmployeeID** and **ServerName**.

5. Change the data type of **EmployeeID** to **int**.

6. Change the data type of **ServerName** to **string**.

7. Save your changes and close the XSD file.

▶ **Save the DataSet when the application closes**

You will now add code to the **MainForm Closing** event to save the application settings stored in the DataSet to an XML file.

Prewritten code is available if you want to use it, at the following locations:

<install folder>\Labs\Lab06_1\Starter\VB\SaveSettingsVB.txt

or

<install folder>\Labs\Lab06_1\Starter\CS\SaveSettingsCS.txt

By using the prewritten code, or by writing code yourself, perform the following tasks in the **MainForm Closing** event handler:

1. Clear any existing rows in the AppSettings table.

2. Add a new row to the AppSettings table by using the values stored in the EmployeeID and ServerName fields.

3. Call the AcceptChanges method to accept the changes that were made to the AppSettings table.

4. Save the DataSet by using the filename OnTheRoad.xml and the DiffGram format. This will ensure that changes to the DataSet are recorded in addition to the original values.

▶ **Test the application settings code**

1. Run and then immediately close the application. An XML file named **OnTheRoad.xml** should have been created in the same folder that contains the executable file.

2. Open the file with Internet Explorer and review its contents.

Exercise 3
Loading and Displaying Employee Information

In this exercise, you will write code for the **Get from central database** menu item, to load employee information from the central database. Errors may occur as you attempt to fill the DataSet, so you will work with a temporary DataSet and store it in the application only if it is created successfully.

Scenario

You will use the DataAdapter named **daEmployees** to fill the Employees table in the DataSet. You will also display the employee information in a list box on the Logon form.

▶ **Start with the solution to the previous exercise**

If you did not complete the previous exercise, open the solution **OnTheRoad** in the folder <install folder>\Labs\Lab06_1\Solution\Ex2\xx\OnTheRoad where *xx* is either VB or CS.

▶ **Fill the DataSet with employees**

Prewritten code is available at the following locations:

   <install folder>\Labs\Lab06_1\Starter\VB\FillDataSetVB.txt

   or

   <install folder>\Labs\Lab06_1\Starter\CS\FillDataSetCS.txt

Perform the following tasks in the **mnuFill Click** event handler:

1. Declare a DataSet named **tempNW** based on the **NWDataSet** schema and class.

2. Write an **If** statement to check the current state of the connection. If it is not open, try to open the connection. If opening fails, catch the exception and display a warning message that suggests that the user try to change the server name, and then exit the subroutine.

3. Write code to try to fill the employees table by using the DataAdapter named **daEmployees**. Catch any exceptions, and display a warning message that informs the user that the employee list failed to be retrieved.

4. Write code to instantiate the **Logon** form. Set the data properties for the form, so that the list box displays a list of employee names, and the bound value is the Employee ID.

5. Add code to highlight the current EmployeeID in the list.

6. Write code to show the **Logon** dialog box, and test if the user clicks **OK** in this dialog box. If so, change the currently stored employee ID to the selected value in the list box, store the temporary DataSet in the **dsNorthwind** DataSet, and finally call a method named **RefreshUI** that you will complete next.

7. Close the database connection.

▶ **Refresh the user interface**

Prewritten code is available at the following locations:

    \<install folder>\Labs\Lab06_1\Starter\VB\RefreshVB.txt

    or

    \<install folder>\Labs\Lab06_1\Starter\CS\RefreshCS.txt

Perform the following tasks in the **RefreshUI** procedure:

1. Set the title bar of the main form to show the full name of the currently selected employee.

2. Append the name of the application. For example, the title bar might show: **Buchanan, Steven – On The Road**.

Note: In Lab 6.2, Exercise 2, Filling a DataSet by Using Multiple DataAdapters, you will complete the rest of the RefreshUI method. You do not need to write code to bind to the grid now.

▶ **Test the code**

1. Run and test your application.

2. On the **File** menu, click **Get from central database**.

3. The **Get from central database** dialog box should appear, displaying a list of employee names. Click any employee name, and then click **OK**.

4. The name you choose should appear in the title bar of the application, along with the name of the application.

5. Close the application.

Exercise 4
Specifying and Using a Different Server Name

In this exercise, you will write code for the **Options** menu item to allow the user to choose a different server. The application will use this server name when it needs to access the central database.

You will also extend the application startup code. When the application is launched, it will try to load application settings and employee information from the XML file **OnTheRoad.xml**.

Scenario

You will modify the database connection string to use the new server name entered by the user in the **Options** dialog box. You will also use the **ReadXml** method to read application settings and employee information into the DataSet at application startup.

▶ **Start with the solution to the previous exercise**

- If you did not complete the previous exercise, open the solution **OnTheRoad** in the folder <install folder>\Labs\Lab06_1\Solution\Ex3\xx\ OnTheRoad where *xx* is either VB or CS.

▶ **Allow the server name to change**

Prewritten code is available at the following locations:

> <install folder>\Labs\Lab06_1\Starter\VB\ChangeServerVB.txt
>
> or
>
> <install folder>\Labs\Lab06_1\Starter\CS\ChangeServerCS.txt

Perform the following tasks in the **mnuOptions** Click event handler:

1. Write code to instantiate the **Options** form.

2. Write code to fill the current server name into the text box on the instance of the **Options** form.

3. Write code to show the **Options** dialog box, and test if the user clicks **OK** in this dialog box. If so, retrieve the value in the **ServerName** field and use it to change the data source parameter in the **ConnectionString** property of the connection object.

▶ **Fill a DataSet when the application starts**

Prewritten code is available at the following locations:

<install folder>\Labs\Lab06_1\Starter\VB\FormLoadVB.txt

or

<install folder>\Labs\Lab06_1\Starter\CS\FormLoadCS.txt

Perform the following tasks in the **MainForm_Load** procedure:

1. Add code to try to open an existing XML file named **OnTheRoad.xml** that uses the DiffGram format.

2. If the file is found (and therefore an exception is not thrown), retrieve default values for the **EmployeeID** and **ServerName** fields.

3. Call the **RefreshUI** method to update the title bar of the form.

4. Write a **Catch** statement. Inside the **Catch** statement, use an **If** statement to ask the user if they want to connect to the central database to create the DataSet and check their response.

5. If the user replies Yes, write code to try to open the connection, and then call the **mnuFill_Click** procedure to simulate the user clicking the **Get from central database** menu item.

6. Write code to catch any exceptions, and if they occur, display a warning message and then exit the procedure.

▶ **Test the code**

1. In Windows Explorer, delete the file named **OnTheRoad.xml** if it exists.

2. Run and test your application. A warning message should appear. Click **Yes** to connect to your local database and retrieve the list of employees.

3. Click any employee name, and then click **OK**. The name you choose should appear in the title bar of the application.

4. Close the application then run it again to see if it correctly opens the XML and remembers the employee you chose.

5. On the **Tools** menu, click **Options**, and then try to change the server name to **London**, the name of the instructor computer.

6. Close the application, and then run it again to see if it correctly opens the XML and loads the employees from the instructor computer.

7. Open **OnTheRoad.xml** and review its contents, which should look similar to the following:

```
<?xml version="1.0" standalone="yes" ?>
<diffgr:diffgram xmlns:msdata="urn:schemas-microsoft-
com:xml-msdata" xmlns:diffgr="urn:schemas-microsoft-
com:xml-diffgram-v1">
<NWDataSet xmlns="http://www.tempuri.org/NWDataSet.xsd">
<Employees diffgr:id="Employees1" msdata:rowOrder="0">
  <EmployeeID>5</EmployeeID>
  <FullName>Buchanan, Steven</FullName>
</Employees>
...
<Employees diffgr:id="Employees9" msdata:rowOrder="8">
  <EmployeeID>6</EmployeeID>
  <FullName>Suyama, Michael</FullName>
</Employees>
<AppSettings diffgr:id="AppSettings2" msdata:rowOrder="0">
  <EmployeeID>7</EmployeeID>
  <ServerName>markpri-srvr-01</ServerName>
</AppSettings>
</NWDataSet>
</diffgr:diffgram>
```

8. On the **Tools** menu, click **Options...** and change the server name back to **(local)**.

9. Close the application.

Lesson: Configuring a DataAdapter to Update the Underlying Data Source

- ■ **Multimedia: How a DataSet Tracks Changes**

- ■ **How Does a DataSet Track Changes?**

- ■ **What Are the Data Modification Commands?**

- ■ **How to Set the Data Modification Commands Using the Data Adapter Configuration Wizard**

Introduction

Although a DataSet is typically a local copy of data from a remote data source, you can create and update data in a DataSet and then use a DataAdapter to update the underlying data source.

Lesson objectives

After completing this lesson, you will be able to:

- ■ Explain how a DataSet tracks changes.

- ■ Use the data modification commands.

- ■ Set the data modification commands by using new stored procedures and the Data Adapter Configuration Wizard.

Multimedia: How a DataSet Tracks Changes

Introduction

This animation shows how a DataSet uses the **RowState** property to identify the state of each row. The animation also shows how the DataSet maintains two versions of data for each row: the Current version and the Original version.

How Does a DataSet Track Changes?

- **Each DataRow has a RowState property**
  - Indicates the status of each row
  - Added, Deleted, Detached, Modified, Unchanged
- **The DataSet maintains two copies of data for each row**
  - Original version
  - Current version

Visual Basic Example   <u>Visual C# Example</u>

Introduction

Each DataRow object in a DataTable has a **RowState** property. The **RowState** property is read-only, and indicates whether the row has been modified, inserted, or deleted from the DataSet since the DataSet was first populated.

The DataSet maintains two sets of data for each row: the current data and the original data. You can specify which version of data you want when you use the DataSet.

Definition of the RowState property

The DataSet maintains the current status of each row in the DataSet. Whenever a DataRow is changed in any way, the DataSet sets the **RowState** property to indicate whether the row has been modified, inserted, or deleted. You can check this property in your code to examine the status of each row in the DataSet.

The **RowState** property has one of the following enumeration values.

RowState property value	Description
DataRowState.Added	The row has been added to the DataSet.
DataRowState.Deleted	The row has been deleted from the DataSet.
DataRowState.Detached	The row has been created, but it has not yet been added to a DataRowCollection in a DataSet.
DataRowState.Modified	The row has been modified.
DataRowState.Unchanged	The row has not changed.

Definition of the Current and Original data versions

The DataSet maintains two copies of data for each row: the Current version and the Original version. This enables you to see exactly how each row has changed in the DataSet. When you access data in a DataRow, you can specify a DataRowVersion parameter to indicate which version of the data you want.

DataRowVersion value	Description
DataRowVersion.Current	The current version of data in the DataRow. This is the default data version if you do not specify an explicit version.
DataRowVersion.Original	The original version of data in the DataRow.

Example of using current and original data in a row

The following example iterates through the rows in a DataSet table, and displays the **RowState** property for each row.

If the **RowState** is **DataRowState.Added** or **DataRowState.Unchanged**, the current version of the row data is displayed. If the **RowState** is **DataRowState.Deleted**, the original version of the row data is displayed. If the **RowState** is **DataRowState.Modified**, the original and current versions of the row data are displayed to show how they differ.

```
' Visual Basic
Dim row As DataRow
For Each row In Me.dsCustomers.Customers.Rows

  Dim msg As String
  If row.RowState = DataRowState.Added Or _
     row.RowState = DataRowState.Unchanged Then

    msg = "Current data:" & vbCrLf & _
       row("CompanyName", DataRowVersion.Current) & ", " & _
       row("ContactName", DataRowVersion.Current)

  ElseIf row.RowState = DataRowState.Deleted Then

    msg = "Original data:" & vbCrLf & _
       row("CompanyName", DataRowVersion.Original) & ", " & _
       row("ContactName", DataRowVersion.Original)

  ElseIf row.RowState = DataRowState.Modified Then

    msg = "Original data:" & vbCrLf & _
       row("CompanyName", DataRowVersion.Original) & ", " & _
       row("ContactName", DataRowVersion.Original) & vbCrLf

    msg = msg & "Current data:" & _
       row("CompanyName", DataRowVersion.Current) & ", " & _
       row("ContactName", DataRowVersion.Current)

  End If
  MessageBox.Show(msg, "RowState: " & row.RowState.ToString())
Next
```

Code continued on the following page

```csharp
// Visual C#
foreach (DataRow row in this.dsCustomers.Customers.Rows)
{
  String msg = "";
  if (row.RowState == DataRowState.Added ||
      row.RowState == DataRowState.Unchanged)
  {
    msg = "Current data:\n" +
      row["CompanyName", DataRowVersion.Current] + ", " +
      row["ContactName", DataRowVersion.Current];
  }
  else if (row.RowState == DataRowState.Deleted)
  {
    msg = "Original data:\n" +
      row["CompanyName", DataRowVersion.Original] + ", " +
      row["ContactName", DataRowVersion.Original];
  }
  else if (row.RowState == DataRowState.Modified)
  {
    msg = "Original data:\n" +
      row["CompanyName", DataRowVersion.Original] + ", " +
      row["ContactName", DataRowVersion.Original] + "\n";

    msg = msg + "Current data:\n" +
      row["CompanyName", DataRowVersion.Current] + ", " +
      row["ContactName", DataRowVersion.Current];
  }
  MessageBox.Show(msg, "RowState: " + row.RowState);
}
```

What Are the Data Modification Commands?

- **A SqlDataAdapter or OleDbDataAdapter object has command properties that are themselves command objects that you can use to modify data at the data source**
  - InsertCommand
  - UpdateCommand
  - DeleteCommand
- **Syntax – essentially the same for both Sql and OleDb DataAdapters and for the series of command objects**

```
public SqlCommand InsertCommand {get; set;}
```

Visual Basic Example   Visual C# Example

Introduction

A DataAdapter uses command objects to modify data at the data source. The DataAdapter uses these commands to save changes in a DataSet back to the underlying data source. These commands contain either SQL statements or stored procedure calls.

Data modification commands

The following table describes the data modification commands that are used by the DataAdapter.

Command	Description
InsertCommand	Used during a call to the **Update** method of a DataAdapter to insert records into the data source that correspond to new rows in the DataSet.
UpdateCommand	Used during a call to the **Update** method to update records in the data source that correspond to modified rows in the DataSet.
DeleteCommand	Used during a call to the **Update** method to delete records in the data source that correspond to deleted rows in the DataSet.

Example of setting the InsertCommand property

The following example programmatically sets the **InsertCommand** property for a DataAdapter. The command inserts a row into a simplified Customers table, which contains columns named CustomerID and CompanyName. The command requires two **SqlParameter** objects to set the column values in the new row.

```vb
' Visual Basic
Dim cmInsert As New SqlCommand( _
    "INSERT INTO Customers VALUES (@ID, @Name)", _
    cnNorthwind)
cmInsert.Parameters.Add(New SqlParameter("@ID", _
    SqlDbType.NChar, 5, ParameterDirection.Input, False, _
    0, 0, "CustomerID", DataRowVersion.Current, Nothing))
cmInsert.Parameters.Add(New SqlParameter("@Name", _
    SqlDbType.NVarChar, 40, ParameterDirection.Input, False, _
    0, 0, "CompanyName", DataRowVersion.Current, Nothing))
daCustomers.InsertCommand = cmInsert
```

```csharp
// Visual C#
SqlCommand cmInsert = new SqlCommand(
    "INSERT INTO Customers VALUES (@ID, @Name)",
    cnNorthwind);
cmInsert.Parameters.Add(new SqlParameter("@ID",
    SqlDbType.NChar, 5, ParameterDirection.Input, false,
    0, 0, "CustomerID", DataRowVersion.Current, null));
cmInsert.Parameters.Add(new SqlParameter("@Name",
    SqlDbType.NVarChar, 40, ParameterDirection.Input, false,
    0, 0, "CompanyName", DataRowVersion.Current, null));
daCustomers.InsertCommand = cmInsert;
```

Example of setting the UpdateCommand property

The following example sets the **UpdateCommand** property for a DataAdapter to update a row in the simplified Customers table. The command requires three **SqlParameter** objects: the new **CustomerID**, the new **CompanyName**, and the original **CustomerID** (to locate the customer record in the data source).

```vb
' Visual Basic
Dim cmUpdate As New SqlCommand( _
    "UPDATE Customers SET CustomerID = @ID, " & _
    "CompanyName = @Name WHERE (CustomerID = @OrigID)", _
    cnNorthwind)
cmUpdate.Parameters.Add(New SqlParameter("@ID", _
    SqlDbType.NChar, 5, ParameterDirection.Input, False, _
    0, 0, "CustomerID", DataRowVersion.Current, Nothing))
cmUpdate.Parameters.Add(New SqlParameter("@Name", _
    SqlDbType.NVarChar, 40, ParameterDirection.Input, False, _
    0, 0, "CompanyName", DataRowVersion.Current, Nothing))
cmUpdate.Parameters.Add(New SqlParameter("@OrigID", _
    SqlDbType.NChar, 5, ParameterDirection.Input, False, _
    0, 0, "CustomerID", DataRowVersion.Original, Nothing))
daCustomers.UpdateCommand = cmUpdate
```

Code continued on the following page

```csharp
// Visual C#
SqlCommand cmUpdate = new SqlCommand(
    "UPDATE Customers SET CustomerID = @ID, " +
    "CompanyName = @Name WHERE (CustomerID = @OrigID)",
    cnNorthwind);
cmUpdate.Parameters.Add(new SqlParameter("@ID",
    SqlDbType.NChar, 5, ParameterDirection.Input, false,
    0, 0, "CustomerID", DataRowVersion.Current, null));
cmUpdate.Parameters.Add(new SqlParameter("@Name",
    SqlDbType.NVarChar, 40, ParameterDirection.Input, false,
    0, 0, "CompanyName", DataRowVersion.Current, null));
cmUpdate.Parameters.Add(new SqlParameter("@OrigID",
    SqlDbType.NChar, 5, ParameterDirection.Input, false,
    0, 0, "CustomerID", DataRowVersion.Original, null));
daCustomers.UpdateCommand = cmUpdate;
```

Example of setting the DeleteCommand property

The following example sets the **DeleteCommand** property for a DataAdapter to delete a row in the simplified Customers table. The command requires one **SqlParameter** object to specify the CustomerID of the row to be deleted.

```vbnet
' Visual Basic
Dim cmDelete As New SqlCommand( _
    "DELETE FROM Customers WHERE (CustomerID = @ID)", _
    cnNorthwind)
cmDelete.Parameters.Add(New SqlParameter("@ID", _
    SqlDbType.NChar, 5, ParameterDirection.Input, False, _
    0, 0, "CustomerID", DataRowVersion.Original, Nothing))
daCustomers.DeleteCommand = cmDelete
```

```csharp
// Visual C#
SqlCommand cmDelete = new SqlCommand(
    "DELETE FROM Customers WHERE (CustomerID = @ID)",
    cnNorthwind);
cmDelete.Parameters.Add(new SqlParameter("@ID",
    SqlDbType.NChar, 5, ParameterDirection.Input, false,
    0, 0, "CustomerID", DataRowVersion.Original, null));
daCustomers.DeleteCommand = cmDelete;
```

How to Set the Data Modification Commands Using the Data Adapter Configuration Wizard

- **You can create data modification commands by using the Data Adapter Configuration Wizard**
- **The wizard can generate the commands in three different ways:**
  - By using SQL statements
  - By creating new stored procedures
  - By using existing stored procedures
- **Practice**

Introduction

You can create data modification commands by using the Data Adapter Configuration Wizard. The Wizard can generate the commands in three different ways:

- By using SQL statements
- By creating new stored procedures
- By using existing stored procedures

Scenario

Developers can use the Data Adapter Configuration Wizard to create new stored procedures on their local computers. This is useful during development because the developer can test the application by using a local scratch database.

When the application is deployed, it is more likely that you will use existing stored procedures on the production database. These stored procedures are usually optimized for performance and security, and are carefully controlled by database administrators.

How to create data modification commands by using the wizard

To create data modification commands by using the Data Adapter Configuration Wizard, follow these steps:

1. Drag a **SqlDataAdapter** control or **OleDbDataAdapter** control from the Toolbox onto your form.

2. On the Welcome screen for the Data Adapter Configuration Wizard, click **Next**.

3. On the Choose Your Data Connection screen, select an existing connection (or click **New Connection** and specify a new connection, if necessary).

4. Click **Next** to move to the Choose a Query Type screen.

5. If you want to use SQL statements for the data modification commands, follow these steps:

   a. Choose **Use SQL statements** and click **Next**.

   b. On the Generate the SQL statements screen, type the SQL statement for the SelectCommand. Click **Advanced Options**, ensure that the check box next to the **Generate Insert, Update, and Delete** statements is selected, and then click **OK**.

   c. On the Generate the SQL statements screen, click **Next**.

   d. On the View Wizard Results screen, click **Finish**.

   e. Examine the generated code in your application to see how the wizard created the data modification commands.

6. If you want to create new stored procedures for the data modification commands, follow these steps:

   a. Choose **Create new stored procedures** and then click **Next**.

   b. On the Generate the stored procedures screen, type the SQL statement for the **SelectCommand**. Click **Advanced Options**, ensure that the check box next to **Generate Insert, Update, and Delete** statements is selected, and then click **OK**.

   c. On the Generate the stored procedures screen, click **Next**.

   d. On the Create the Stored Procedures screen, enter names for the new stored procedures, and then click **Next**.

   e. On the View Wizard Results screen, click **Finish**.

   f. In the Server Explorer, examine the stored procedures.

   g. Examine the generated code in your application to see how the wizard created the data modification commands.

7. If you want to use existing stored procedures for the data modification commands, follow these steps:

   a. Choose **Use existing stored procedures** and then click **Next**.

   b. On the Bind Commands to Existing Stored Procedures screen, choose existing stored procedures for the **Select**, **Insert**, **Update**, and **Delete** commands, and then click **Next**.

   c. On the View Wizard Results screen, click **Finish**.

   d. Examine the generated code in your application to see how the wizard created the data modification commands.

Practice

Northwind Traders needs to allow users to make changes to the product catalog that is published on the company's Web site. In this practice, you will create a new Windows Application that uses a **SqlDataAdapter** to query and modify the Products table.

You will use the Data Adapter Configuration Wizard to generate four new stored procedures to achieve this task. The DataAdapter will call these stored procedures in its data modification commands (**SelectCommand**, **InsertCommand**, **UpdateCommand**, and **DeleteCommand**).

▶ **Create new stored procedures by using the Data Adapter Configuration Wizard**

1. Create a new Windows Application solution named **CatalogEditor** at the following location:

   \<install folder>\Practices\Mod06_2\

2. Drag a **SqlDataAdapter** control from the Toolbox onto the form. Use the Data Adapter Configuration Wizard to set the following properties.

Property	Value
Server Name	(local)
Log On	Use Windows NT Integrated security
Database	Northwind
Query Type	Create new stored procedures
Load Statement	SELECT * FROM Products
Advanced Options	All options enabled
Stored Procedure Names	**SelectProducts** **InsertProducts** **UpdateProducts** **DeleteProducts** Let the wizard create these in the database for you.

3. Select the new DataAdapter named **SqlDataAdapter1**. In the Property window, set the following properties.

Property	Value
(Name)	daProducts
DeleteCommand (Name)	cmDeleteProducts
InsertCommand (Name)	cmInsertProducts
SelectCommand (Name)	cmSelectProducts
UpdateCommand (Name)	cmUpdateProducts

4. In the Server Explorer, examine the four new stored procedures in the Northwind database. The stored procedures are named **SelectProducts**, **InsertProducts**, **UpdateProducts**, and **DeleteProducts**.

5. In the Code View window, examine the code that has been generated by the Data Adapter Configuration Wizard.

6. Save all of the files in your application.

The solution for this practice is located at
\<install folder>\Practices\Mod06_2\Lesson3\CatalogEditor\

Lesson: Persisting Changes to a Data Source

- **Multimedia: How the DataAdapter's Update Method Modifies the Underlying Data Source**

- **When to Use the GetChanges Method of a DataSet Object**

- **How to Merge Changes into the DataSet**

- **How to Update a Data Source by Using a DataSet**

- **How to Accept Changes into the DataSet**

Introduction

After you have created a DataSet in a typical multiple-tier implementation and made changes to the DataSet, follow these steps to persist the changes to a data source:

1. Invoke the **GetChanges** method to create a second DataSet that features only the changes to the data.

2. Invoke the **Merge** method to merge the changes from the second DataSet into the first DataSet.

3. Call the **Update** method of the **SqlDataAdapter** (or **OleDbDataAdapter**) and pass the merged DataSet as an argument.

4. Invoke the **AcceptChanges** method on the DataSet to persist changes. Alternatively, invoke the **RejectChange** method to cancel the changes.

Lesson objectives

After completing this lesson, you will be able to persist changes to a data source, and be able to:

- Use the **GetChanges** method of a DataSet object.

- Use the **Update** method of a DataAdapter object.

- Use the **Merge** method to merge changes into the DataSet.

- Use the **AcceptChanges** method.

Overloading a method

Many of the methods that you use on a DataAdapter object allow different combinations of parameters and data types for a method. The ability to create different versions of a method is called *overloading*. The methods that you will learn about in this lesson all have the ability to be overloaded.

Multimedia: How the DataAdapter's Update Method Modifies the Underlying Data Source

Introduction	This animation shows how the **Update** method of a DataAdapter object can modify the underlying data source.

When to Use the GetChanges Method of a DataSet Object

- **Use the GetChanges method when you need to give the changes to another class for use by another object**
- **Code example**

```
If dsCustomers.HasChanges(DataRowState.Modified) Then
    Dim dsTemp As DataSet
    dsTemp =
    dsCustomers.GetChanges(DataRowState.Modified)
    DataGrid1.DataSource = dsTemp.Tables(0).DefaultView
End If
```

- **Use the GetChanges method to get a copy of a DataSet that contains all changes made to the DataSet**
  - Since it was loaded, or
  - Since the last time the AcceptChanges method was called.

Introduction

When you work in a disconnected environment, you can make changes to data in a DataSet and then transmit those changes to a data source. You use the **GetChanges** method of a DataSet object to produce a new DataSet object that contains a copy of only the changed rows in the original DataSet. You then can merge the new copy back into the original DataSet.

Syntax

The following is the Microsoft Visual C#® syntax for the **GetChanges** method of a DataAdapter object:

```
public DataSet GetChanges(
    DataRowState rowStates
);
```

Use the **rowStates** argument to specify the types of changes the new object should include. You can create subsets of subsets containing only changes of a certain type, (for example, deleted rows).

When to use the GetChanges method

You use the **GetChanges** method when you need to give the changes to another class for use by another object.

While updating, the sequence in which inserts and deletes are performed is important for parent/child related tables, such as Customers and Orders. When inserting a new order for a new customer, the customer (parent) record must be inserted before the order (child) record. However, when deleting a customer, child orders must be deleted before the customer (parent) record.

Example of getting changes in a DataSet

The following example tests a DataSet named dsCustomers to see if it has any modified rows. If it does, the modified rows are copied to a temporary DataSet named dsTemp. The modified rows are displayed in a DataGrid.

```
' Visual Basic
If dsCustomers.HasChanges(DataRowState.Modified) Then
  Dim dsTemp As DataSet
  dsTemp = dsCustomers.GetChanges(DataRowState.Modified)
  DataGrid1.DataSource = dsTemp.Tables(0).DefaultView
End If
```

```
// Visual C#
if (dsCustomers.HasChanges(DataRowState.Modified))
{
  DataSet dsTemp;
  dsTemp = dsCustomers.GetChanges(DataRowState.Modified);
  dataGrid1.DataSource = dsTemp.Tables[0].DefaultView;
}
```

How to Merge Changes into the DataSet

- **Use the Merge method to merge two DataSets – an original, and one containing only the changes to the original**

- **Code example**

```
aDataSet.Merge(anotherDataSet)
```

- **The two merged DataSets should have similar schemas**

Introduction

When you make changes to a DataSet, you typically create a new DataSet that contains only the changes that you made to the original DataSet.

Definition of the Merge method

The **Merge** method of a DataSet object merges the contents of the DataSet to which the method is applied, with a second DataSet that typically contains only the changes to the original DataSet. Similarly to other methods that deal with changes to a DataSet, the **Merge** method can be overloaded.

Syntax

The following is the Visual C# syntax for the **Merge** method, where *dataSet* is the DataSet whose data and schema will be merged:

```
public void Merge(
   DataSet dataSet
);
```

When to use the Merge method

You use the **Merge** method to merge two DataSet objects that have similar schemas. You typically use a **Merge** method on a client application to incorporate the latest changes from a data source into an existing DataSet. This allows the client application to have a refreshed DataSet with the latest data from the data source.

The **Merge** method is typically called at the end of a series of procedures that involve validating changes, reconciling errors, updating the data source with the changes, and finally refreshing the existing DataSet.

How to Update a Data Source by Using a DataSet

- **The Update method of a DataAdapter object calls the appropriate statement for each changed row in a specific DataTable:**
  - INSERT
  - UPDATE
  - DELETE
- **Code example**

```
aDataAdapter.Update(aDataSet, aDataTable)
```

Visual Basic Example   Visual C# Example

Introduction

The **Update** method of a DataAdapter object calls the respective **INSERT**, **UPDATE**, or **DELETE** statements for each inserted, updated, or deleted row in the specified DataSet from a DataTable named Table.

The **Update** method of a DataAdapter object is different from the **UpdateCommand** property of a DataAdapter object, which gets or sets a SQL statement or **OleDbCommand** that updates records in the data source.

Syntax of the Update method

The following is the Visual C# syntax for the **Update** method of the DataAdapter class:

```
public abstract int Update(
    DataSet aDataSet, DataTable aDataTable
);
```

In this syntax, *aDataSet* and *aDataTable* identify the DataSet and DataTable that are used to update the data source.

How to call the Update method

When an application calls the **Update** method, the DataAdapter examines the **RowState** property and executes the required **INSERT**, **UPDATE**, or **DELETE** statements based on the order of the indexes configured in the DataSet. For example, the **Update** method might execute a **DELETE** statement, followed by an **INSERT** statement, and then another **DELETE** statement, because of the ordering of the rows in the DataTable data. An application can call the **GetChanges** method in situations where you must control the sequence of statement types (for example, **INSERT** statements before **UPDATE** statements). For more information, see Updating the Database with a DataAdapter and the DataSet.in the Visual Studio .NET online books.

If **INSERT**, **UPDATE**, or **DELETE** statements have not been specified, the **Update** method generates an exception. However, you can create a **SqlCommandBuilder** or **OleDbCommandBuilder** object to automatically generate SQL statements for single-table updates if you set the **SelectCommand** property of a .NET data provider. The **CommandBuilder** then generates any additional SQL statements that you do not set. This generation logic requires key column information to be present in the DataSet. For more information, see Automatically Generated Commands in the Visual Studio .NET documentation.

The **Update** method retrieves rows from the table listed in the first mapping before performing an update. The **Update** method then refreshes the row by using the value of the **UpdatedRowSource** property. Any additional rows that are returned are ignored.

After any data is loaded back into the DataSet, the **OnRowUpdated** event is raised, allowing the user to inspect the reconciled DataSet row and any output parameters that are returned by the command. After a row is updated successfully, the changes to that row are accepted.

Example of updating a data source

The following example shows how to use the **Update** method to update a data source. The example uses a DataSet named dsCustomerOrders that has two tables named Customers and Orders. The Customers table is initially filled by the **daCustomers** DataAdapter, and the Orders table is filled by the **daOrders** DataAdapter.

The objective is to allow the user to delete customers and all orders placed by those customers. The orders must be deleted first to avoid foreign key constraint errors when the customers are deleted.

To achieve this effect, the **GetChanges** method is called to get the deleted rows in the Orders table. These rows are deleted first. The **GetChanges** method is then called a second time to get the deleted rows in the Customers table. These rows can now be safely deleted without any errors.

```
' Visual Basic
' Fill the Customers and Orders tables initially
daCustomers.Fill(dsCustomerOrders.Customers)
daOrders.Fill(dsCustomerOrders.Orders)
DataGrid1.DataSource = dsCustomerOrders.Customers.DefaultView
...
' Update the data source with any changes
Dim deletedOrders As DataTable = _
   dsCustomerOrders.Orders.GetChanges(DataRowState.Deleted)
daOrders.Update(deletedOrders)

Dim deletedCustomers As DataTable = _
   dsCustomerOrders.Customers.GetChanges(DataRowState.Deleted)
daCustomers.Update(deletedCustomers)

// Visual C#
// Fill the Customers and Orders tables initially
daCustomers.Fill(dsCustomerOrders.Customers);
daOrders.Fill(dsCustomerOrders.Orders);
dataGrid1.DataSource = dsCustomerOrders.Customers.DefaultView;
...
// Update the data source with any changes
DataTable deletedOrders =
   dsCustomerOrders.Orders.GetChanges(DataRowState.Deleted);
daOrders.Update(deletedOrders);

DataTable deletedCustomers =
   dsCustomerOrders.Customers.GetChanges(DataRowState.Deleted);
daCustomers.Update(deletedCustomers);
```

How to Accept Changes into the DataSet

- **The AcceptChanges method of the DataSet commits all changes made to a specific DataSet since it was last loaded, or since AcceptChanges was called**

- **Code example**

  ```
  aDataSet.AcceptChanges()
  ```

- **You can invoke AcceptChanges for an entire DataSet or for a each DataRow in each DataTable**

- **Practice**

Visual Basic Example   <u>Visual C# Example</u>

Introduction

When you make changes to a DataSet, you typically create a new DataSet that contains only the changes that you made to the original DataSet. When you have merged the two DataSets and updated the contents, you can call the **AcceptChanges** method of any of the following objects: DataSet, DataTable, and DataRow.

Choosing an AcceptChanges method

There is an **AcceptChanges** method for the DataSet, DataTable, and DataRow objects.

When you call the **AcceptChanges** method on a DataSet, you also invoke the **AcceptChanges** method on all subordinate objects with a single call. A call to **AcceptChanges** on a DataSet object also calls **AcceptChanges** on each DataTable in the DataSet, and on each DataRow object in each DataTable. However, you can call **AcceptChanges** on an individual DataTable or DataRow.

Syntax

The following is the Visual C# syntax for the **AcceptChanges** method of the DataSet class:

```
public void AcceptChanges();
```

The syntax is the same for the DataTable and DataRow objects.

Example of merging DataSets

The following example shows how to use the **Merge** and **AcceptChanges** methods in a client application.

The client application has a DataSet named **dsCustomers**. The DataSet is bound to a DataGrid to allow the user to change the data locally. When the user is ready to send the changes to the data source, the application calls **GetChanges** to get the changes to the DataSet. The application sends this (smaller) DataSet to a middle-tier component, such as an XML Web service method.

The code for the XML Web service method is not shown, but it could use stored procedures to update the data source with the DataSet changes. The XML Web service method returns a new DataSet, which contains the latest data from the data source. (For example, the data source might have assigned default values to null columns in the DataSet.)

The client application receives this sanitized DataSet and merges it into the main **dsCustomers** DataSet. The client application then calls **AcceptChanges** to mark these new records as "unchanged" in the **dsCustomers** DataSet.

```
' Visual Basic code, at the client
' Get changes made by the user to the dsCustomers DataSet
Dim dsChanges As DataSet = dsCustomers.GetChanges()

' Send changes to an XML Web Service, get latest data back
' again
Dim service As New MyWebService()
Dim dsLatest As DataSet = service.MyUpdateMethod(dsChanges)

' Merge latest data back into the dsCustomers DataSet
dsCustomers.Merge(dsLatest)

' Mark all rows as "unchanged" in the dsCustomers DataSet
dsCustomers.AcceptChanges()


// Visual C# code, at the client
// Get changes made by the user to the dsCustomers DataSet
DataSet dsChanges = dsCustomers.GetChanges();

// Send changes to an XML Web Service, get latest data back
// again
MyWebService service = new MyWebService();
DataSet dsLatest = service.MyUpdateMethod(dsChanges);

// Merge latest data back into the dsCustomers DataSet
dsCustomers.Merge(dsLatest);

// Mark all rows as "unchanged" in the dsCustomers DataSet
dsCustomers.AcceptChanges();
```

Practice

▶ **Continue to build a Windows Application to edit the Northwind Traders online product catalog**

1. Open the Windows Application solution you used in the previous practice, or the solution named **CatalogEditor** at the following location:

   <install folder>\Practices\Mod06_2\Lesson3\CatalogEditor\

2. In the Form Designer, right-click the **daProducts** control and then click **Generate Dataset**. Set the name of the new DataSet to **ProductDataSet**, and select the **Products (daProducts)** table.

3. Drag a **DataGrid** onto the form.

4. Drag a **Button** onto the form, and change the text of the button to **Fill**.

5. Add the following code to handle the **Click** event of this button:

```
daProducts.Fill(ProductDataSet1.Products)
DataGrid1.DataSource = ProductDataSet1.Products
```

6. Drag another **Button** onto the form, and change the text of the button to **Get modified rows**.

   Add the following code to handle the **Click** event of this button. This code is provided in GetModifiedRows.txt, located at

   \<install folder\>\Practices\Mod06_2\Lesson4.

   The code gets a copy of all modified rows and displays the current and original ProductName and UnitPrice for each row.

```
If (ProductDataSet1.HasChanges(DataRowState.Modified)) Then
  Dim ds As ProductDataSet = _
    ProductDataSet1.GetChanges(DataRowState.Modified)

  Dim row As DataRow
  For Each row In ds.Products.Rows
    Dim str As String = "Current:   " & _
      row("ProductName", DataRowVersion.Current) & ", " & _
      row("UnitPrice",   DataRowVersion.Current) & vbCrLf

    str = str & "Original:  " & _
      row("ProductName", DataRowVersion.Original) & ", " & _
      row("UnitPrice",   DataRowVersion.Original)

    MessageBox.Show(str, "Modified row")
  Next
Else
  MessageBox.Show("No modified rows", "Information")
End If
```

7. Drag a third **Button** onto the form, and change the text of the button to **Update**.

8. Add the following code to handle the **Click** event of this button. This code updates the data source by using the current and original data in the DataSet.

```
daProducts.Update(ProductDataSet1.Products)
```

9. Build and run the application.

10. Click **Fill** to fill the DataSet and display the data in the DataGrid.

11. Change the **ProductName** and **UnitPrice** values for some rows, and then click **Get modified rows** to display the current and original data in these rows.

12. Click **Update** to send all updates to the data source.

13. In the Server Explorer, verify that the products have been updated.

14. Return to your application and click **Get modified rows**. There are no modified rows in the DataSet now because any pending modifications have been saved to the data source.

The solution for this practice is located at
\<install folder\>\Practices\Mod06_2\Lesson4\CatalogEditor\

Lesson: How to Handle Conflicts

- **What Conflicts Can Occur?**
- **How to Detect Conflicts**
- **How to Resolve Conflicts**

Introduction

When you write a disconnected application, you might experience data conflicts when you try to update the data source. This happens if the data source has been changed by another application or service while your application was disconnected from the data source.

In this lesson, you will learn how to detect potential data conflicts before they happen. You will see how to use the **HasErrors** property to detect errors in a DataSet, DataTable, or DataRow. You will also learn how to resolve these conflicts in your application.

Lesson objectives

After completing this lesson, you will be able to:

- Explain when conflicts can occur.
- Define optimistic concurrency.
- Detect and resolve conflicts by using the **HasErrors** property.

What Conflicts Can Occur?

- **Disconnected applications use optimistic concurrency**
  - Releases database locks between data operations
- **Data conflicts can occur when you update the database**
  - Another application or service might have already changed the data
- **Examples**
  - Deleting a previously deleted row
  - Changing a previously changed column
- **Practice**

Introduction

Disconnected ADO.NET applications use optimistic concurrency. This can cause conflicts when the application tries to update the data source. You can write code to detect these conflicts, and handle them accordingly.

Definition of optimistic concurrency

In *optimistic concurrency,* database locks are released as soon as data retrieval operations or data update operations are complete. Disconnected applications use optimistic concurrency so that other applications can query and update the database concurrently.

This differs from connected applications, which often use pessimistic concurrency. The database is kept locked while a series of related data operations are performed. This stops other applications from accessing the database until the related operations have been completed, preventing conflicts at the expense of temporarily denying database access to other applications.

Scenario

A disconnected application retrieves customer records from the central database at the start of the day. During the day, a mobile worker modifies, adds, and deletes records while disconnected from the database.

At the end of the day, the mobile worker connects to the corporate network and tries to update the central database with these changes. Unfortunately, a coworker has already modified some of the customer records in the database. The application needs to detect which customer records are in conflict, and must resolve these conflicts in an appropriate way.

Practice

Group Discussion: What specific conflicts can occur when the disconnected application tries to update the data source? How can the disconnected application resolve these conflicts?

How to Detect Conflicts

- **The Data Adapter Configuration Wizard can generate SQL statements to detect conflicts**

- **When you update the database:**

  - Data modification commands compare the current data in the database against your original values

  - Any discrepancies cause a conflict error

Visual Basic Example   Visual C# Example

Introduction

The Data Adapter Configuration Wizard can generate SQL statements to detect conflicts. The wizard adds SQL tests to the **InsertCommand**, **UpdateCommand**, and **DeleteCommand**. These tests check to see if the data in the database has not been changed since you retrieved it into your application.

How the wizard supports optimistic concurrency

When you use the Data Adapter Configuration Wizard to create a DataAdapter that uses SQL statements, you can specify **Advanced Options** by using the Generate the SQL statements screen. One of these options is **Use optimistic concurrency**.

- If you choose this option, the wizard will add tests to your SQL statements to detect conflict errors that arise because of optimistic concurrency.

- If you do not choose this option, the wizard will not add conflict tests to your SQL statements. Any changes your application makes to data in the database will overwrite changes made by other users.

Example of how the wizard supports optimistic concurrency

The following example shows how the Data Adapter Configuration Wizard helps detect conflicts that arise because of optimistic concurrency. The example sets the **UpdateCommand** for a DataAdapter. For simplicity, the example uses a simplified Customers table containing only two columns: CustomerID and CompanyName.

The **UpdateCommand** object requires the following five parameters:

- The first and second parameters specify the current CustomerID and CompanyName for the row.

- The third and fourth parameters specify the original CustomerID and CompanyName for the row. The SQL statement has a WHERE clause to ensure that the row in the database still contains these original values.

- The final parameter is used in a **SELECT** statement to retrieve the updated row from the database. This ensures that the application has the very latest row data, after any trigger operations or default values assignments by the database.

```
' Visual Basic
Me.cmUpdate.CommandText = _
    "UPDATE Customers " & _
    "SET CustomerID=@CustomerID, CompanyName=@CompanyName " & _
    "    WHERE (CustomerID  = @Original_CustomerID) " & _
    "    AND    (CompanyName = @Original_CompanyName); " & _
    "SELECT CustomerID, CompanyName FROM Customers " & _
    "    WHERE (CustomerID = @Select_CustomerID)"

Me.cmUpdate.Parameters.Add(New SqlParameter( _
    "@CustomerID", _
    SqlDbType.NChar, 5, ParameterDirection.Input, False, _
    0, 0, "CustomerID", DataRowVersion.Current, Nothing))

Me.cmUpdate.Parameters.Add(New SqlParameter( _
    "@CompanyName", _
    SqlDbType.NVarChar, 40, ParameterDirection.Input, False, _
    0, 0, "CompanyName", DataRowVersion.Current, Nothing))

Me.cmUpdate.Parameters.Add(New SqlParameter( _
    "@Original_CustomerID", _
    SqlDbType.NChar, 5, ParameterDirection.Input, False, _
    0, 0 , "CustomerID", DataRowVersion.Original, Nothing))

Me.cmUpdate.Parameters.Add(New SqlParameter( _
    "@Original_CompanyName", _
    SqlDbType.NVarChar, 40, ParameterDirection.Input, False, _
    0, 0, "CompanyName", DataRowVersion.Original, Nothing))

Me.cmUpdate.Parameters.Add(New SqlParameter( _
    "@Select_CustomerID", _
    SqlDbType.NChar, 5, ParameterDirection.Input, False, _
    0, 0, "CustomerID", DataRowVersion.Current, Nothing))
```

Code continued on the following page

```csharp
// Visual C#
this.cmUpdate.CommandText =
    "UPDATE Customers " +
    "SET CustomerID=@CustomerID, CompanyName=@CompanyName " +
    "   WHERE (CustomerID = @Original_CustomerID) " +
    "   AND   (CompanyName = @Original_CompanyName); " +
    "SELECT CustomerID, CompanyName FROM Customers " +
    "   WHERE (CustomerID = @Select_CustomerID)";

this.cmUpdate.Parameters.Add(new SqlParameter(
    "@CustomerID",
    SqlDbType.NChar, 5, ParameterDirection.Input, false,
    0, 0, "CustomerID", DataRowVersion.Current, null));

this.cmUpdate.Parameters.Add(new SqlParameter(
    "@CompanyName",
    SqlDbType.NVarChar, 40, ParameterDirection.Input, false,
    0, 0, "CompanyName", DataRowVersion.Current, null));

this.cmUpdate.Parameters.Add(new SqlParameter(
    "@Original_CustomerID",
    SqlDbType.NChar, 5, ParameterDirection.Input, false,
    0, 0 , "CustomerID", DataRowVersion.Original, null));

this.cmUpdate.Parameters.Add(new SqlParameter(
    "@Original_CompanyName",
    SqlDbType.NVarChar, 40, ParameterDirection.Input, false,
    0, 0, "CompanyName", DataRowVersion.Original, null));

this.cmUpdate.Parameters.Add(new SqlParameter(
    "@Select_CustomerID",
    SqlDbType.NChar, 5, ParameterDirection.Input, false,
    0, 0, "CustomerID", DataRowVersion.Current, null));
```

How to Resolve Conflicts

- **Use the HasErrors property to test for errors**
  - Test a DataSet, DataTable, or DataRow
- **Choose one of these strategies to resolve conflicts:**
  - "Last in wins"
  - Retain conflicting rows in your DataSet so you can update the database again later
  - Reject conflicting rows and revert to the original values in your DataSet
  - Reject conflicting rows and reload the latest data from the database
- **Practice**

Visual Basic Example   **Visual C# Example**

Introduction

You use the **HasErrors** property to resolve conflicts when you update data in a disconnected application. You can use this property to find the location and nature of the error in your DataSet.

Definition

The DataSet, DataTable, and DataRow classes each provide a **HasErrors** property. You can use this property on any of these objects to identify conflicts and other errors at any level of granularity in your data. The DataRow class also has a **GetColumnsInError** method to get the columns in error for a particular row.

How to resolve conflicts

To resolve conflicts, choose one of the following strategies:

- Use a "last in wins" approach, so that data changes made by your application overwrite any database changes made by other applications. This approach is effective for administrative applications that need to force changes through a database.

  To achieve this effect, do not choose **Use optimistic concurrency** when you create the DataAdapter in the Data Adapter Configuration Wizard.

- Do not force conflicting data changes on the database. Retain the conflicting changes locally, in your DataSet, so that the user can try to update the database again later.

  This is the default behavior when you choose the **Use optimistic concurrency** option in the Data Adapter Configuration Wizard.

- Reject the conflicting data changes in the local DataSet, and revert to the data originally loaded from the database.

  To achieve this effect, call the **RejectChanges** method on the conflicting DataSet, DataTable, or DataRow.

- Reject the conflicting data changes in the local DataSet, and reload the latest data from the database.

  To achieve this effect, call the **Clear** method on the DataSet, and then call the **Fill** method on the DataAdapter to reload the latest data.

Example of resolving conflicts

The following example shows how to resolve conflicts in a disconnected application.

After an Update operation, the **HasErrors** property is tested to see if the DataSet has any errors. If there are errors, a loop is used to check each table in turn. If a table has errors, another loop is used to check each of its rows. If a row has errors, the **GetColumnsInError** method is used to find the columns in error. The **ClearErrors** and **RejectChanges** methods are then called to clear the error status and reject the conflicting data in each row.

```vb
' Visual Basic
Try
  daCustomers.Update(dsCustomers)
Catch ex As System.Exception
  If dsCustomers.HasErrors Then
    Dim table As DataTable
    For Each table In dsCustomers.Tables

      If table.HasErrors Then
        Dim row As DataRow
        For Each row In table.Rows

          If row.HasErrors Then
            MessageBox.Show("Row: " & row("CustomerID"), _
                          row.RowError)

            Dim column As DataColumn
            For Each column In row.GetColumnsInError()
              MessageBox.Show(column.ColumnName, _
                          "Error in this column")
            Next
            row.ClearErrors()
            row.RejectChanges()
          End If
        Next
      End If
    Next
  End If
End Try
```

Code continued on the following page

```csharp
// Visual C#
try
{
  daCustomers.Update(dsCustomers);
}
catch(System.Exception ex)
{
  if(dsCustomers.HasErrors)
  {
    foreach(DataTable table in dsCustomers.Tables)
    {
      if(table.HasErrors)
      {
        foreach(DataRow row in table.Rows)
        {
          if(row.HasErrors)
          {
            MessageBox.Show("Row: " + row["CustomerID"],
                               row.RowError);

            foreach(DataColumn col in row.GetColumnsInError())
            {
              MessageBox.Show(col.ColumnName,
                                 "Error in this column");
            }
            row.ClearErrors();
            row.RejectChanges();
          }
        }
      }
    }
  }
}
```

Practice

In this practice, you will continue to build a Windows Application that allows the user to edit the Northwind Traders online product catalog.

▶ **Build a Windows Application that allows the user to edit the Northwind Traders online product catalog**

1. Open the Windows Application solution you used in the previous practice, or the solution named **CatalogEditor** at the following location:

   <install folder>\Practices\Mod06_2\Lesson4\CatalogEditor\

2. Run the application. Change the name of a product. Do NOT click **Update** yet.

3. Use the Server Explorer to change the same product name to a different value.

4. Return to the running application, and click **Update**.

   What happens?

   Why?

   What must the user do to force a change through to the underlying data source?

5. Stop the running application.

6. Modify the **Click** event handler for the **Update** button as follows. Check for a **DBConcurrencyException** to indicate a conflict error. If this occurs, clear the error status and accept the latest value for the conflicting row from the database.

```
Try

    daProducts.Update(ProductDataSet1.Products)

Catch ex As System.Data.DBConcurrencyException

    MessageBox.Show( _
      "Conflict with an existing record. " & _
      "You have lost your changes for product: " & _
       ex.Row("ProductName").ToString(), _
      "Warning!")

    ' Clear the error status for the conflicting row
    ex.Row.ClearErrors()

    ' Accept the latest value for this row from the database
    ex.Row.AcceptChanges()

End Try
```

7. Run and test your application. Conflicts are now automatically handled by resetting conflicting values to the central version, and the user can immediately reenter the value they want.

The solution for this practice is located at
<install folder>\Practices\Mod06_2\Lesson5\CatalogEditor\

Review

■ **Configuring a DataAdapter to Retrieve Information**

■ **Populating a DataSet Using a DataAdapter**

■ **Configuring a DataAdapter to Update the Underlying Data Source**

■ **Persisting Changes to a Data Source**

■ **How to Handle Conflicts**

1. How do you create and configure a DataAdapter to provide a disconnected application with read-only access to a Microsoft SQL Server™ 2000 database?

2. What is the most efficient way to populate a DataSet by using a DataAdapter?

3. How do you configure a DataAdapter to allow a data source to be updated from the contents of a DataSet?

4. How do you persist data changes back to the data source? How do you control the order in which different types of changes are persisted?

5. What types of conflicts can occur when you update a data source in a disconnected application? How do you detect and resolve these conflicts?

Lab 6.2: Retrieving and Updating Customers and Orders Data

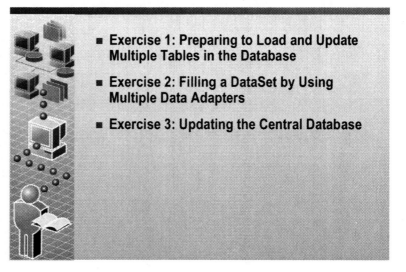

- Exercise 1: Preparing to Load and Update Multiple Tables in the Database
- Exercise 2: Filling a DataSet by Using Multiple Data Adapters
- Exercise 3: Updating the Central Database

Objectives

After completing this lab, you will be able to:

- Create DataAdapters to access multiple tables in the Northwind database.
- Define corresponding tables in a DataSet in your application.
- Specify relationships and constraints in the DataSet tables.
- Populate the DataSet and display its data in a DataGrid.
- Update the data source from the DataSet.

Prerequisites

Before working on this lab, you must have:

- Visual Basic or Visual C# programming skills.
- Familiarity with the Visual Studio .NET development environment.
- Basic knowledge about SQL stored procedures.

For more information

See the DataSet and SqlDataAdapter topics in the Visual Studio .NET documentation.

Scenario

In Lab 6.1, Retrieving Data into a Disconnected Application, you started writing a Windows Application to help salespeople at Northwind Traders work with customer data while they are away from the office.

So far, you have written code to download employee names from the central database. You have also written code to save employee names and application data locally in an XML file.

In this lab, you will extend the application so that it can retrieve and update customer and order data from the central database. The salesperson will download this data at the start of the day, and work with the data while he or she is disconnected from the central database. At the end of the day, the salesperson will connect to the central database and update any records that have been changed during the day.

Estimated time to complete this lab: 60 minutes

Exercise 1
Preparing to Load and Update Multiple Tables in the Database

Northwind Traders salespeople need to use the Windows Application to create new orders during the working day. To achieve this task, the application needs a local copy of the products, customers, orders, and order details information from the central database.

Scenario

In this exercise, you will create DataAdapters to access the Products, Customers, Orders, and Order Details tables in the Northwind database. You will then add four tables to the DataSet in your application, to correspond with the data returned by these DataAdapters.

▶ **Continue building the application**

1. Start Visual Studio .NET.

2. Open the solution you created in Lab 6.1, or open the solution **OnTheRoad** in the folder <install folder>\Labs\Lab06_2\Starter\xx\OnTheRoad, where *xx* is either VB or CS.

▶ **Create the Products table**

1. Open the **MainForm** class in Designer view and drag a **SqlDataAdapter** from the Toolbox onto the form.

2. Choose a data connection to the Northwind database on your local computer running SQL Server.

3. Click **Use SQL statements**, and then click **Next**.

4. Enter the following statement:

```
SELECT
    ProductID, ProductName, UnitPrice
FROM
    Products
```

5. Click the **Advanced Options** button and clear the **Generate Insert, Update and Delete statements** check box. Click **OK**.

6. Click **Finish**. The wizard will now create a DataAdapter with a command that will be used to populate the Products table in the data set.

7. Change the name of the new DataAdapter to **daProducts**, and change its associated **SelectCommand** to **cmSelectProducts**.

8. Right-click the **daProducts** DataAdapter and then click **Generate Dataset**.

9. Choose the existing DataSet called **OnTheRoad.NWDataSet**, clear the **Add this dataset to the designer** check box, and then click **OK**.

10. Right-click the **dsNorthwind** DataSet and then click **View Schema** to verify that the Products table has been added to the DataSet schema.

▶ **Create the Customers table**

1. Open the **MainForm** class in Designer view and drag a **SqlDataAdapter** from the Toolbox onto the form.

2. Choose a data connection to the Northwind database on your local computer running SQL Server.

3. Click **Create new stored procedures**, and then click **Next**.

4. Type the following statement. (This SQL statement is available as CustomersSQL.txt in the folder <install folder>\Labs\Lab06_2\Starter.)

```
SELECT
    Customers.CustomerID, CompanyName, ContactName, City,
Phone
FROM Customers INNER JOIN Orders ON
    Customers.CustomerID = Orders.CustomerID
WHERE (Orders.EmployeeID = @EmployeeID)
ORDER BY CompanyName
```

5. Click **Next**.

6. Change the names of the stored procedures to **SelectCustomers**, **InsertCustomers**, **UpdateCustomers**, and **DeleteCustomers**.

7. Click **Finish**. The wizard will now create a DataAdapter with four commands that will be used to populate and modify customers.

8. In the Server Explorer, modify the **SelectCustomers** stored procedure by adding DISTINCT after the SELECT keyword. This will prevent duplicate customer rows. The wizard cannot auto-generate DML statements based on SELECT DISTINCT statements.

9. Change the name of the new DataAdapter to **daCustomers**, and change its associated **XxxCommands** to **cmSelectCustomers**, **cmInsertCustomers**, **cmDeleteCustomers**, and **cmUpdateCustomers**.

10. Right-click the **daCustomers** DataAdapter and click **Generate Dataset**. Click the existing DataSet named **OnTheRoad.NWDataSet**, clear the **Add this dataset to the designer** check box, and then click **OK**.

11. If a message box appears, telling you that **NWDataSet.xsd** has been modified outside the source editor, click **Yes** to reload the file.

▶ **Create the Orders table**

1. Open the **MainForm** class in Designer view and drag a **SqlDataAdapter** from the Toolbox onto the form.

2. Choose a data connection to the Northwind database on your local computer running SQL Server.

3. Click **Create new stored procedures** and then click **Next**.

4. Type the following statement. (This SQL statement is available as OrdersSQL.txt in <install folder>\Labs\Lab06_2\Starter.)

```
SELECT OrderID, OrderDate, EmployeeID, CustomerID
FROM Orders WHERE (EmployeeID = @EmployeeID)
```

5. Click **Next**.

6. Change the names of the stored procedures to **SelectOrders**, **InsertOrders**, **UpdateOrders**, and **DeleteOrders**.

7. Click **Finish**.

8. Change the name of the new DataAdapter to **daOrders**, and change its associated **XxxCommands** to **cmSelectOrders**, **cmInsertOrders**, **cmDeleteOrders**, and **cmUpdateOrders**.

9. Right-click the **daOrders** DataAdapter and then click **Generate Dataset**. Click the existing DataSet named **OnTheRoad.NWDataSet**, clear the **Add this dataset to the designer** check box, and then click **OK**.

10. If a message box appears, telling you that **NWDataSet.xsd** has been modified outside the source editor, click **Yes** to reload the file.

▶ **Create the Order Details table**

1. Open the **MainForm** class in Designer view and drag a **SqlDataAdapter** from the Toolbox onto the form.

2. Choose a data connection to the Northwind database on your local computer running SQL Server.

3. Click **Create new stored procedures**, and then click **Next**.

4. Type the following statement. (This SQL statement is available as OrderDetailsSQL.txt in <install folder>\Labs\Lab06_2\Starter.)

```
SELECT
    [Order Details].OrderID, ProductID, UnitPrice, Quantity
FROM [Order Details] INNER JOIN Orders ON
    [Order Details].OrderID = Orders.OrderID
WHERE
    (Orders.EmployeeID = @EmployeeID)
```

5. Change the names of the stored procedures to **SelectOrderDetails**, **InsertOrderDetails**, **UpdateOrderDetails**, and **DeleteOrderDetails**.

6. Click **Finish**.

7. Change the name of the new DataAdapter to **daOrderDetails**, and change its associated **XxxCommands** to **cmSelectOrderDetails**, **cmInsertOrderDetails**, **cmDeleteOrderDetails**, and **cmUpdateOrderDetails**.

8. Change the **TableMappings** property of the **daOrderDetails** DataAdapter so that the DataSet table name does not include a space between Order and Details.

9. Right-click the **daOrderDetails** DataAdapter, click **Generate Dataset**, and then choose the existing DataSet named **OnTheRoad.NWDataSet**. Clear the **Add this dataset to the designer** check box, and then click **OK**.

10. If a message box appears, telling you that **NWDataSet.xsd** has been modified outside the source editor, click **Yes** to reload the file.

▶ **Add primary keys to the custom DataSet schema and class**

1. Right-click the **dsNorthwind** DataSet, and then click **View Schema** to verify that the Customers, Orders, and Order Details tables have been added to the DataSet schema.

2. In the **Customers** table, right-click the **CustomerID** field, and then click **Add – New key**.

3. Change the name to **PK_Customers** and click **OK**.

4. In the **Orders** table, right-click the **OrderID** field, and then click **Edit key**.

5. Change the name to **PK_Orders** and click **OK**.

6. In the **OrderDetails** table, right-click the **OrderID** field, and then click **Add – New key**.

7. Change the name to **PK_OrderDetails**, add **ProductID** to the list of fields, and then click **OK**.

8. In the **Employees** table, right-click the **EmployeeID** field, and then click **Edit key**.

9. Change the name to **PK_Employees** and click **OK**.

10. In the **Products** table, right-click the **ProductID** field, and then click **Edit key**.

11. Change the name to **PK_Products** and click **OK**.

▶ **Add relationships to the custom DataSet schema and class**

1. Right-click the **Orders** table and then click **Add – New Relation**.

2. Select **Employees** for the parent element and **Orders** for the child element. Select **EmployeeID** in the drop-down menu under **Foreign Key Fields**, and then click **OK**.

3. Right-click the **Orders** table and then click **Add – New Relation**.

4. Select **Customers** for the parent element and **Orders** for the child element. Select **CustomerID** in the drop-down menu under **Foreign Key Fields**, and then click **OK**.

5. Right-click the **OrderDetails** table and then click **Add – New Relation**.

6. Select **Orders** for the parent element and **OrderDetails** for the child element, and make sure the name is **OrdersOrderDetails**. Select **OrderID** in the drop-down menu under **Foreign Key Fields**, and then click **OK**.

7. Right-click the **OrderDetails** table and then click **Add – New Relation**.

8. Select **Products** for the parent element and **OrderDetails** for the child element, make sure the name is **ProductsOrderDetails**, select **ProductID** in the drop-down menu under **Foreign Key Fields**, and then click **OK**.

9. Save and close the XSD file.

▶ **Test your code**

• Build your application and correct any errors. You are not ready to execute the application yet, because you have not written any code to fill the DataSet from the DataAdapers.

Exercise 2
Filling a DataSet by Using Multiple Data Adapters

When a Northwind Traders salesperson is connected to the company's central database, he or she can download data for products, customers, orders, and order details. This information will be held in a local DataSet within the application, so that the user can continue to use the data while the application is disconnected from the database.

Scenario

In this exercise, you will use the **Fill** method on the DataAdapters to fill the various tables in the DataSet. You will also bind the DataSet to a DataGrid, to display the data on the screen.

▶ **Start with the solution to the previous exercise**

- If you did not complete the previous exercise, open the solution **OnTheRoad** in the folder
  <install folder>\Labs\Lab06_2\Solution\Ex1\xx\OnTheRoad, where *xx* is either VB or CS.

▶ **Refresh the DataGrid**

1. In the **MainForm**, add code to the **RefreshUI** method to bind the DataGrid to the **Customers** table in the DataSet.

   ```
   ' Visual Basic
   Me.grd.SetDataBinding(Me.dsNorthwind, "Customers")
   ```

   ```
   // Visual C#
   this.grd.SetDataBinding(this.dsNorthwind, "Customers");
   ```

2. Locate the **mnuFill_Click** procedure, and insert a new line after the line that retrieves the selected employee ID into the field. For example:

   ```
   ' Visual Basic
   If frmLogon.ShowDialog(Me) = DialogResult.OK Then
      Me.EmployeeID =
   CInt(frmLogon.lstEmployees.SelectedValue)
      ' insert new code here
   ```

   ```
   // Visual C#
   if (frmLogon.ShowDialog(this) == DialogResult.OK)
   {
      this.EmployeeID =
         (int)frmLogon.lstEmployees.SelectedValue;
      // insert new code here
   ```

3. Write code to try to fill the new tables you just added to the DataSet (Products, Customers, Orders, OrderDetails) by using the DataAdapters created by the wizard. Catch any exceptions and display a warning message.

   Prewritten code is available if you want to use it, at the following locations:

   > <install folder>\Labs\Lab06_2\Starter\VB\FillTablesVB.txt

   > or

   > <install folder>\Labs\Lab06_2\Starter\CS\FillTablesCS.txt

   Note that the following two lines of existing code should be inside but at the end of the **Try** block because the temporary DataSet should only be used if it has been successfully loaded with data:

```
' Visual Basic
Me.dsNorthwind = tempNW
Me.RefreshUI()
```

```
// Visual C#
this.dsNorthwind = tempNW;
this.RefreshUI();
```

▶ **Test the filling and saving of the complete DataSet**

1. Build the application and correct any build errors.

2. Open the **MainForm** class in Code view and set a breakpoint at the beginning of the **mnuFill_Click** procedure.

3. In the Server Explorer, set breakpoints on the first line of the **SelectCustomers**, **SelectOrders**, and **SelectOrderDetails** stored procedures.

4. Run the application.

5. If a message box appears at start up, asking if you want to connect to the central database, click **No**.

6. On the **File** menu, click **Get from central database**.

7. Step through the code line by line until the form appears.

8. Choose **Fuller, Andrew**, and then click **OK**.

9. Continue to step through the code line by line. Notice the value of the EmployeeID field.

10. When stepping through the code that fills the Customers table, notice that the debugger steps into the correct stored procedure, and that the value passed to the stored procedure for the @EmployeeID parameter is the same value as the EmployeeID field.

11. Continue to step through the code line by line until the main form appears with the DataGrid full of customers and orders taken by Andrew Fuller.

12. Close the application, and in Internet Explorer, check that the **OnTheRoad.xml** file contains all records in the DataSet.

13. Run the application again and notice that the DataSet is correctly reloaded automatically.

Exercise 3
Updating the Central Database

When a Northwind Traders salesperson reconnects to the company's central database, he or she can persist any changes made to the Products, Customers, Orders, and Order Details tables in the DataSet.

Scenario

In this exercise, you will use the **Update** method on the DataAdapters to update the central database.

To update the database, you must separate the insert, update, and delete changes made to the DataSet so that they can be applied to the three tables (Customer, Orders, Order Details) in the correct order. For example, insertions of customers must occur before insertions of orders, but deletions of customers must come *after* deletions of orders.

▶ **Start with the solution to the previous exercise**

• If you did not complete the previous exercise, open the solution **OnTheRoad** in the folder
<install folder>\Labs\Lab06_2\Solution\Ex2\xx\OnTheRoad, where *xx* is either VB or CS.

▶ **Update the central database**

You will now add code to the **mnuUpdate_Click** event handler, to update the central database. Prewritten code is available at the following locations:

<install folder>\Labs\Lab06_2\Starter\VB\UpdateVB.txt

or

<install folder>\Labs\Lab06_2\Starter\CS\UpdateCS.txt

By using the prewritten code, or by writing code yourself, perform the following tasks in the **mnuUpdate_Click** event handler:

1. Write code to declare nine local DataTable variables named **dsInsertCustomers, dsInsertOrders, dsInsertOrderDetails, dsUpdateCustomers, dsUpdateOrders, dsUpdateOrderDetails, dsDeleteCustomers, dsDeleteOrders**, and **dsDeleteOrderDetails**.

2. Instantiate the DataTables with the results of calling the **GetChanges** method of the three tables in the **dsNorthwind** DataSet, passing a **DataRowState** parameter to separate insert, update, and delete changes.

3. Write code to try to call the **Update** method of each of the three DataAdapters for the insert, update, and delete changes made to the DataTables in the correct order, if the DataTables exist.

4. Write code to accept changes to the **dsNorthwind** DataSet if the updates are successful.

5. Write code to catch any exceptions by displaying a message box and exiting the procedure.

6. Write code to ask the user if he or she wants to refresh the DataSet, and if so, call the **mnuFill_Click** procedure.

▶ **Test the updating of the central database**

1. Clear all existing breakpoints in your application.

2. Set a new breakpoint at the beginning of the **mnuUpdate_Click** procedure.

3. Create two watch expressions to monitor the value of the OrderID field of the first row in the Orders and OrderDetails tables:

```
' Visual Basic
dsInserts.Tables("Orders").Rows(0)(0)
dsInserts.Tables("OrderDetails").Rows(0)(0)


// Visual C#
dsInserts.Tables["Orders"].Rows[0][0]
dsInserts.Tables["OrderDetails"].Rows[0][0]
```

4. In the Server Explorer, set breakpoints on the first line of the **UpdateCustomers**, **UpdateOrders**, **UpdateOrderDetails**, **InsertOrders**, **InsertOrderDetails**, **DeleteOrders**, and **DeleteOrderDetails** stored procedures.

5. Run your application.

6. Make changes to the DataSet. For example:

   a. Change the contact name for an existing customer.

   b. Change the order date for an existing order.

   c. Insert some new order detail rows for an existing order.

7. Insert a new order (and order details) for an existing customer that has an OrderID assigned by the DataSet that will not match the OrderID that will be assigned by SQL Server when the order is inserted into the central database.

   a. Click on a blank order line as if inserting a new order. Notice the automatically assigned OrderID.

   b. Click on an existing order, then click back on the blank order row. Notice that the automatically assigned OrderID has incremented by one. Repeat this step several times.

   c. Enter valid information for a new order, including some order detail rows. Note the OrderID assigned by the DataSet.

8. On the **File** menu, click **Update to central database**.

9. Step through the code and stored procedures. Note the values of parameters passed to the stored procedures, and use the watch expressions to monitor what happens to OrderIDs when they are assigned by SQL Server.

> **Note** Notice that after the **InsertOrders** stored procedure is executed, the OrderID assigned by SQL Server is returned to the DataSet, and is then used by the DataSet to update the related OrderDetails table before inserting the related rows.

10. Close your application.
11. Restart the application and try to delete the order you added previously.
12. On the **File** menu, click **Update to central database**.
13. Step through the code and notice which stored procedures are run, and the values of parameters passed.
14. Close the application.

msdn training

Module 7: Building and Consuming a Web Service That Uses ADO.NET

Contents

Microsoft

Overview

- **Building and Consuming a Web Service That Returns Data**

- **Lab 7.1: Troubleshooting an ADO.NET Application**

Introduction

Web services allow applications to communicate regardless of operating system or programming language. Web services can be implemented on any platform and are defined through public standards organizations. Sharing data through Web services allows the Web services to be independent of each other while simultaneously enabling them to loosely link themselves into a collaborating group that performs a particular task.

In this module, you will learn how to create a Web service that returns data.

Objectives

After completing this module, you will be able to:

- Build a Web service.

- Consume a Web service in a client application.

- Troubleshoot errors in a Microsoft® ADO.NET application.

Lesson: Building and Consuming a Web Service That Returns Data

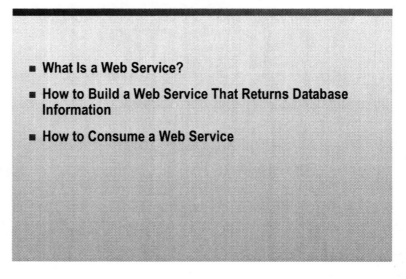

- **What Is a Web Service?**
- **How to Build a Web Service That Returns Database Information**
- **How to Consume a Web Service**

Introduction

Web services are making possible a new era of distributed application development. By using ADO.NET, you can build Web services that return data, and these Web services can be consumed by multiple applications locally or across the Internet.

Lesson objectives

After completing this lesson, you will be able to:

- Explain what a Web service is.
- Build a Web service that returns data.
- Consume a Web service.

What Is a Web Service?

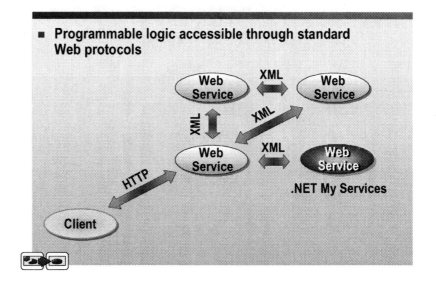

Definition

A Web service is a unit of programmable logic that is accessible by using standard Web protocols such as HTTP and XML. A Web service can be used locally by a single application, or published on the Internet for use by many different applications.

Web services allow applications to share data and functionality, and use XML-based messaging to communicate between systems that use different component models, operating systems, and programming languages. Developers can create applications that combine Web services from a variety of sources in much the same way that developers traditionally use components when creating a distributed application.

Using XML-based messaging to communicate between a Web service and a client application frees both the Web service client and the Web service provider from needing any knowledge of each other beyond inputs, outputs, and location.

Example

A Web service can provide reusable functionality that many clients can share.

For example, a challenge faced by e-commerce applications is the need to calculate charges for a variety of shipping options. Such applications would require current shipping cost tables from each shipping company to use in these calculations.

Alternatively, an application could send an XML-based message over the Internet, using a standard transport protocol such as HTTP, to the shipper's cost-calculation Web service. The message might provide the weight and dimensions of a package, origin and destination locations, and other information such as class of service. The shipper's Web service would then calculate the shipping charge by using the latest cost table, and then return this amount to the calling application in a simple XML-based response message for use in calculating the total charge to the customer.

How to Build a Web Service That Returns Database Information

- **Web services that return database information typically:**
  - Establish a connection to a data source
  - Define the structure of a Typed DataSet (by using an .xsd file)
  - Create an empty instance of the Typed DataSet
  - Run a query or perform calculations, and fill the DataSet; a DataAdapter is commonly used to fill the DataSet
  - Return the DataSet to the client application for further processing

Visual Basic Example

Introduction

Creating a Web service is similar to creating any component that provides programmatic access to its application logic. To create a Web service, you need some functionality that constitutes the service you want to expose, a service description that defines how to use the service, and an infrastructure to support receiving and processing requests and sending responses. Fortunately, much of the required infrastructure is generated automatically by Microsoft Visual Studio® .NET.

Building a Web service that returns data

To build a Web service that returns data, you first create a new Web service by using Visual Studio. NET. Typically, this Web Service will:

- Establish a connection to a data source.
- Define the structure of a typed DataSet (by using an .xsd file).
- Create an empty instance of the typed DataSet.
- Run a query or perform calculations, and fill the DataSet. A DataAdapter is commonly used to fill the DataSet.
- Return the DataSet to the client application for further processing.

Example

The following example defines a Web method that takes a customer's city as input, queries the Customers table in the Northwind database, and returns a DataSet with information about all of the customers in that city.

```
'Connect to the Northwind DataBase
Dim myCn as New SqlConnection()

myCn.ConnectionString = "data source=localhost;" & _
"initial catalog=Northwind;" & _
"integrated security=SSPI;persist " & _
"security info=false"

myCn.Open()
```

This example assumes that a **SqlDataAdapter** object has been defined with the following parameterized query:

```
SELECT CustomerId, CompanyName, ContactName, Address, City,
Region, PostalCode, Country, Phone, Fax
FROM Customers
WHERE (City like @city)
```

Note When you create parameterized queries by using the **SqlDataAdapter** object, use named arguments to mark parameters.

When you create parameterized queries by using the **OleDbDataAdapter** object, use the "?" character to mark parameters.

```
'Example of a Web Service that returns a DataSet
Imports System.Web.Services
Public Class Service1
  Inherits System.Web.Services.WebService

  'This method accepts a city name as a query parameter
  <WebMethod()> Public Function GetCustomers( _
    ByVal city As String) As CustDS

    'Create an instance of a typed DataSet to hold the
    'information retrieved from SQL Server
    Dim ds As New CustDS()

    'Set the city parameter of the query, 0 is the first in
    'the collection
    SqlDataAdapter1.SelectCommand.Parameters(0).Value = city

    'Fill the local DataSet with the results
    SqlDataAdapter1.Fill(ds)

    'Pass the results to the calling program
    Return ds

  End Function

End Class
```

Practice

A salesperson for Northwind Traders travels to various cities to visit customers and take orders. Because customer information changes frequently, the Customer Information application uses an XML Web service to retrieve information about customers in a particular city from the company's central database. The salesperson then uses the application to generate the list of customers to visit in a particular city.

▶ **Create a Web service**

1. Start Visual Studio .NET and create a new project on the local server. Use the information in the following table.

Option	Value
Project Type	Microsoft Visual Basic® or Microsoft Visual C#™
Template	ASP.NET Web service
Location	http://localhost/2389/Practices/Mod07/ClientRosterService

2. Use the Server Explorer to add a new connection to the Northwind database on your local Microsoft SQL Server™.

3. In the Solution Explorer, double-click **Service1.asmx**. This displays the design surface for the Web service.

4. Click the **Data** tab of the toolbox, and then drag a **SqlDataAdapter** object onto the design surface. Use the information in the following table to configure the **SqlDataAdapter** object by using the wizard.

Option	Value
Connection	Localhost.Northwind.dbo
Query type	Use SQL statements
Query	SELECT CustomerId, CompanyName, ContactName, Address, City, Region, PostalCode, Country, Phone
	FROM Customers
	WHERE (City like @city)

5. Right-click the new DataAdapter, and then click **Generate DataSet**. Use the information in the following table.

Property	Value
New DataSet Name	CustDS
Tables	Customers
Add this dataset to the designer	Checked

6. Right-click the new DataSet named **CustDS1**, and then click **View Schema**. Examine the generated schema.

► **Create a Web method that returns a DataSet**

1. View the code for Service1.asmx.

2. Create a new Web method by inserting the following code after the commented example:

```vb
'Visual Basic

<WebMethod()> Public Function GetCustomers( _
    ByVal city As String) As CustDS

  Dim ds As New CustDS()
  SqlDataAdapter1.SelectCommand.Parameters(0).Value = city
  SqlDataAdapter1.Fill(ds)
  Return ds
End Function
```

```csharp
// Visual C#

[WebMethod()] public CustDS GetCustomers(String city)
{
    CustDS ds = new CustDS();
    sqlDataAdapter1.SelectCommand.Parameters[0].Value
        = city;
    sqlDataAdapter1.Fill(ds);
    return ds;
}
```

3. In the **Solution Explorer**, double-click the **Web.config** file.

4. After the line that sets the authentication mode (<authentication mode="Windows" />), add a line to enable impersonation.

```
<identity impersonate="true" />
```

5. On the **Build** menu, click **Rebuild Solution**, and fix any errors that are found.

► **Disable anonymous access to the XML Web service**

1. Start the **Internet Services Manager**. It is one of the Administrative Tools installed with Windows 2000 Server.

2. Expand the **Default Web Site**.

3. Right-click the \2389\Practices\Mod07\ClientRosterService\ virtual directory and then click **Properties**.

4. Click the **Directory Security** tab.

5. In the **Anonymous access and authentication control** section, click **Edit**.

6. Unselect the **Anonymous access** check box. Click **OK**.

7. Click **OK**.

8. Close the **Internet Services Manager**.

► **Test the Web service**

1. Right-click Service1.asmx, and then click Browse With. Select Microsoft Internet Explorer from the list and then click Browse.

2. Examine the default page that is generated to describe the Web service.

3. Click GetCustomers.

4. Test the Web method by using London as the parameter value. Click Invoke.

5. Examine the XML returned by the Web service. Notice that it contains both schema information and data.

6. Close both Internet Explorer windows.

7. Close your solution in Visual Studio .NET.

Note   A sample solution is provided for this practice. To use the solution, use the following steps.

▶ **Use the XML Web service solution**

1. Open the solution named **ClientRosterService.sln** in the folder **<install folder>\Practices\Mod07\Lesson1\ClientRosterService**.

2. On the **Build** menu, click **Rebuild Solution**, and fix any errors that are found.

3. Start the **Internet Services Manager**. It is one of the Administrative Tools installed with Windows 2000 Server.

4. Expand the **Default Web Site**.

5. Right-click the \2389\Practices\Mod07\Lesson1\ClientRosterService\ virtual directory, click **All Tasks**, and then click **Configure Server Extensions**.

6. In the wizard, click **Next** until the wizard gets to the last page, and then click **Finish**.

7. Follow the steps described above in the procedure **Disable anonymous access to the XML Web service**.

How to Consume a Web Service

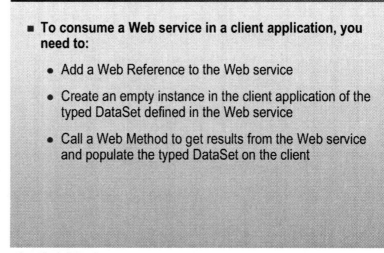

- **To consume a Web service in a client application, you need to:**
  - Add a Web Reference to the Web service
  - Create an empty instance in the client application of the typed DataSet defined in the Web service
  - Call a Web Method to get results from the Web service and populate the typed DataSet on the client

<u>Visual Basic Example</u>

Introduction

Because Web services are accessible by using Uniform Resource Locators (URLs), HTTP, and XML, applications running on any operating system and in any language can access these services. The decentralized nature of Web services enables both the client and the Web service to function as autonomous units. Therefore, there are countless ways to consume a Web service.

For example, you can include a call to a Web service in a Web application, a middleware component, or even another Web service. No matter what type of Web service client is used, calling a Web service only requires the sending of a properly formatted request message that conforms to the published service description for that Web service. Depending on the nature of the Web service being called, it may send a response message in return. The originator of the request must have the ability to extract the necessary information from this message.

To consume a Web service

To consume a Web service in a client application, you need to:

- Add a reference to the Web service in the client application.
- Create an instance in the client application of the typed DataSet defined in the Web service.
- Call a Web method to get results from the Web service and populate the typed DataSet on the client.

When you create a Web reference to a Web service, the classes and methods defined in the Web service are then available for use in the client application. Web services that are designed to return database information usually define a typed DataSet that is used to return results to the client. When you add a Web reference, Visual Studio .NET imports the definition of the resulting DataSet into the client application. You typically create an instance of this DataSet on the client to capture results from the Web service. Finally, you call a Web method to return data to the client and populate the DataSet.

You can use Universal Description, Discovery, and Integration (UDDI) to find out what methods are available from the Web service. When you find the Web service that you want to access, you need to add a Web reference to that Web service within the client application. This allows you to access the Web service's classes and method as if they were local to your client application.

Security

If the XML Web service has been secured so that callers of the XML Web service must be authenticated, credentials must be passed to the XML Web service before methods can be successfully executed.

Example

The following example retrieves a DataSet from a Web service. In this application, a client form sends the city where customers live as a parameter to a Web service. The Web service connects to SQL Server and executes a query to retrieve a list of the customers in that city. The results are sent to the client as a strongly typed DataSet.

The client application receives the DataSet and uses it to populate the local cache. This cache is a DataSet of the same type defined by the Web service. The application binds a DataGrid control to the local cache to display the results.

The form in the client application contains a text box to record the choice of city, a DataGrid to display results, and a button to process the request for information.

```
Public Class Form_ClientList
  Inherits System.Windows.Forms.Form

  'Create a new strongly typed DataSet based on the one
  'declared in the Web service.

  'Web reference to the Web service that defines CustDS
  'already exists.

  Public CustDS1 As New ClientList.localhost.CustDS()
  Private myCity As String
  .
  .
  'Contact the Web Service, execute the query and retrieve the
  'results

  Private Sub Btn_GetClients_Click( _
    ByVal sender As System.Object, _
    ByVal e As System.EventArgs) _
      Handles Btn_GetClients.Click

    'Create a variable to point to a Web Service in order to
    'use the methods defined in the service.
    Dim ws As New ClientList.localhost.Service1()

    'Pass current user security context to XML Web service
    ws.Credentials = _
      System.Net.CredentialCache.DefaultCredentials

    'Get the city parameter from the form
    myCity = txt_city.text

    'Use the Web method to retrieve results.
    'Merge the results into the local cache.
    CustDS1.Merge(ws.GetCustomers(myCity))

  End Sub

End Class
```

Practice

A salesperson for Northwind Traders travels to various cities to visit customers and take orders. Because customer information changes frequently, the Customer Information application uses an XML Web service to retrieve information about customers in a particular city from the company's central database. The salesperson then uses the application to generate the list of customers to visit in a particular city.

In this practice, you will build a simple client Microsoft Windows® Application to consume the Web service.

► **Create a client form**

1. Start Visual Studio .NET and create a new project. Use the information in the following table.

Option	Value
Project Type	Visual Basic or Visual C#
Template	Windows Application
Name	ClientList
Location	<install folder>\Practices\Mod07

2. Add a button to the form. Use the information in the following table.

Property	Value
Name	btnGetClients
Text	List Customers
Dock	bottom

3. Add a text box to the form. Use the information in the following table.

Property	Value
Name	txtCity
Text	Enter a city
Dock	Top

4. Add a DataGrid to the form. Use the information in the following table.

Property	Value
Name	dgrCustGrid
Dock	Fill

► **Add a Web reference**

1. In the Solution Explorer, in the **ClientList** project, right-click the **References** folder, and then click **Add Web Reference**.

2. Enter http://localhost/2389/Practices/Mod07/ClientRosterService/Service1.asmx in the **Address** box.

3. Click **Add Reference**.

4. In the Solution Explorer, in the **ClientList** project, expand the **Web References** folder and then expand **localhost**. Notice that CustDS.xsd describes the schema of the DataSet returned by the Web service.

5. In the **Class View**, expand **ClientList** and then expand **localhost**. Notice that a class named CustDS has been created. In the next procedure, you will create a strongly typed DataSet based on this class.

▶ **Use the methods and classes from a Web service**

1. From the **Data** tab of the toolbox, add a new DataSet to the form. Use the information in the following table.

Option	Value
Typed DataSet	Selected
Name	ClientList.localhost.CustDS

2. Set the **Data Source** property of the DataGrid to **CustDS1.Customers**.

3. Copy the following code to the **btnGetClients_Click** procedure:

```
Dim ws As New ClientList.localhost.Service1()
ws.Credentials = _
  System.Net.CredentialCache.DefaultCredentials
CustDS1.Merge(ws.GetCustomers(txtCity.Text))
```

4. Save the form and build the solution.

▶ **Test your application**

1. Start the ClientList application in Debug mode.

2. Type **London** in the text box, and then click **List Customers**.

3. Examine the results.

4. Close the application.

Note   A sample solution is provided for this practice.
Open the solution named **ClientList.sln** in the folder **install_folder\Practices\Mod07\Lesson2\ClientList**. To test this application, follow the steps described above in the procedure **Test your application**.

Review

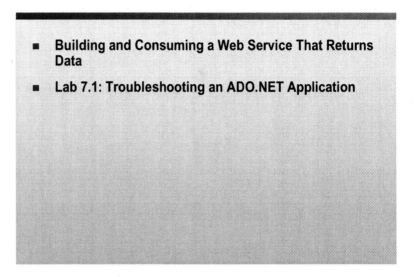

- **Building and Consuming a Web Service That Returns Data**
- **Lab 7.1: Troubleshooting an ADO.NET Application**

1. You are building a Web Service to return database information to a client application. How should you pass back query results to the client application?

2. You are building a client application that calls a Web service. What must you do before calling a Web method to return a DataSet?

Lab 7.1: Troubleshooting an ADO.NET Application

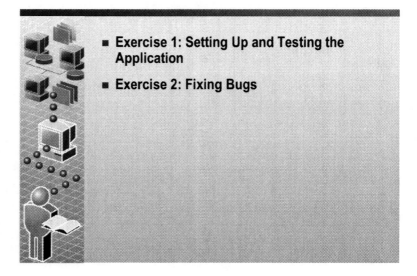

- **Exercise 1: Setting Up and Testing the Application**
- **Exercise 2: Fixing Bugs**

Objectives

After completing this lab, you will be able to:

- Debug a Windows application and an XML Web service that use ADO.NET.

Prerequisites

Before working on this lab, you must have:

- Experience testing and debugging .NET solutions.

Estimated time to complete this lab: 120 minutes

Exercise 1
Setting Up and Testing the Application

Before completing this lab, ensure that the environment is set up correctly and test the lab solution.

▶ **Set up the XML Web service**

1. Start the **Internet Services Manager**. It is one of the **Administrative Tools** installed with Windows 2000 Server.

2. Expand the **Default Web Site**.

Note If the 2389 virtual directory does not exist, run the **cvd2389.vbs** file in the <install_folder>\Labs\ folder.

---

3. Right-click the \2389\Labs\Lab07\Solution\VB\OnTheRoadWS\ virtual directory or the \2389\Labs\Lab07\Solution\CS\OnTheRoadWS\ virtual directory, and then choose **Properties**.

4. Click **Create** to make the virtual directory into an application.

5. Click the **Directory Security** tab.

6. In the **Anonymous access and authentication control** section, click **Edit**.

7. Unselect the **Anonymous access** check box. Click **OK**.

8. Click **OK**.

9. Right-click the **OnTheRoadWS** virtual directory, click **All Tasks**, and then click **Configure Server Extensions**.

Note When you create an XML Web service by using the Visual Studio .NET development environment, these steps are completed automatically. When you deploy an XML Web service to a production Web server, you need to manually configure the Web service, although automation by using scripting is possible.

---

10. In the wizard, click **Next** until you see the final step, and then click **Finish**. The default options for configuring the server extensions will be used.

11. Close the Internet Services Manager.

▶ **To set up the stored procedures**

1. Start the Microsoft SQL Server Query Analyzer.

2. Open the script named **lab6setup.sql** in the folder

   <install path>\2389\Labs\Lab06_1\

3. Run the script.

4. *On the Instructor machine only*: Open the script named **setuplab7.sql** in the following folder: <install path>\2389\Labs\Lab07\

5. *On the Instructor machine only*: Run the script.

6. Close the SQL Server Query Analyzer.

▶ **To open, rebuild, and test the XML Web service**

1. Start the Microsoft Visual Studio .NET development environment.

2. Open the existing solution named **OnTheRoad**, located at
   <install path>\2389\Labs\Lab07\Solution\xx\OnTheRoad\

3. View the **Solution Explorer** and browse the two projects. Notice that the
   XML Web service project is named **OnTheRoadWS**. The Windows
   Application project is named **OnTheRoad**.

4. Open the file **NWDataSet.xsd**. This file defines the schema used by the
   DataSet in this solution.

5. Open the file **SalesManager.asmx**. Right-click and select **Line Up Icons** if
   all of the data controls are not visible.

6. If the Instructor computer is not named London, select the
   cnNorthwindInstructor connection object and change the **data source**
   parameter to the name of the Instructor computer. For example, to use the
   local SQL Server, type **(local)**.

7. Right-click and select **View Code**. Notice that the class has two
   WebMethods named **GetDataSet** and **UpdateDatabase**.

8. To rebuild the XML Web service project, on the **Build** menu, click **Rebuild
   OnTheRoadWS**.

9. In the **Solution Explorer**, right-click the file **SalesManager.asmx** and click
   Set As Start Page.

10. In the **Solution Explorer**, right-click the project **OnTheRoadWS** and click
    Set as StartUp Project.

11. On the **Debug** menu, click **Start**.

Note The **SalesManager** Web service should now appear in Internet Explorer.
You will see a Web page that describes the Web service and lists the two
available methods. To manually test, run Internet Explorer and navigate to
http://localhost/2389/Labs/Lab07/Solution/xx/OnTheRoadWS/SalesManager.as
mx.

---

12. Click the **GetDataSet** link.

13. Enter **2** for the **iEmployeeID** value and **(local)** for the **sServerName** value.

14. Click the **Invoke** button.

15. The XML Web service should return an XML document containing all
    orders taken by that employee (Andrew Fuller).

16. Close the Internet Explorer windows.

▶ **To rebuild and test the Windows application**

1. In the Windows Application project named **OnTheRoad**, expand the **Web References** folder.

2. In the **Solution Explorer**, right-click **localhost** and choose **Delete**. Click **Yes** to confirm.

3. In the **Solution Explorer**, right-click the **Web References** folder and choose **Add Web Reference**.

4. Enter the URL for the XML Web service, http://localhost/2389/Labs/Lab07/Solution/xx/OnTheRoadWS/SalesManager.asmx, then click **Add Reference**. Notice that a copy of the Web service XSD file has been added to the project, and that WSDL and other files have been created.

5. In the **Solution Explorer**, right-click the project **OnTheRoad** and click **Set as StartUp Project**.

6. Open the **MainForm** class and notice the **mnuFill_Click** procedure that declares and calls the Web service.

7. To rebuild the solution, on the **Build** menu, click **Rebuild Solution**.

8. Close the Visual Studio .NET development environment.

▶ **Test the Windows client application**

1. Open Windows Explorer and navigate to one of the following paths:

   <install path>\Labs\Lab07\Solution\VB\OnTheRoad\bin\

   <install path>\Labs\Lab07\Solution\CS\OnTheRoad\bin\Debug\

2. You should see two files named **OnTheRoad.exe** (the application executable file) and **OnTheRoad.pdb** (the program debug database). If there is a file named **OnTheRoad.xml**, delete it. (This is where the data set is saved while you are working on the road.)

3. Double-click the file **OnTheRoad.exe** to start the application.

4. You will see a warning message saying that a data set was not found, and offering to connect to the central database to create one. Click **Yes**. This will connect to the central database, and download a list of employees from the database.

Note Notice the ninth employee, John Smith. The list of employees is populated from a table on the instructor computer. All other tables used by this Web service are located on your local computer running SQL Server.

5. In the **Get from central database** dialog box, choose any employee name (except John Smith, who has no customers), and then click **OK**. You will see all of the customers managed by that employee, in addition to their orders and order details.

6. Close the application. This saves your employee ID and database settings to an XML document.

7. In Windows Explorer, notice that a file was created named **OnTheRoad.xml**. Double-click the file to open it in Microsoft Internet Explorer.

8. Restart the application again. This time, you will not be asked to select employee details, because your application reads this information from the XML document. The application displays the customers for the employee you specified earlier.

9. In the data grid, expand a customer and one of his or her orders.

10. Add a new order detail row. Use any product ID (1-77), unit price, and quantity.

11. Click the first order detail row to make sure that the change is made to the data set.

12. Write down the Order ID number of the order to which you added the order detail row.

13. On the **File** menu, click **Update to central database**. In the central database, one row will be added to the OrderDetails.

14. Click **No** when prompted to refresh the DataSet. Refreshing is only necessary in a multi-user environment.

15. Start the Microsoft Visual Studio .NET development environment.

16. Use the Server Explorer in Visual Studio .NET to check that the additional row was successfully added.

Now that you know how the solution is supposed to work, you are ready to fix the bugs in the starter solution.

Exercise 2
Fixing Bugs

In this exercise, you will fix bugs in a broken Visual Studio .NET solution. The solution includes an XML Web service and a Windows client application that both use ADO.NET to allow salespeople to track customer orders when they are away from the office and the central sales database.

Scenario

You work as a programmer in the Northwind Traders information technology department. The previous programmer left behind an application project that contains many bugs. Your first task is to fix the bugs in the application.

The instructor will play the role of the database administrator (DBA) for the Northwind Traders IT Department. If you find DBA-related problems, ask the DBA questions and negotiate with the DBA as you would in the real world.

1. Start the Microsoft Visual Studio .NET development environment.

2. Open the solution in one of the following locations:
   <install path>\Labs\Lab07\Starter\VB\OnTheRoad\ or
   <install path>\Labs\Lab07\Starter\CS\OnTheRoad\

3. Opening the solution file should open two projects: **OnTheRoad** (the Windows client application) and **OnTheRoadWS** (the XML Web service). If not, make sure that you have opened the *solution* (.sln) file, not the *project* (.vbproj or .csproj) file.

4. Rebuild the solution.

5. You will get many error messages. Find and fix the bugs.

Note   It might be easier to fix the two projects separately, for example, open and fix the XML Web service project first, then open and fix the Windows application, after refreshing the Web Reference to the XML Web service.

Fixes for the bugs

If you have difficulty finding or fixing the bugs, either open the fixed solution that is provided, or review the list of bugs and fixes below.

▶ **Solutions for the broken application**

- *Problem.* The OnTheRoadWS XML Web service virtual directory needs to be made into an ASPX application and anonymous access must be disabled.
  Solution. Run the Internet Services Manager and expand the **Default Web Site**. Right-click the \2389\Labs\Lab07\Starter\VB\OnTheRoadWS\ virtual directory or the \2389\Labs\Lab07\Starter\CS\OnTheRoadWS\ virtual directory and click **Properties**. Click **Create** to make the virtual directory into an application. Click the **Directory Security** tab. In the **Anonymous access and authentication control** section, click **Edit**. Unselect the **Anonymous access** check box. Click **OK**, and then click **OK** again. Right-click the \2389\Labs\Lab07\Starter\VB\OnTheRoadWS\ virtual directory or the \2389\Labs\Lab07\Starter\CS\OnTheRoadWS\ virtual directory and click All Tasks, and then click **Configure Server Extensions**. Click **Next** until the wizard gets to the last page, and then click **Finish**.

- *Problem.* The OnTheRoad project is missing a reference to the System.XML.dll assembly. This causes six build errors related to classes defined in the System.Xml namespace.
  Solution. Right-click the **OnTheRoad** project, click **Add Reference**, select the **System.XML.dll** assembly, click **Select**, and then click **OK**.

- *Problem.* The **SalesManager.asmx** class is missing an **Imports** (VB) or a **using** (C#) statement for the System.Web.Services namespace. This causes two "Type is not defined: 'WebMethod'" build errors, because the <WebMethod()> attribute is defined in the System.Web.Services namespace.
  Solution. Add the following code to the top of the **SalesManager.asmx** class.

```
' Visual Basic
Imports System.Web.Services

// Visual C#
using System.Web.Services;
```

- *Problem.* The call to the **Fill** method when filling the Employees table has accidentally swapped the DataSet and DataAdapter, giving a compile error; for example, ds.Fill(da.*tablename*) is wrong.
  Solution. Swap the DataSet and DataAdapter references.

- *Problem.* A new employee started recently. His name is John Smith, but the name does not appear in the application.
  Solution. The problem is that the connection string for the cnNorthwindInstructor connection in the **SalesManager.asmx** class uses (local) as the server name. Therefore, the database that is used is on the same server as the Web service. This must be changed to the instructor computer name, London, because this is the only server that contains the EmployeesLatest table. This error frequently occurs when moving from a development or test environment to a production environment.

- *Problem*. The connection string for the cnNorthwindInstructor connection in the SalesManager.asmx class uses a SQL login named **MaryJoe** with a password of **secret** that does not exist on the server.
  Solution. This problem frequently occurs when moving between servers; for example, when moving from a test server to a production server. The solution is to either create a new login with the correct permissions, or to use another login name and password. Use the **MaryJane** login instead because this employee has the same password.

- *Problem*. The code that calls the **GetDataSet** Web method is missing a well-written exception handler, so it is much harder to determine what is wrong when the code fails.
  Solution. Add the following exception handling code *as a minimum*. If you have time, write more code to catch specific exceptions and display friendly error messages to the user.

```
' Visual Basic
Try
    tempNW = wsSalesMgr.GetDataSet( _
        Me.EmployeeID, Me.ServerName)
Catch Xcp As System.Exception
    MessageBox.Show(Xcp.ToString(), "Exception")
End Try
```

```
// Visual C#
try
{
    tempNW = wsSalesMgr.GetDataSet(
        this.EmployeeID, this.ServerName);
}
catch (System.Exception Xcp)
{
    MessageBox.Show(Xcp.ToString(), "Exception");
}
```

- *Problem*. The instructor can put the Northwind database on the London server into single-user mode (or run a stored procedure) to limit the number of concurrent connections to fewer than the total number of students.
  Solution. Contact the DBA and make sure that the database does not limit connections for either reason.

- *Problem*. The **cmSelectCustomers** command uses the **SelectClients** stored procedure, which now has the wrong name.
  Solution. Users can fix the name in their code. It should be changed to **SelectCustomers**.

- *Problem*. A stored procedure has a parameter type mismatch.
  Solution. The **cmInsertCustomers** command needs the parameter definition line for the @CustomerID parameter altered from a 4-byte integer to a 5-byte NChar.

- *Problem*. Before calling the **Fill** method of the **daOrderDetails** DataAdapter, the parameter value for the EmployeeID is not set properly, so the order detail rows that are displayed to the user are wrong.
  Solution. Change the variable name to use **iEmployeeID** instead of **EmployeeID** (which is always 0).

- *Problem*. DataGrid binding code uses a child table (Orders) instead of a parent table (Customers).
  Solution. Change the code in the **RefreshUI** method to bind to the Customers table.

- *Problem*. The XSD file does not define a relationship between the Orders and OrderDetails tables, so the DataGrid also does not recognize the relationship.
  Solution. Users need to use the XSD Editor to manually edit the XSD file. Open the NWDataSet.xsd file. Right-click the **Orders** table, click the **Add** menu, and then click **New Relation**. Set the **Parent** element to **Orders**, set the **Child** element to **OrderDetails**, and then click **OK**.

- *Problem*. Not using Merge method when trying to combine two DataSets, instead assigning one to the other thereby destroying the first.
  Solution. Change the code in the **mnuUpdate_Click** method to use the **Merge** method.

```
' Visual Basic
dsChanges.Merge(Me.dsNorthwind.AppSettings)

// Visual C#
dsChanges.Merge(this.dsNorthwind.AppSettings);
```

- *Problem*. Code incorrectly calls the **AcceptChanges** method before calling **Update**. Therefore, marked changes are "lost" and are not sent to the central database. On the next call to the **Fill** method, the DataSet will revert to the underlying values.
  Solution. Delete the call to the **AcceptChanges** method before calling the **GetChanges** method in the **mnuUpdate_Click** procedure.

- *Problem*. The **CommandText** property of the **SelectCommand** of the **SqlDataAdapter** daEmployees has been incorrectly fixed, so there is a missing space character before the ORDER BY clause.
  Solution. Manually add the space back, or run the wizard again to regenerate the statement.

Course Evaluation

Your evaluation of this course will help Microsoft understand the quality of your learning experience.

To complete a course evaluation, go to http://www.metricsthatmatter.com/survey.

Microsoft will keep your evaluation strictly confidential and will use your responses to improve your future learning experience.

Notes

Notes

Notes

Notes

Notes

Notes